Lois & Clark

Lois & Clark ™

A SUPERMAN NOVEL

C.J. Cherryh

Prima Publishing

PRIMA PUBLISHING and colophon are registered trademarks of Prima Communications, Inc.

Library of Congress Catalog Card Number: 96-67725

ISBN: 0-7615-0482-6
Printed in the United States of America
96 97 98 99 00 AA 10 9 8 7 6 5 4 3
How to Order:
Single copies may be ordered from Prima Publishing, P.O. Box 1260BK, Rocklin, CA 95677; telephone (916) 632-4400. Quantity discounts are also available. On your letterhead, include information concerning the intended use of the books

Chapter 1

Morning in the *Planet* offices: "Where's the City Hall article?" and "Chief, the copy machine repairman's downstairs!" vied for urgency with "Where's the City Hall photos?" and "There's ten pairs of scissors in this office! Why can't I find just one?"

The place, a central room lined with offices and conference rooms, had a comfortable untidiness, wooden railings rescued from the *Planet*'s old newsroom and refurbished, desks a little on the eclectic side and sporting here a photo of kids and spouse, there the inevitable pothos vine, a scatter of disks, printout, file cards, folders, and notepads—around computers wired to the world.

It was a newsroom: it was a nerve center: it was wired in, plugged in, and it put out one of the finest newspapers in the world. Desktop computers spilled the latest from Baghdad and the Poconos for the benefit of any reporter who urgently needed to know.

But today the wire feed was as slow as the news in Metropolis. The Vice President was due to attend a fund-raiser in Philadelphia. A labor dispute in the Metropolis Public Works Department was headed for arbitration. Someone had dumped a load of trash in front of City Hall. So far it was the lead.

"The coffee's out," Letitia complained. "Where's the coffee service?"

No one answered. No one wanted to be responsible. Nobody wanted to suggest to Letitia Frenk, society columnist, that she might risk her manicure on the job.

Kent arrived for the day, late, and shed his raincoat onto the coat-tree in the less trafficked corner. Lane's coat, likewise on the tree, was still dripping. So the *Planet's* other star reporter was late, too. And he'd had trouble getting a cab.

"Supper at six-thirty," Lois Lane said, intercepting him on his way past the wooden railing. She looked as if rain had never fallen on her, gray striped suit, immaculate hair—she was one of those women whose looks outshone her clothes, never extravagant, but just—elegant. Even on a day like this.

"What supper?" He'd been known to forget things. This woman could pass hints right past his absent attention, and he was afraid he'd slipped something this time, when he was listening elsewhere or using faculties that weren't quite . . . apparent to the world around him.

A little absentminded, was how the rest of the office characterized Clark Kent. But as he followed her back to her desk, into the center of the heartbeat of the newspaper, she cast him an over-the-shoulder glance with a little self-satisfied smile that said, no, this was news she was telling him—happy news, wonderful news, I've-got-a-secret kind of news.

"There was a cancellation," she said, "at The Twelve Tables."

He was too wise to ask, *Are we going?*

But maybe not wise enough to look thoroughly delighted.

"Clark, you have to know how lucky we are! This place is absolutely booked solid, just absolutely impossible to get a reservation! We'll need to leave my apartment at six. At six, latest. Don't *tell* me you've got another engagement!"

"Great," Clark said. And told himself he meant it. Dinner and theater in London or a trattoria in Rome had always been in reach for him, personally. The world's best theaters. The most exclusive restaurants. *He* could always go globe-hopping. But he only rarely indulged that kind of whim—for one thing, because a reporter's salary didn't extend to meals at Alfredo's, and for another, because he'd grown up with harvest-hand breakfasts and suppers back home, and American country cooking was what he truly favored. There was a roadside cafe on old Route 66 that served up chili cheeseburgers to die for.

But Metropolis's latest and trendiest restaurants were Lois's personal passion from before they'd dated, and by what she said, and what he'd heard of the place, reservations were hard to come by. It was a quest, an acquisition, a moment of glamor *she* aspired to. And as surely as he loved the ground she stood on, they were going to go, tonight, to a tiny, exclusive, and expensive place called The Twelve Tables (aptly named, since that was the number of tables), which was the rave of Metropolis.

He suspected the chairs were going to be frail, the premises crowded, the flowers edible, and the portions more like a sample than a satisfaction.

But *she* was going to be happy. And a man in love rated that goal above other considerations. She was the kind of woman who could enjoy that Route 66 cheeseburger, too.

She loved him. She knew everything about him—everything—and she loved him anyway. And there wasn't a thing wrong with the world. The Twelve Tables, it was. He memorized the appointment. Her apartment at six. Early supper.

Maybe a movie, then. Maybe they'd just watch television and sit and talk. Her apartment. She had a television.

She flashed him a look, and a grin, as he sat down at his desk, which was directly facing hers.

She was pleased. He could see that much in the enthusiasm with which she attacked the keyboard.

"Who's seen the coffee filters?" Perry White came back complaining. The editor-in-chief was on a quest. Coffee was an operational necessity in the newsroom.

Clark turned his computer on and punched keys from memory as the bootup sequence proceeded. He wanted weather reports for the evening, for starters. They'd take a taxi tonight. It was raining outside, a cold, end-of-April downpour. Lois wouldn't appreciate a sky tour in the soggy weather, and by what he saw on the weather, it wasn't going to clear. The fronts were stacked up and waiting. Springtime.

Lunch in the deli around the corner was the likely choice today, a course that didn't leave the shelter of awnings and overhangs.

Meanwhile the computer was pulling up stories he'd been tracking, topics he'd preselected, a steady stream of crises, court cases, and miscellany.

Perry was investigating counter cabinets, opening and slamming doors. Lois, at the next desk, punched a key with reckless authority as lightning flashed outside the windows, and Jimmy Olsen came up with the missing filters.

Coffee would come welcome, Clark thought. The McKenzie lawsuit over school districting was the local lead story and the headline if it wasn't the city workers' dispute or the far more photographic City Hall trash episode. The national news was the vice presidential speech and the international feed was the World Economic Conference in Brussels, which Clark followed and studied. It did have a foreseeable impact on Metropolis and on the state. But Perry wanted him on a brewing controversy regarding the power plant.

He wanted to do a feature on the proposal to demolish the old Miller Building in favor of municipal parking, and Perry called it taking sides. But with a little reportorial query as a nudge, the Historic Sites Committee had this week become aware and was stirring to action in protest of the quiet and marginally legal sale of the building. He'd heard rumors that was the case, and he was keeping a close eye on the matter, waiting for the break.

The mayor's office was in favor of the parking garage, the HSC was about to come down on the other side, and his source hinted the end of next week for a news conference and a counterproposal. His fault? He was glad to have it his fault. It was a beautiful old building of the art deco period.

Meanwhile he was searching up clippings on the building's murals and unique architecture that were otherwise doomed to urban salvage.

"Want some coffee?" Lois asked. She'd made the pilgrimage to the machine while he'd been sunk in his information flow and oblivious. He held out his hand. The cup arrived in it. He drank a sip and stared at the photos of the mural. He wanted those run in color. Full-page local feature. He wondered how he could talk Perry into it, and he needed to write down the web address for a reference on architecture he thought he could use.

A computerized desk never had a pen. He took a sip of coffee and, simultaneously searching the side drawer that held such things, came up with a pen. He wrote *www,* or tried to, on the notepad, and the pen ran out of ink—victim, he remembered now, of one of his fast-and-furious note-takings during a phone conversation last week.

The computer wire feed scroll, minimized to run in the background, beeped at him and came up with a highlighted item: DAM FAILURE THREATENS TOWNS.

Tbilisi was the dateline, the origin of the wire feed; the story was from the remote Caucasus, part of the former Soviet Union. He called it up, *dam* and *flood* being two words he'd set as Page-Me criteria in the fancy new software program, Electronic Desk, Perry had been sold on. A keystroke got the dam article full-screen.

The situation had been chancy in that district of the world since the quake last January. Engineers in the region had been acutely concerned, particularly about the highest dam, whether it would withstand the thaw in the hills, when snowmelt would swell the rivers that fed into the lake it held.

It wasn't withstanding the surge of water that it was under-going now. What came up from the wire was almost as dire as it could get, excluding another quake. Beyond the initial para-graph siting the disaster in the Caucasus Mountains, near the Caspian Sea, it said:

A powerful storm system has sent nine inches of rain down on a river already swollen by spring floods. Engineers last week ordered the dams in the area to open spillways and lower water levels in an attempt to reduce pressure against the dams, but the rainfall amounts combined with snowmelt and strong prevailing winds have produced an imminent threat to the first and most compro-mised of the dams. Built as part of a modernization push by the former regime, the dam . . .

The computer didn't produce text as fast as he could read it, and he knew what the rest of the article would say. He had an atlas on his desk. He took it with him in a calm, ordinary walk to the hall that led to the conference rooms, a far more reliable refuge than most nooks in the *Planet* offices.

Then, out of sight of his coworkers, he could move at the speed he wanted. He opened the atlas and scanned the European map at a flash. The area map he took with him, as providing detail he might need.

Then he shed the glasses, the brown suit, and the self that moved like ordinary men, and left that end-of-the hall conference room at a speed that riffled the pages of the atlas. The pressure of air thumped the windows of dark, adjacent conference rooms—windows that reflected red and blue off their disturbed substance.

He opened the stairwell door ever so carefully compared to the speed at which he wanted to move. He pulled it shut at a speed that didn't blow the hydraulic cylinder, and then looked up, and up, feet leaving the ground, course spiraling faster and faster up the stairwell with all senses alert to anyone using those stairs, no sense of power at first, not even of speed, just a lightness of being, just an impatience to be up the stairs and moving, and a knowledge that using the steps at superspeed would shake the spine of the building. It was a sinuous twist of body and a flight path up, up the stairwell as floor numbers, painted on the walls, blurred past: 33, 34, 35 . . . 50 and higher: fast, but not, even yet, fast enough for the air shock to rattle doors and set off alarms.

The door at the very top of the stairwell, carefully handled, afforded him an exit onto the roof in a gray soup of blowing rain. With all of Metropolis spread around him, blurred in mist, he delayed only to drop the packet that was Clark into a heavy-lidded hiding place that looked like (but wasn't) a feature of the *Planet* Building's roof-access cupola. Lightning whitened the roof, threw details of the cupola into stark light and shadow, and before the light faded from his eyes or the thunder rolled, Superman was up into the storm.

There was no restraint now to his speed. It was like plowing through a lake, the rain a steady sheet around him. No need to calculate direction. The *Daily Planet* was his launch point and his compass rose. He knew his heading and he knew his course.

And there was no need from this starting point to worry about traffic: he rose high and higher, and struck out to enter an ascending air corridor *he* used and none of Metropolis's airports assigned or allowed to any craft.

He had no way to breathe in the sheeting rain, but no need to breathe yet, either. The potential for lightning was in the clouds he sped through. Lightning attended him in a crazed cloud-to-cloud display as he climbed.

Then he broke through the gloomy gray clouds into the brilliant day that existed above the storm, rising into increasing cold and thinner air. Here he breathed like a swimmer in surf, water streaming off him and then freezing in his wake. Snow might have followed him, however briefly. He'd never seen the phenomenon. Today he had a map he couldn't, because of the speed he used, resort to for guidance; but he knew the general course he was taking toward Europe, and he could see the morning sun for a guide. Clouds obscured the shore and the sea, but he knew that he had the ocean below him now, and he knew to a nicety the moment he could break out and fly at a convenient speed.

Faster still. Past the sound barrier—and traveling a course that didn't rely on the jet stream or the prevailing winds. Aerodynamics counted, and the substance of the opposing air streamed around him, battered at him, failed to resist him. When he took to skies untroubled by aircraft and unfettered by considerations for sonic booms and traffic, nothing on Earth flew faster, higher, or further.

Lives were at stake on the far side of the world; and no person on Earth except Superman stood a chance of helping those people if that dam went. Four more dams were downriver. That whole region, rocked by earthquake and deluged by spring rains, was in imminent danger.

A cup of coffee cooled on Clark's desk. Lois thought nothing of it for ten, fifteen minutes. Clark might have had a dozen reasons for walking away.

Sixteen minutes, however, was at least reason to notice.

Seventeen was reason to look around the office and wonder whether Clark was in conference with Perry in his office, or on some other phone.

Twenty was reason to conclude something was unusual. It was half past ten, or thereabouts. Clark had left his computer running. That said he meant to come back.

Ordinarily it said so. And the copy machine was fixed. Ron reported it to the office. He wasn't tied up there.

A quarter of, and Jimmy Olsen stopped by to ask where Clark was.

She'd used to be put off by the excuses. Now she made them up for him. "Oh, around." The simplest ones were the best. Followed by diversion. "I've got to get this article written. It's thrilling. All about the garbage strike."

"You going out to lunch?"

"Pastrami on rye, if you're going to make a deli run."

"I don't know." Clearly that wasn't Jimmy's hope. "There's awnings most of the way to Foggarty's."

"It's wet out there. Have you noticed? The sky's falling."

"I've got an umbrella."

"Sure. Look. Have you got an assignment?"

"Nothing's doing yet."

"Good." She put on her brightest grin and leaned her chin on folded hands, classic deb pose. "Hot mustard. Hold the pickle."

Jimmy knew when he was being ragged. "Maybe Ron's game for a swim."

"Oh, okay, I'll think about it." She'd worn moderately practical shoes because of the weather, but if it was an expedition, she had a pair of tennies in her desk she could change into. She had a big, special dinner coming. That was the real consideration.

So was Clark's unscheduled absence.

But it was a gray, gloomy lunch, in the third consideration, and the reservations for this evening had put her in a celebratory mood. "Foggarty's is tempting. Don't leave without me."

Jimmy went off on his own mission. She got up, curious about Clark's whereabouts. Clark's computer had gone to screen saver, pictures of country meadows and a ramshackle barn. She punched the key and got nothing of significance, just the parking garage controversy and Clark's notes.

So Clark hadn't shut down his computer: either he thought he was coming back soon or he'd had no chance to come back. His raincoat was still hanging on the coat-tree by the door. A dozen times before she'd known for certain what his reasons were for such forgetfulness, Clark had left that brown raincoat in the office. And there it was. *Not* forgetfulness. He'd not needed it or couldn't come back for it.

And he'd been gone for half an hour.

She walked back to the conference rooms. There was an atlas open on a table in the endmost room, and she gathered it up. There was a page missing.

That was ominous. It was the foreign section of the atlas, in the G's. Gambia? That map was still there. Greenland? The same. What country or area started with a G?

She walked back to the desk and put the atlas back in Clark's stack of books, wondering where and why. She could turn his computer off. She could cover that small fact. But what was she supposed to do with his coat? Leave it there, conspicuous, after all the other coats had found homes at the end of the shift?

It wouldn't be the first time that coat had hung there. The staff made jokes about Clark forgetting his head if it wasn't part of him. He'd leave the copy machine on, leave the computer on, leave his coat, leave his reference books. Something was missing? You looked where Clark would have left it.

On one hand the sometimes real forgetfulness was charming, in a man who could do so much—who *saw* and *heard* so much no one else did that it distracted him.

But the absences, as he went flying off to some emergency . . . that was the scary part of their relationship. Love left her trying to think of clever excuses, covers, patches, and it wasn't just the coat. It was "Where's Clark?" at lunch, and "Where's Clark?" regarding that coat hanging there, and "Where's Clark?" all day long. She could joke about it, she could say he was on an interview, at the barber's, downstairs. She could say he had a meeting, that he was at the airport, checking out a lead. And when he did show up he tried to slip into whatever she'd said and look as if it were true, but he didn't give her warning, and she didn't always know which was the right excuse.

Not her responsibility, she told herself from time to time, and it was better if she pretended to know nothing. Clark had handled his secret all his life. It wasn't her responsibility, and if she started taking it on, people were bound to talk and ask her more questions she couldn't answer. Clark was forgetful. That was the line she had to take.

No matter that sometimes she worried. No matter that love made her imagine disaster in every half hour beyond reasonable expectation. He had enemies, powerful enemies who'd stop at nothing to be rid of him. There was at least one substance that harmed him. But there might be others. She could never be sure. There were natural disasters. He'd come unscathed out of all of them, but there was always the next one, the next test of his abilities, the next undertaking of ill-defined limits. There'd never been anyone like him and nobody knew what his limits were. Neither did he.

"Pastrami on rye?" Jimmy asked her glumly, having found, evidently, no takers for Foggarty's.

She gave him a look, telling herself she'd set it up, she'd suggested it to Jimmy, and now she was doomed to lunch from a sack.

"You suppose I should get one for CK?" Jimmy asked. Clark was CK to Jimmy. Persistently. And Jimmy concluded, after the second look she shot him, "No, I guess not."

"He can—"

—*take care of himself*, was what she was about to answer.

The whole building shook. Swayed. Stopped. Sound had rumbled through bone and flesh and everybody in the office stopped where they stood for that heartbeat, then looked at the ceilings, at the floor.

"My God," someone said. Someone else: "What was that?" And irresistibly, then, the general movement toward the windows. Lois was moving toward that helpless vantage before conscious thought caught up: it wasn't *this* building, she was sure it wasn't this building. But something monstrous had happened.

Information wasn't in here, in the office. Perry, Jimmy, Ron, Burns, everybody was moving toward the windows that afforded a limited view of the street, give or take the overhang.

Not enough.

In the sudden, proprietary search for first crack at a story—which, so help her, Clark had better not have failed to tell her about—she snagged her purse off the chair, detoured past the coat-tree on her way to the door, and checked the cell phone in her coat pocket as she passed down the hall.

She didn't wait for the elevator. She took the stairwell down, running, in the practical shoes the weather had dictated.

"Hey!" she heard behind her. She'd been the first to think "story," but not the only one. That was Burns. There might be others taking the elevator.

She hastened her pace and kept ahead of the pack, down to the door marked Lobby.

Cold, damp air hit as she pushed that door open and exited into the lobby of the *Planet* Building. Cold wind and gray daylight came from the glass doors. There wasn't a soul in the lobby. She ran across the terrazzo floor, and her steps raised echoes. She thought only belatedly about the rain, her hair, and her umbrella still upstairs as she shoved her way out the chrome and glass doors and came out under the dripping overhang of the *Planet* Building emblem.

Traffic on the street had stopped. Burglar alarms were going off. Sirens were blowing, the security kind. Men in raincoats were running toward uptown, two kids in sneakers were threading the traffic, running toward downtown, and people all up and down the block stared in the direction the men were running—toward a billowing of dust and a column of black and white smoke coming up from . . . it looked like midway down their block.

Someone blew a car horn. A bus near the curb blocked her view. Its exhaust went up, odorous and white against the gray chill.

But beyond that, down the street, brown smoke billowed out. Brown smoke. Or dust.

Cars coming toward her were coated in pale, rain-pocked mud, and down the block they sat frozen still, coated to a uniform paleness and carrying shattered pieces of concrete on hoods and tops. Traffic in the intersection wasn't moving.

The whole observation might have taken half a dozen heartbeats. "Lois!" she heard Burns shout after her, but she started to run, like the men ahead of her, like others on the block, toward that pillar of smoke and dust boiling up so unlikely in the rain.

And over all, that mingled pillar of dust and smoke went up and up into a deluge that washed it out of the sky somewhere among the towering skyscrapers. Down here, heading into it, it stung the eyes and nose.

Through it, in her jolted vision, she saw the tumble of concrete where a major building had stood. She didn't know which building, at first, then realized it was the hotel: a new hotel, the Maernik, and where the Maernik's beautiful frontage had stood, a gap sent out smoke and dust and tattered, bloody refugees.

Sirens foretold ambulances. A woman in a black suit and stylish high heels staggered toward her over the carpet of crushed glass. Her nylons were in bloody rags. Lois offered a hand to guide the dazed woman, but the woman said, "Others! I'm all right," and pointed back into the boiling pale haze from which others were emerging.

"Lois!" Jimmy had caught up, camera in hand. "God, was it a bomb?"

"I don't know!" she said, and at the same time a man was calling out, "Billy! Andy, where are you?" The smoke had started her eyes watering, and Jimmy snapped pictures, his flash coming off the smoke and the dust, limiting his range and all but blinding her.

Burns might be with her. She had no idea. She ventured into the gap on a reporter's mission, with the thought as well that people might be dazed and needing the sense of direction she maintained toward the outside and safety. "That way!" she shouted at two men she met and pointed a coughing chamber-maid toward the frontage and daylight.

Then, about where the elevators were, came kids, three, four of them, the fourth one hauling along a sports bag as big as he was, all of them with faces stark and shocked. Dust made a coating over freckles, the blue of sports team shirts.

"Keep going!" she shouted at them. "The exit's that way! Go for the light, you can walk right through!"

"Billy and them's still downstairs," the freckled kid said in a shaky voice. "They were going to get stuff from the car! We just got up in the elevator—"

Kids. A sports team. The parking garage.

She knew the layout of the hotel, and there was a garage, valet parking, underneath the glass tower. "Get out to the side-walk!" she shouted. "Get yourselves out of here! Are you a team? Is the whole team in here?"

"Yes!" the boys shouted at the same time, and something about their coach checking in at the desk.

"Anybody who can has already run outside!" Sirens from outside nearly drowned her voice. "Go! Get help! Tell the police what you told me! Now!"

They believed her. In shock, or in the strange priority of kids, they took their sports bag and dragged it through the glass and the dust, headed for murky daylight.

She tried not to breathe the stuff, and feared for her lungs, but there were other kids in the building, maybe lost, maybe trapped. A stairwell behind the elevators went down from here to the garage: she'd been on assignment in the Maernik, and she knew the geography. She reached that stairwell through a tan-gle of fallen ceiling tiles, and it looked intact, but the only light through the brown haze of dust came from emergency lanterns bracketed at the landing. From behind her, against the shattered walls, red light strobed into the dusty air, heralding the arrival of emergency vehicles on the street outside.

She was at the stairway, and she didn't know what was below, whether boys were trying the stairs in the blinding dust, or whether they might be trapped in the elevators, or worse. But she was in a position to find that out with a fast look, to report to the emergency services—or direct them out, if she could find them.

She reached for support as she started down the steps. She recoiled from moisture, and saw liquid running down the wall and down the steps . . . of course: rain, from the outside, from the shattered roof.

But a turn further down dashed all her hope of finding the boys within easy reach. She saw darkness, devastation, chunks of concrete, tilted slabs crushing parked cars. There were skeins of hanging cables, picked out by the emergency light against a cavity otherwise dark.

Electrical cables. She was suddenly alarmed and checked her feet. She was standing on a dry spot. The stairwell on which she stood was the only whole structure, a stairway from which the light found only the edges of concrete and the shapes of crushed cars.

"Hey!" she yelled. "Anybody hear me?"

She thought a voice yelled back. She wasn't sure. It was a toss-up in her mind whether to run back up the steps and get the emergency crews on it—but those were *kids*. With electrical cables down and water pouring down the walls and the steps.

"You stay put, hear me? There are *live wires!* Do you hear me?"

There *were* voices. "We're down here!" she heard high, anxious voices with the edge of panic.

"Stay *put!*" Kids. God. She didn't know what to do, didn't dare let them panic and go scrambling around in the dark. She had her purse. She had—God!—her cell phone.

She dialed 911.

Line busy. Jammed. You could figure it.

"Where are you!" someone called, a young voice, desperate with fear. A youngster in that place below was asking to know her location, maybe trying to go to her through a world otherwise dark. *"Where are you?"* the faint voice called.

"I'm at the stairs! You wait!" She traded the cell phone back to her purse in favor of the pocket flashlight, turned it on, and essayed a careful step down onto what looked like solid floor.

A chunk of concrete fell, unexpectedly, from the sagging concrete ceiling. It was only the web of rebar, the metal reinforcing rods set within the concrete, still holding it up. That, and the tilted slabs that had been part of the floor, and crushed, dusty cars. She hoped the cars had all been parked.

"Can you see where I am?" she asked into the dark.

"No," the voices came to her. "It's dark down here! Billy's stuck, and we can't get him out!" And another voice: "Get my dad! Please get my dad!"

She tried the cell phone again, balancing it with the flashlight, trying to shine it on the floor ahead.

Busy.

She dialed the *Planet.* Nobody was answering the phone. Of course. They were all investigating the disaster. They were all outside.

Ring. Ring. Ring. *Come on, somebody pick up the phone . . .*

Water leaked down the wall, a steady flow that turned the dust to mud underfoot and dripped down from the ceiling. Water meant dust would run off, not pack down and support the slabs.

She tried the next autodial, any number at all on the buttons in the dark.

And got through, to Nathan, the restaurant reviewer: *"Daily Planet."*

"Nathan, for God's sake, who's there?"

"Is that Lois?"

"Yes! I'm in the stairwell of the Maernik Hotel parking garage. The emergency lines are jammed. Kids are trapped in the parking garage underneath the rubble. If I get stuck I want somebody to know where those kids are! I'm going to hang up now. I'm going down after those kids. There's wires and water all over the place! Tell the fire department!"

"Lois!" Nathan objected, but she didn't have time for discussion. She folded the phone and tucked it into her purse, slung her purse to the side, and shouted up the stairs.

"Help! Anybody hear me? There are *kids* down here! Help!"

She yelled, and wished to all the stars that Superman would show up. Clark had to know by now . . . if he was anywhere in sight. His superhearing might have picked up the sound of the collapse. He might hear her. She expected him, she believed in him, that at any instant he'd show up in a whoosh of disturbed air and that Superman would save those kids.

But it wasn't Superman who came scuffing ponderously down the steps above her. It was a shape from outer space that loomed in the yellow light at the top of the pile, carrying a blinding beam: a man wearing the oxygen tanks, face mask, and hazard-yellow reflective stripes of the fire department rescue team. He pulled the mask down and called out to her, "Are you hurt, ma'am?"

"No! But there are kids trapped down here! A soccer team . . . there's a bunch of kids in this hotel! One's stuck, or trapped! We may need paramedics!"

"Are you a doctor, ma'am?"

"No, I'm a reporter for the *Planet!* Can you get a medic down here? And there's wires hanging all over the place!"

"The power and the gas are getting cut off right now! I'd rather have you out of there, ma'am. I'll give you a hand up . . ."

"I'm not leaving these kids! They're scared, and I know where they are!"

"All right, ma'am." This was a man in a hurry. And she claimed line-of-sight knowledge of survivors. "You stay put! You stay right there, and don't touch anything. Those lines aren't off yet, and concrete is still coming down!"

He was going for help. Thank God.

"Go! I'm all right!" She watched him turn, ponderously, and ascend the stairs, taking his emergency light with him. He likely had a radio. He'd get help organized down that stairwell. She'd mark the place for him, steer help to the voices she heard. He left her because it was the expedient thing, to have a witness, on-site, who knew what she'd heard, if those voices should go silent.

"Where are you?" the young voice called out to her.

The kids she was looking for. They were nearer. And that meant they were moving around. Risking their lives among the fallen wires and the puddles. They might have seen the fireman's light flare out across the tangled wires and shattered concrete— and seen it go away again, and feared they were being left.

She had her little light, her light that was only for finding her keys in her apartment hallway. But with it she found a safe way across the floor and heard them clambering over concrete rubble below her.

She shined the light over the rim of stable floor and saw a pale young face down a slope of crumbled concrete. Then a second boy looked up out of the destruction and the dark, toward a figure that could only be a shadow with a pinprick of light in their darkness.

"All right, it's all right. The firemen are coming." She kept the light on them, to relieve their panic. They were maybe eight or nine years old. Scared out of their minds.

"I want my dad."

"Is he in here?"

"He's in New Jersey."

It was all but grimly funny. "Then he's all right, isn't he? And you're all right. What are your names?"

"Andy and Mike. But Billy and Gene is both stuck."

"Where?"

"Back over there!"

Her little flashlight wasn't strong enough to reach much further. There was a pile of rubble. That was all she could see. Billy and Gene, wherever they were, weren't visible, and her heart sank.

"You get up here," she said. "You climb up right now, to me, and you be careful. There are electric wires all over. They'll *kill* you, you understand, if you step in water or if you touch a wire. I'm not kidding! Get up here!"

They scrambled, knocking rock down. But they weren't that badly off, scrapes and bruises, a bloody forehead. From the level where she was, there was a staircase visible. Salvation. The strobing red lights of emergency vehicles for a guide. And, please God, rescue personnel.

"You walk straight to the stairs and you don't step in any water! Hear?"

"We can't leave Billy and Gene," the other boy said.

"I won't leave them. You get up and tell the firemen to get down here!" She'd gone beyond the place the fireman had told her to wait. But she sent two boys out in her stead. And *they* could be her messengers, across a floor clear of electric lines, toward a lighted stairs. "Tell them! We need help!"

They went. The light of that stairway drew them. They flinched together as another chunk of concrete came down, and a sifting of dust followed, gray powder that had been solid concrete. But she saw them make it as far as the stairs; she saw them advancing up and up the steps, being careful all the way of the hanging wires.

"Where'd you go?" a ghostly faint voice asked from her other side, out of the depths of crushed cars and fallen concrete, down the slope from which she'd come. "Where are you guys?"

If two boys had been able to climb up the rubble slope to get to her, then she could get down it. The occasional sifting of dust advised her there might not be time to wait for jacks and equipment. There were kids down in that dark place, kids with no light, no help: she left the stairs, over the side, kept a hand on the slope and went down, gradually, gradually—slipped as rubble gave, and scraped her knee, but the raincoat saved her from most of the rough edges.

"Guys?" she called into the dark, and heard a faint, fearful, "Yeah?"

"My name's Lois Lane. Your friends got out. They're safe. They made it to the stairs. How are you doing? Can you see the light I'm holding?"

"No. We're in a hole!"

Bad news. Disheartening news. She caught her breath. "How are you?"

"Pretty scared. And Billy's foot's stuck or something, and there's water coming in."

That didn't sound good. That didn't sound good at all. She didn't want to tell the kid what the extent of his danger could be. She hoped that they had the power cut off, and that there wasn't a line near that water.

And she couldn't wait for firemen, if a woman's strength might be able to pull rock off or free a frightened eight-year-old. She navigated the dark by question and answer, and by the faint glow of her light—listening, over the noise of running and dripping water, the occasional fall of a pebble, until she followed that voice to a narrow gap between slabs. There a major support and a slab still held up the floor of the garage above—against a horrific weight of concrete. The improbable wreckage of a car, of which one wheel and a concrete-dusted bumper were visible, sheltered a kind of tunnel, a passageway into the deepest dark yet.

"I'm here," she said, squatting down, shining the light in. "Who have we got here? Can you move?"

"Sort of."

She could see just faintly a young black face, a boy trying so hard to be brave. "What's your name?" she asked.

"Gene."

"Gene what?"

"Gene Pratt."

Gene Pratt, she discovered through rapid and gentle questions, was eight. Gene couldn't make it out the opening that was left, which was mostly small pebbles and dust. Andy and his friend had gone for help because they couldn't move the rock that separated them from Gene and Billy. And when she tried it—she couldn't, either. She didn't know what it might be propping up. That big slab over their heads was possibly relying on something this skull-sized rock held in place.

"That's all right," she said. "Firemen are coming. We'll get you out." She'd gotten down flat on her stomach with her raincoat for padding, and was grateful the boys hadn't pulled things at random. She could feel where it was mostly dust. "How much do you weigh, Gene?"

"About eighty pounds."

"That's good. We don't have to dig so much for eighty." She scooped out a fistful of gritty wet dust. "You dig and I'll dig," she said. She'd propped the flashlight where she could get a little light past her body. "You push the stuff toward me and I'll rake it out. All right?"

"Yeah." Gene had been trying to shove stuff out. She started clearing it back, raking it past her right side.

The *cell phone* rang.

"God." She got it out and unfolded it, hoping for Clark. She didn't care what city he was calling from. "Hello?" Here she was lying on cold ground in near dark with the sound of dripping water and the constant, ominous sift of gravel down from overhead—and the phone rang. "Hello? This is Lois."

"Ms. Lane, this is Carmen Alverado, LNN. We understand you're in the Maernik Hotel and you've seen trapped kids. There are desperate parents wanting information, Ms. Lane. Can you tell us anything?"

LNN. Television. A rival news organization.

But parents wanting news of trapped kids . . .

"Yes! I'm in the parking garage underneath the Maernik Hotel, I think about the second or third level. I'm in touch with two young boys, they're in a pocket with concrete and cars holding up a slab. Their names are . . ." She didn't want to make a mistake, not with parents' hopes riding on her accuracy. Her voice was wobblier than she'd have expected. Professional calm, she told herself. "Billy and his friend Gene Pratt. What's Billy's last name, Gene?"

"Anderson," came the shaky, scared voice. "Is that my mom?"

"Gene Pratt. Billy Anderson. Two kids just climbed out: that was Andy from New Jersey and his friend Mike. Is Billy awake, Gene?"

"Yeah." She heard another voice. "Yeah, I'm okay, I'm just kind of stuck."

"Billy Anderson just answered. He's in a predicament, and the other boys couldn't pull him out. I'm trying to dig, here." She was giving information to frightened parents and tried to preface bad news with good, remembering that not only the parents but the boys themselves could hear what she was saying.

"You're saying one boy is pinned in the collapse . . ."

"Yes." With all the structural steel about, and below ground level, she wasn't sure of the quality of the transmission. "Can you hear me clearly? I'm staying with the boys. I've talked to a fireman who's gone after equipment and help. Right now the area seems stable. There are electric lines down all over, but the fireman told me they're cutting off utility connections to remove the danger of the lines. Are you hearing me?"

"Yes! Please stay on the line! Please don't break the connection. Phone service to the area is interrupted. Can you talk to the boys?"

"I have talked to them." She'd have liked to hang up and call Nathan at the *Planet* and see—if news was at issue—whether she could turn in a story from where she was. But LNN was a sure route for information to get out of this basement, and right now LNN was where scared parents were calling for information. "I'm on the level just a little above where Billy is, and I can hear them." To whatever parents were listening, "They're good kids. They sound in good spirits."

"Were you *in* the explosion?"

"I was in the *Planet* Building, and I should correct that: it didn't sound like an explosion. The *Planet* Building shook. I ran outside and saw smoke, or steam, and dust, a lot of dust, even in the rain." The environment of dark and strange-smelling stone, this small hole she was in and trying to widen, was so complete she'd forgotten how to imagine the rain outside for the moment, the safe, ordinary streets of Metropolis outside, where there'd be fire trucks and ambulances and police and a gathering horde of news services.

Her concern was for the youngsters below: at a shaky, gut-deep level she knew there must be lives lost in this mess. She hadn't seen whether the whole hotel had gone down or whether the collapse was confined to this area in particular: but *she* had two more precious lives located, people were relying on her for information critical to the boys' rescue—and somewhere in the equation, she held a position that every reporter out there would ache to have.

If they had her telephone feed on the air, and knowing LNN she'd bet they did, she was going to get in a point for Perry and the home team, paper journalists that they were. "I should say, by the way, that this is Lois Lane, reporter for the *Daily Planet.*"

Chapter 2

In the high, thin reaches of the stratosphere Superman flew above the weather, up where the brilliant blue faded to a deeper shade, and where air resistance was minimal. Cloud cover over the ocean was solid, but he had a feeling for time and distance that didn't depend on seeing where he was going. The same way a practiced runner had a sense of his speed and distance, Superman didn't need his special vision to know he was still over ocean, and he had a fair sense of how fast he was traveling.

More, he knew his flight path, having flown this route to Europe many times just this year. Knowing this emergency could come, he'd studied in advance that local map he'd torn from his atlas. He took it as insurance, a chart to show him the fine details once he reached the distant Caucasus. But in the main, he knew the important landmarks on the routes he used, and equally important, he made it his constant business to know the current course of the jet stream and the state of world weather. He knew all manner of things: the height and extent of mountain ranges, the behavior of the sun, the calculations of speed and height and temperature of the winds aloft, the barometric highs and lows, the fronts, and everything else that he could gain from sources pilots used. He kept his information up to date constantly, never knowing when an emergency he hadn't studied was going to turn up to send him halfway around the world.

This situation with the unstable dams had entered the news with the earthquake weeks ago, and he'd done his study the first time the matter of how those dams were constructed came over the wire. In the earthquake, they'd held, cracks in walls, no one injured. The more grave matter was the question of the dams, five in succession, which (two in particular, hanging like stair steps in the high valley) were under examination by an international committee of engineers—as they should have been more deeply studied before they were built, from what the UN said. The old regime had been very quick to put up those high dams, his sources hinted, to shore up a shaky local government by bringing in electrical power, but there had been another motive in that hasty construction: to afford local officials a means of breaking up a coalition of ethnic groups in an area only uneasily ruled by the old regime.

Land had been flooded when those dams were built, creating new lakes. Farmers of certain ethnic origins, who had lived where those imperiled lakes now stood, had been moved and placed under close government supervision. It was a new government, now, but those dams were a dangerous legacy of bad old times and a regime that had, for various reasons, concealed incredibly bad decisions from the outside world.

He didn't interfere in politics. But this wasn't politics. This was nature straightening out the kink in her tail . . . or bidding fair to. Earthquakes happened frequently in the region; and this one was a tremor only moderately sharper than average. A test of the dams' integrity was bound to have come someday. Because it came now, after the collapse of the old regime, after glasnost, it attracted international interest—and international interest in a bad decision stirred touchy local habits of secrecy and protective bureaucracy.

All of that was simmering along as engineers tried to reason with political interests and regional pride.

Then Mother Nature came in with another punch: spring, and an unusually heavy snow last winter, a correspondingly heavy melt in the mountains, and a strong front moving out of Europe. Rain had started, a lot of rain. The engineers had had a plan ready—but rain was bad news for those plans that had come over the wire this morning. It was very bad news.

He was flying into night now, moving away from the sun. The stars were brightening, and below him, as he whisked along past the planetary terminator and into the side of the earth away from the sun, the view ahead showed him the coast of Europe lit up like some exotic fabric.

He corrected course, a mere two degrees. Clouds, after the gap along the French coast, closed in again, soft gray to his night-adapted eyes. Soon the peaks of the Alps were coming up above the sea of cloud.

Jungfrau, and Matterhorn: navigational markers. He put them at his back and made a little change of course, setting the right stars in front of him.

Greece. The Turkish frontier and the Black Sea. He flew high, high above political boundaries where his radar signature might trip alarms and scramble aircraft. He might have been a falling satellite. A piece of space junk. A cosmic piece of debris above the ancient and disputed land of Anatolia.

Then he was approaching the Caspian, a body of water heavily abused by politics and pollution, but not yet in sight of it.

He began his descent and felt more substance to the air. The sky below and ahead, the ridge of the Caucasus, ancient home of myth, modern home of ethnic strife, looked like spun-glass floss lit with lazy flashing lights. That was a thunderstorm seen from above, at night.

The peaks of mountains thrust above the storm. He identified Ebrus, on the Balkarian-Georgian frontier, and used the more than eighteen-thousand-foot summit for a navigation point as he dropped below the speed of sound, looking for the faint lights of villages, of the city of Vladikavkaz, with its airport. The mountain ridge itself, Mquinvartsveri, distinct in its height, gave him his bearings as he veered off north and west.

There was the high valley, up from Kislovodksk and other towns long unheard of in Metropolis—towns remote in their mountains and now caught between the political push for the Caspian's oil and the ethnic bitterness of centuries, Chechens and Russians, Ossetians and Georgians, and nationalities most of the West had never remotely heard of.

In these valleys the last regime, determined on industry, had built the ill-considered dams, stopping the snowmelt on its way to the Caspian, quick construction, sufficient to get electrical power.

And to hang above the heads of thousands already suffering from years of war, pollution, and ethnic strife.

Now was the time for precision. Now among all the deceptive folds of the mountains that looked as alike as trees in a forest, and different from every angle, he had to pick the right one.

At this speed and in the dark and the driving rain that had come down since his passage below the clouds, he couldn't hope to consult the map he'd brought: he relied instead on the memory he'd established from that map and on the memory he'd refreshed when he'd looked at the atlas back in the office half a world away. The names, the contours, the seams in the earth that were the source of the quake, jostled for place in his estimation of location.

There! The curve, the sharp bend of a river and the dam that checked its flow, the white plume of open floodgates and the froth on the river shining bright to his eyes. He'd found the river, and he followed it through the folds in the mountain flanks to the next in the chain of dams. He chased that thread of river and used his night vision, seeing warmth, not daytime light, scanning that dam for any flaw, any seepage of cold, deep lake water against sun-warmed concrete—but brightest was the discharge plume.

That one proving sound, he flew on, still following the river, passing the burning-hot spots in the storm-drowned night that were villages and livestock. Nine inches of rain and still coming down.

If word of the impending disaster had gone out to the villages above, then the people in the most threatened village might not be sleeping. He hoped they might be trying to get to higher ground—fleeing as people in the remote regions had always fled, afoot, carrying their goods on their shoulders, or in carts or wagons.

But the road that might have led them along the mountainside, a road that might have stayed high and dry above disaster, grew more narrow and more precarious—and he saw no movement, no indication of general flight on this isolated strip of gravel, in a darkness where bus or car engines would have shone like fires in his amplified vision.

The high-country residents then didn't know their danger. The thought that registered that conclusion lasted a split second of the seconds it took him to blaze along a lake surface in a valley and chase the climbing road to the next dam. His hands in front of him, battered by the rain, created a wind pocket that let him both see downward and breathe. He could feel the building charge of lightning grow around him and shut his eyes and locked his arms tightly across them so as not to be blinded as the exchange of energies blazed past.

When the electrical fury was gone, a second along in his flight, he made a wild dodge to avoid a mountain, and in that turn simultaneously saw the dim glow of a town beside a lake. The dam that made that lake was not so great as he'd imagined from its function—but it was hydroelectric. He couldn't pronounce the name of the place, but he knew it was the next to last of the chain.

Closer and closer in two beats of his heart . . . and he saw in this dam, as at the others, what the wire service had reported as their best hope: that plume of white. As spring melt and rains were at this very moment pouring a freak abundance of water into the system, this lake was spilling water down to the other dams in a roaring discharge column out the spillway, this one the most impressive yet.

This dam created power for the small town that sprawled up the hillside below the dam at the level of the road, out of the reach of ordinary floods and, he hoped, of this one. Their power lines ran from the hydroelectric plant: he could hear their presence singing to the lightning, and reminded himself they were there, huge towers along the mountainside, a hazard to his flight and most of all to helicopters and other rescuers.

The Red Cross was working in the town—at least they'd been there last week; and *they* knew the danger. Two weeks ago, the date of his best information, scientists had overflown the area, trying to assess damage. They likely were still trying to assess it, back in their labs with their aerial photographs; but whoever had taken the definitive professional risk to order those open gates to take the lake levels way down, both to study the dam and to try to reduce the pressure, was in his estimation heroic. It was the one piece of good planning he'd found; and in the press of other emergencies, reassured that the spillways were reducing the threat on an ordinary time scale, he'd thought he could leave this situation to the Red Cross and the international relief agencies for a number of days, until wiser heads than his—including representatives at the UN—figured out what, ultimately, to do about dams that shouldn't have been built in the first place and lakes that shouldn't have been sited where they were.

The trouble was, aftershocks had continued to make the relief work and the assessment difficult. Political forces were still wrangling over responsibility for having built the dams, the engineers hadn't reported a solution for what was proving a tough situation, and now the signs of collapse, the report said, were undeniable—in the dam upriver from this one.

Chasing his road, he rose into the teeth of a rain-laden gale, along slopes scarred with recent landslides, legacy of the quake, in pale areas of ruin that had tumbled trees down with boulders. It went on for miles, a river running briskly under an old iron bridge, and the thread of a road going on after that on the other side of the river, a road sometimes lost in trees and at one place completely wiped out by landslide.

There was no chance people could have gotten past that. He could have cleared it and shored up the road in minutes, but if imminent collapse of that dam threatened, there wasn't time for people to use that route, even if they would. The residents of the high villages, remote from the rest of the world, had already refused, in what contact anyone from the relief agencies had had with them, to be relocated to a town they didn't trust.

The highest dam, that remained the question: the dam set above the river where the road crossed. If it went—and took out this one—the catastrophe to the region would involve more than a village cut off by a rockfall.

He didn't have the engineers' knowledge, but he could deliver them a report that they'd be glad to have. They looked at individual photographs and readouts on paper: *his* vision, on the scene, was binocular, dimensional, and integrated into his brain in a way as ordinary as the act of breathing and as quick as a glance; and maybe if he could see the damage and find local authorities, they could establish a plan of action that might include fixing that road. But it was a case of first things first and a situation that, with all those successive dams involved, could be more complicated than anything he'd tackled before. He'd seen the tragedy of unbridled industry in Eastern Europe, and he didn't want to act as the previous government had, without consideration, spreading toxic materials that might be piled up in the silt behind one low-country dam down to land already ravaged by ill-considered industry, a river already polluted and flowing into a damaged sea.

And, pale wall that it was in the dark ahead, he suddenly saw the dam they said was critical—more, he immediately *saw* that irregularity where the stresses on the dam had made seepage around the floodgate.

He wanted finer detail as he came in. He sharpened the focus of his eyes on a smaller area . . . unlike the engineers, *he* didn't have to organize another plane, another picture taking and placement of instruments. He *saw* things immediately he didn't like at all, things that, whatever his level of expertise, told him that the concrete that was supposed to hold back vast acre-feet of water was starting to go in a significant way.

He maneuvered for a better angle, telling himself now that he should have followed his instincts and come here directly after the quake.

Now, in the freak direction of the storm, in the worst luck that could befall the region and the situation, the force of the wind was coming at the lake in such a way that the water was actually overtopping the dam as a torrential rain poured down on the mountains. The gates were just inadequate.

And that wasn't the worst. The worst was the anomaly in the dam face, the thing that drew the acute focus of his vision. It didn't even require his conscious thought: that sharp glance just instantly was, and the sight of the leakage *was*, and he knew there wasn't a way in the world to stop it. Everything he'd ever read and all the knowledge he had gained in similar crises told him that once the water had begun to flow through cracks that extensive, it would only increase, too rapidly and at too many angles to stop. The concrete, inexorably, was going to give way.

Divert it elsewhere? Water ran downhill no matter what Superman could do, and downhill was the next dam, prepared, yes, with that lowered lake level to sustain the flood crest that by the time it reached the lake would be a watery monster with teeth of uptorn stone and wood, a gravity-driven surge that would slam into its lake and drop that load—but that might not be enough to dispel its force. And if *that* dam gave—

Freeze it? A gamble. He had superspeed, but the sheer mass was daunting. Even to put a patch on that crumbling con-crete—freezing *expanded* liquid water, and freezing a patch onto that already uncertain dam might be the same as driving a wedge into the crumbling concrete, and hasten the process, not hinder it.

Boil it off? Again, it took time, it was a huge mass, and what would happen when that much rising steam hit a cold and already charged atmosphere? Rain was already sheeting down so thick it choked and blinded. Rain was already falling on mountains and pouring down to augment the disaster. And chemical changes would follow, and the biomass of all that lake of fish and algae and who knew what else would rot, doing further damage.

A vortex of wind, a tornado straight to the stratosphere? Worse and worse.

Break the spillway wider, try to lessen the abrupt force of the flood to come? The whole dam might go at once, *before* he was able to get people out of its path.

Everything he thought of was another disaster with increasingly outré events and ramifications. Water was coming through that gap while he hovered in doubt of what to do. When it cut loose it would come fast, one of those processes in nature that, once started, would operate so fast even he couldn't hope to stop it.

Superspeed was for only one thing, in this situation—for rushing down along that slope to the faint glow of life he'd passed on the way to the dam, a glow that shone like a firefly in the dark. Not an electric light in the place.

And no way to escape.

Life. Helpless life. He couldn't save the creatures of the mountain woods, those whose instincts would, if they were frightened at night and in the storm, lead them to burrow deeper. Their instincts to hide, ordinarily their salvation, would kill them tonight.

And there was nothing he could do to save the creatures that would hide and not run.

But for that brightest glow, that resolved from one glow into a huddle of firefly lights down the valley—for them, he could make a life-and-death difference.

He didn't land. He passed like a storm wind through the streets, pounded at every door fit to wake the dead—or those in danger of dying.

"Wake up!" he shouted to the winds and the mountain-side—in Russian, which in a region of languages he didn't speak he thought his best hope. "The dam is breaking! Danger! Come out, come out now!"

Doors opened, sending light out onto the puddled, rain-pocked ground. People had been asleep and stood amazed, sure-ly, at the unprecedented visitor in their street, a visitor who flew and paused and shouted at them about danger and the dam.

They understood. He saw the terrified glances toward a men-ace out of sight in the dark and the storm, hanging literally over their heads.

They began shouting at each other in a language among the fifty or so in the region he didn't know, and other doors opened to hails and shouts he couldn't understand. Villagers poured out of dimly lit houses, some struggling into coats and others car-rying and leading children. He saw a farm wagon sitting idle by a shed and snatched up a woman and a little girl and set them into the wagon bed, snatched up a man and did the same.

Then the villagers understood that was the way to safety, and almost as fast as he could pile them in, they were running and trying to board, ten, fifteen maybe, before he shoved the others back at superspeed, so quickly and so firmly they might not know what had pushed them.

He shouted in Russian, "I'll come back!" and "Wait!" and dived under the wagon and took off with it, not as fast or as high as he could fly. The wagon would never take it. But it was faster than that wagon had ever moved, for certain, and there were childish squeals and adult outcries from above him, some excited, some crying out in alarm and—he hoped, as wind hit his unstable load—holding on tight and keeping their heads down.

He dared not gain any altitude, for fear that one of his charges might take a fatal fall unnoticed. Dodging random trees and outcrops of rock, he scanned the dark for a safe spot to establish these people.

He found it at the edge of a high woods, above any threat of rushing water—set the wagon down and urged the villagers out, quickly, lifting down the ones that didn't immediately jump for the ground. They called out names to him, and he knew they were names of fathers, mothers, children.

"I'm hurrying!" he cried, and seized up the wagon and left again as fast as the wagon structure could bear.

Frightened people were still standing in the dark and the rain, believing his promise, bringing out far too many of their household goods, with their children, a struggling dog, a crate of pigs. He didn't have the ability to argue with them in their language. He just took whatever children and anxious relatives the wagon could safely hold and made another trip.

And a third. This trip an old man held a crate of rain-soaked chickens, and they went into the wagon. He had no time to argue with the man. Another man was trying to get a goat cornered. People came first, but he couldn't dissuade the ones with baggage or livestock in their arms. He just took the tightest-packed load he dared, carrying each wagonful to a growing knot of people on the edge of the forest, all huddled in what blankets they'd managed to save. By now they understood the drill and shouted to each other in their language, urging people to jump down, or get up, or whatever the situation required. He lost count of his trips. He thought there might be a hundred people.

But when he'd carried the last wagonload of people, something still seemed missing, to their distress. People pointed down the mountain, and said a word to him, and one young man tried very hard to tell him in broken English what he couldn't understand in the local dialect. Grandmother, he finally understood, in Russian, from a young woman. *Babushka!* And something about the village and a cow.

Someone was missing. Someone he hadn't saved. Someone had gone after livestock and was still in danger down there.

"I go with!" the young man cried in Russian, pulling at his arm, pointing into the storm-lashed heavens. "Go, go, go, please!"

He snatched the youth under one arm and jumped for the sky, shielding him from the bitter windchill and rain-choked breaths of his rapid course as best he could with his cape and his shoulder. The young man's clothes were immediately soaked, and his hands and feet, Superman was sure, must be chilled through by the time he reached a hovering stand above the threatened village.

"There, there!" the young man cried, pointing down. True enough, his own eyes saw the illusory glow of body warmth— two such glows, in fact, one quite large and four-footed, and one small, on two.

He whisked down onto the path in front of a rain-battered old woman leading a cow by a halter and trying to keep a coat and scarf about her.

"Nana!" the boy cried as they landed on the hillside among the trees. But the old woman clutched her shawl close as if fearing contagion or capture and refused his offers, if one could read the gestures, to lead the cow himself. She struck away his attempts to separate her from the rope, and no matter how strange or intimidating the caped, brightly clad figure involved in the process might seem to her, she would have no rescue, clearly, that did not also save the milk cow.

"Nana!" the youth pleaded, and won nothing.

There was no way to talk it through: the dam was failing. Superman expected it at any moment, and in a quick decision, he snatched up the young man and the old woman, each under an arm, and flew back to the gathering point with, to him, agonizing slowness and great gentleness. He was fearful of putting stress on the old woman's joints with any speed; and he was fearful, too, of crushing her, with her struggling and shouting and kicking all the way—blows that hit mostly the air and occasionally him.

A formidable woman, he thought, as to the cheers of the village he set foot on the ground and set down his two charges safe and sound.

But the old woman cried and struck at him with her stick and waved gestures down the mountain.

He was a farm boy himself. He understood. A howling blizzard came down on you and you got out in the pickup and carried feed to the cattle; you had a newborn calf in a driving cold rain and you carried that calf in your arms back to the house and warmed it by the kitchen stove.

And if you were an old farm woman with one single cow to your name you risked your neck and led that patient, unassuming creature the slow way up the mountain, no matter if your arthritis was aching and the rain chilled you and a flood was about to sweep you both away.

He knew, and he was instantly off into the night, this time as fast as he *could* move—because even Superman couldn't find a balance point on a scared wet cow with his bare hands.

He opened the shed door, grabbed up canvas and rope from inside, and scanned the area on his way up the hillside, looking for strays. There were loose chickens, a barking dog, a pony in its pen behind a house; and having taken note of their locations in the village, he went uphill fast, before a lost and confused cow could lose itself in the woods.

It had snagged its halter rope in the brush, and he jerked it free of that impediment. He slung the canvas under the cow's ribs, reinforced it with rope, and hauled the startled creature up the mountain with all the speed he could.

He set it down carefully and let it go to, he trusted, a grateful and happy old woman. Then he took his canvas sling and went back after the pony, which didn't want to be caught. But it had no choice, matched against superspeed and Superman's rising impatience to get downriver.

The whole village was glad to see the horse; and the mangled Russian-English converse he had with the soaked, shivering villagers assured him there were no outlying houses but Granny's, and no villages but those safely *above* the dam.

But livestock—there was precious livestock, there were treasured goods, there were appeals for help and for rescue of all they owned in the world.

If the dam should go this instant, he had confidence he'd lodged them high enough that no effects could reach them. It was sustenance they lacked—clothing, shelter, and the animals and their livelihoods, without which they were destitute.

So back he went down the threatened hillside, this time at a speed that launched a storm wind in the trees and rattled rocks loose on the hillside. He found feed sacks and bagged two pigs, and chickens, and finally caught the barking dog; he made trip after trip with animals shielded from the effects of his speed in sacking or, in the case of the dog, his cape.

He was asking himself all the while what he was going to do when the dam did break, simultaneously trying to think of answers and keeping an ear out for what he feared he'd hear at any moment: the thunder of all that water let loose.

But he had his next load lined up and he had the gratitude of his rain-soaked refugees to encourage him. He made a reckless last dive downhill with the wagon and set it down in the midst of the village.

Then he visited every house so quickly he *did* do damage, and piled on the wagon bed every piece of canvas and rope he could find, axes, kitchen knives, jewel boxes, bowls, pots, and food, everything of use he could drag out of the houses, right down to matches, quilts, and a couple of hoes and a shovel.

In one house, where the kitchen fire was still burning, he found a wooden box full of kittens and under the kitchen stove a mama cat who took great exception to a stranger and more exception to being caught.

But just then came a strange rumble that might have been thunder. He shoved the frantic cat in with the kittens, wrapped the whole box up in a tattered quilt, and whisked his wagonload, cats, kittens and all, up the mountain as the rumble continued.

It was a last load of everything a farm boy from America's heartland thought other farmers might most want to save . . . and a last living prize in the lot that someone might be glad to see.

He reached the villagers. Just as he set his load down, the roar he'd dreaded came rolling up out of the valley, the dark down there turned boiling white, and a chilling spray came up at them despite the rain as the ground itself shook. The villagers cried out in shock.

A herd of deer rushed past them, panic-stricken, saving their lives. The horse bolted a distance away and stopped in confusion. To Superman's vision, perhaps to that of others, the boil of water down in the valley, the length of a football field below them, became a thing of strange, lacy beauty, as the flaw in the dam became a general collapse.

Superman leapt for the sky and chased that wave front of death and destruction, flying in the dark and the chaos along its leading edge, looking for life in its path; but the rumbling in the earth warned wildlife into an unlikely flight into the dark. He saw a trio of deer—he thought they were deer—leaping along the valley road and up the slope, and hoped they made it.

The white line of destruction roared and rumbled behind him; and in an instant there was no village. There was only seething white where the village had stood.

No more land, no more fences, no more woods. A plume of water maybe thirty, forty feet high went shooting up above the flood where the deluge hit a spire of rock.

He dived through that plume on his way down the valley. The bridge vanished as he watched, just vanished under the boiling white torrent. The road that led to the bridge was inundated, maybe eroded utterly, he couldn't tell and didn't wait to see. He flew in a burst of speed so great it warmed his skin. The flood surge was restrained only by the friction of water over the land and the resistance, however brief, of obstacles, and he outflew that mile-a-minute rush of water as it pursued a crooked course ten, maybe twenty miles to the lake below.

How did one protect the next dam? The hydroelectric dam had had the floodgates open, preparing the lake to receive the spate of rain and spillage from the dam above. He had that leeway to work with.

He spotted the lights of a little watchman's station at the side of the floodgate. This dam was at least three times the size of the one that had failed, with maybe—*maybe*—a chance to hold the tree-toothed monster that was coming.

He landed in front of the office and knocked—incongruous act—at a door that wouldn't receive many visitors. The blare of music inside ceased. Possibly the gatekeeper was taking time to tidy up, in fear of a supervisor pulling a surprise inspection. He bashed the door with the flat of his hand and broke the latch, bursting it from its hinges.

The watchman saw him appear out of the dark and rain, a bright red and blue figure that the man had never, for certain, seen before.

"I'm Superman." He made his two-word introduction in Russian and pointed up toward the higher valley. "The dam has gone."

"Gone?" It was not a stupid question. The language interface wasn't a good one here, any more than with the villagers. Clearly Russian wasn't this man's language. But the man, maybe in his forties, mimed a structure falling flat.

"Yes," Superman confirmed and kept his word choice down to the absolute simplest terms. "The dam has broken. Telephone! Quickly! Tell the people, tell the town, tell the other dams!"

The man might have asked if he'd dropped in from Mars. That Superman was known throughout the world didn't necessarily include a power station in the Caucasus any more than it had included that village up there.

But, white-faced, primed and ready to believe implicitly in this particular disaster, the man snatched the telephone and called someone in a spate of the local language, not panic, but urgency trembling in every syllable.

Then he pushed a button, and a siren blared out into the night.

That sound had to be an authorized warning, reaching everyone in town at once. Summoning help. Warning the dams downstream.

Superman's acute attention was on the map on the wall, a contour map. He could see villages designated, he could see two other small towns downstream that were definitely in danger if this second dam went. The gatekeeper was talking urgently with someone on the phone, and Superman looked with equal urgency for any place hinted at in the contour lines of that map to divert the disaster that was going to hit this dam in a massive surge.

There was no such place visible, even on this detailed a scale.

The watchman had put the phone down and said something beyond Superman's fluency. The man was afraid for his life. That took no guesswork. The dam would hold now or it would not. This man, probably the operator of the floodgate, had staunchly come up here, held his post, and made his call of warning to the towns downriver.

And could do nothing more.

Superman didn't wait. He flung an edge of his cape about the man, against speed and windchill, snatched the man's coat off the peg by the door, and whisked him out the door and through the night at all the speed he judged the man could bear as far as the first lights of the town.

From there, the man was on his own, on two feet, and in reach of shelter and telephones.

Superman still had time left before that deadly wave broke out of its valley and surged across the lake. He leapt for the air, climbed through the storm and above the dam, searching the far distance across the lake for any sign of the disaster. But it was a wide lake—the best hope of all the dams to sustain the flood surge. Here, the ruin of one small dam was pouring down on a vastly bigger one.

If a piece of debris, some log traveling on the force of that surge, didn't follow the outflowing current straight for this dam's vulnerable crest, it could knock a hole in it.

If *that* happened, then a disaster of twice the scope was going to pour down on the dam below this one, which would have far less chance of withstanding the onslaught. He only hoped the officials the man had called would sound the civil defense warnings downstream without clearing it with higher-ups in the capital; and he couldn't guarantee that would be the case. If there was no evacuation, and if this dam failed, there would be human tragedy on a vaster scale: lost homes, lost businesses and farms.

He had to hold it here. This time, with a sound dam to work with, he had to *stop* a destructive force that came—he could see it now in the distance, at the other end of the large lake—not as a towering wall, but as a line like a ripple proceeding across the lake, deceptively calm.

He didn't have a map for the topography of the land beneath the lake, the land before the dams were built. If it shelved, if there was a submerged rock, the wave might break and go chaotic before it hit the dam. In the narrows of the valley the flood would have been a high, white froth that would skim at a mile a minute over the surface of the slower water of the river, a swiftly moving storm of air and water scouring trees and boulders from the valley walls.

At this point, the floodwater having hit the lake edge, it was less traveling water than traveling force: that hump in the lake was all the terrible force of the incoming water shoving lake water up into a moving wave. With the wind at its back for good measure, that wave was coming right toward the dam, where irresistible force would meet man-made object, and if that wave was too high, it would overtop the crest. If an overflow started, floating debris, whole trees, would be sucked along toward the dam. If the force of the breaking wave failed to damage the crest, the hammering impact of debris would finish the job.

There wasn't leverage to use against a mile-wide wave. But *this* concrete and steel, at this dam, being sound, uncompromised—it *could* hold, if no wave topped it. If it held, the debris would travel more slowly, and the floodgate wasn't at the crest on this hydroelectric dam, but low, where it wouldn't jam with floating debris.

The lake level being down, thanks to the engineers, ten feet of algae-blackened concrete showed behind the dam crest, marking where the water had stood before they took that precaution. That meant the lake could absorb ten feet of water; and ten feet in acre-feet, water spread out over all the surface of the lake and surrounding shore, was very meaningful indeed. The lake in the valley above, behind the dam that had failed, hadn't been as deep, or as wide.

And with a lift of his spirits, Superman saw in that set of circumstances not a sure thing, but a fighting chance—for a man who wasn't an engineer, wasn't a mathematician, wasn't a scientist, but who knew enough to know that for every action there was an equal and opposite reaction.

For every displacement of matter by *his* body, the substance he displaced had to go somewhere; and if he hit something liquid very fast, the force would dissipate in a . . .

Wave.

Hit the lake dead-on, and he'd generate a wave in all directions from his point of impact. But not to hit the water at all was a better idea . . . remembering how the direction of the wind had complicated the problems of the dam above.

He shot skyward like a rocket. And dived for the rain-scarred waves with hands locked in front of him, as fast as he could fly.

Pulled up just short of the surface and rose, rose, rose; and accelerated all the way until he came down at a speed that sent his bow shock into the teeth of the wind and against the crest of that deadly oncoming ripple. He was tempted to watch what he *thought* would happen, but he repeated the plunge, hammering the water again and again and again with a fist of air until he saw the shock meet the wave, until water plumed white and high into the lightning-lit dark.

Then he hung in midair, amazed by the sight he'd wrought and watching to be sure the wave followed the line he thought it would.

A grin broke out on his face. The wave was continuing to break as if two opposing lines of surf had met belly-to-belly, a white line proliferating in symmetry to either hand.

It wasn't stopped, not yet. But against a monster made of water he'd thrown up a wall of like substance, a wall capable of absorbing the shock so that, checked of its momentum at its entry into the lake, the monster had to drop its weapons of sharp-edged debris. And now, like a mob with its forward motion blocked, what had been a moving hump of water was a moiling confusion of eddies impeding its own path.

Smallville High and high school physics were in his mind: the little frame with the swinging balls, click, click, click. There'd be a gouge on the lake floor as there'd been a plume in the air: the force had to go somewhere, and it had gone. Now his circling hammerblows at the water could come at greater intervals, slow rise to admire his own handiwork, then a burst of downward speed that sent another wave proliferating down into the lake bed and into the path of the oncoming water. Thump! Whump! And thump again.

He kept up his assault on the flood coming in, until the distant shores of the lake showed white as the wave kicked up and broke—doing damage to fishing boats, perhaps. There was a village on the far shore that might have suffered flood damage to its waterfront as that wave broke. But without loss of life. The debris would drop where the fast-moving flood hit the still waters of the lake. Floating debris was a problem. But the dam would survive. Even the fish would.

So would people in the towns below this one.

And Superman could let go a sigh, hanging rain-drenched and still overheated above a living lake.

Chapter 3

T hat's right, that's right . . . they're clear."
Firemen were on the scene now, and Lois,
sitting on a slanted concrete slab in the
bowels of the ruin, drew back to catch her breath,
grimy fingers clenched on her cell phone. She had
a link to the parents of Gene Pratt, who were listening to LNN, and was acutely aware that Billy's
parents were listening, too. The first boy was in the
hands of firemen passing him toward the stairs in
the flare of emergency lights. Gene had cried out
when he came free, but he had come out with no
damage but a broken leg.

And firemen were trying to see, now that Gene's
body wasn't blocking their view, what Billy's situation was.

"They're getting Gene up toward the stairs now.
He's awake and talking." Crying, but she wasn't
going to alarm parents whose nerves had been
through enough, or embarrass a boy who'd been
brave throughout. And after the pain he'd been
through, getting through the narrow opening,
Gene was as brave as you could ask of a kid.

"They've been very brave kids. They're lifting Gene now. They're passing him from hand to hand toward the stairs . . ."

Where she'd been, she could barely fit herself in, had to stoop even to sit here, in the tunnel of slabs and cars, and firemen had stripped off protective gear to be able to reach and widen the opening to get Gene out.

"Are you still in touch with the other boy?" the voice from LNN wanted to know.

"Yes." She kept her answers generally short. She tried to stay out of the way of the firemen, but they signaled that they needed her now, and she tucked the phone into her muddy purse, got down, and inched toward the hole on elbows and hip.

She accepted a sealed light they took forward when they worked up there—a light she'd established for them once before, and which they'd had to move back out of the hole in order to get Gene out.

Now they needed it put back, and none of them could get up to the hole.

"I'll try to see," she told the fireman who put it in her hand. He gave her a fire department mike and an earpiece which she fitted in her ear.

They wanted her to look for what she could see, not—they'd said emphatically when they'd accepted her help in the first place—to move rock. They'd dug, with rods, with the fullest stretch of their fingers, scraping out compacted dust, while concrete sifted down above them. They'd shored up the big slab over them: that had taken a long, careful effort. Maybe ten minutes ago they'd let her take a rescue rope in as far as the hole.

She'd done it, because widening the tunnel to get a man in could endanger the boys. She stayed because no rescue personnel they could call on was smaller, no one else could fit the area they had to reach, and she and the firemen had long passed by the argument of a civilian in danger. Now, in getting that essential light back to the second boy, who remained trapped in total dark when that light was withdrawn, she'd reached another point of her usefulness.

She got onto her knees, took their light and a rope as well as her bundled raincoat, and flattened down as she wormed her way to that narrow opening. She bunched up her coat for an armrest (the position she held when she was most of the way in was excruciating otherwise) and crawled along the rubble.

Nobody, not the firemen and not the EMTs, could hope to fit through that child-sized opening—just one cold and soggy reporter, in a situation that, over the last hour, had become critical. And her faint hope was that, if Gene's small body had dragged any dirt with him on his way out, maybe she could get a look at the second boy when she delivered the light to the hole.

Gene, Mike, Andy—and Billy—the boys were all eight years old. They were in town for the soccer clinic. They'd been the first team to check into the hotel—and the scope of the disaster that might have occurred even two hours later, after noon, was horrifying. The hotel had been in its morning lull, yesterday's guests mostly gone or about town on business, the weekend clinic guests yet to come. Hundreds of kids of like age were scheduled to be here by now but, LNN had said, were being turned back and advised of the catastrophe, and kids were phoning home to anxious parents, giving them reassurance.

This carload had come in maybe an hour early. One father—also a coach—had been upstairs at the reception desk, with his kid. *They'd* made it out. Two people behind the desk hadn't been so lucky. But they didn't tell the kids down here how bad it was up there—or tell them anything but good news about their teammates: they're safe, they'd say, and name names the trapped boys knew, keeping their spirits up. "They're cheering for you," she'd said to Gene when she'd delivered the rope. "I've got your parents on the phone. And your team—your team wants you to beat this one. All right? You tie this on, and we'll get you out."

"Yeah," Gene had said, small fingers reaching for the rope. "Yeah."

Gene was safe now, relatively unharmed. Beautiful kid. Parents were coming from New Jersey, probably breaking speed limits all the way. *This* kid was the question mark. Gene had blocked their view of his situation. Gene had tried his best and couldn't move the rock he said had caught Billy. And Billy was in the dark, alone now. What could a kid think, alone, in this dreadful place, his friends all gone?

Her body chilled fast on the concrete. You never knew where mud came from in places like this, but there was mud, maybe just waterlogged concrete dust, maybe stuff that had boiled up as dust when the building came down. She used her knees and feet to drive her to the opening, into which she shone the vital light. It lit the edges of concrete, the sagging web of rebar holding back tons of concrete overhead.

"Billy?"

"Ms. Lane?" She heard a weak, frightened voice, faint, very faint, above the persistent sound of water that reminded them it was still raining outside. Water seeped down the walls from the riven roof and made a small lake Gene had reported, but they hadn't been able to see past him.

"Where are you?" She couldn't find him with the light.

From here it was maybe eight feet sloping down the rubble to the side, the light down there showing her bent metal, the side of a tire, and the edges of concrete slabs.

And when she set the light through the hole onto the place where Gene had been lying and wriggled forward to get her head and one arm through, she could see to the left and down into the blackness. Her faint light shone on muddy water.

In that water, almost hidden by two huge slabs of concrete, a boy's pale face looked desperately up at her, flinching from the glare after the deep dark he'd been in.

"Billy, can you crawl up to me?"

A despairing shake of Billy's head, that immediately dropped in weariness and weakness toward the water. She could see one shoulder above the surface, Billy's left side. His right, and the lower half of his body, were in water-drowned rubble, deeply shadowed by those two tilted slabs.

Came another thump. A sound of concrete sliding. It happened now and again. The ruin was settling.

"Ms. Lane," said a voice in her earpiece, "get out of there. Get back. Now."

Billy's head lifted. His face grimaced in a fierce effort to pull his lower body up. It wasn't working. The kid was scared and hurting, she could see it.

More dust sifted down and made a pale film on the dirty water.

"Back off, back off," a live voice called through the opening. "Ms. Lane, move back. We're going to have to move nonessential personnel out of here for safety's sake."

"Who's going to reach him?" They were back at the "all civilians out" argument. She thought they'd passed that point.

And she foresaw, after she was clear, a more desperate, disruptive attempt coming on the part of the firemen. After this they'd have no choice but to move the rock that was so precariously balanced above a pale, frightened kid with his face half in the water. She could see him so close, and the hole was wider than it had been.

The firemen couldn't get to this point. They couldn't see what she saw. "Look, I think I can get past the opening. I can see Billy. I've got the rope. He'll fit going out if I fit going in, and then you don't have to move that rock! There's water down here. I don't know how fast it's coming in, but we haven't got a lot of time!"

She knew moving any rock was a point of controversy, and something they didn't want to do. It required meticulous planning and shoring up that took a lot of time—time in which the whole ruin could collapse on the kid and them or the cold alone could kill him. She didn't want to raise and dash the kid's hopes. She didn't know whether in fact she could even get through the opening. She heard objections in her earpiece and felt a fireman's cautioning hand on her ankle, but that hand didn't pull her back: the man just behind her, the only one who could haul her back, gave her leg an encouraging pat, a tacit go-ahead, go now. *Move!* He was on her side, and maybe with that shifting of concrete a moment ago the whole effort was a heartbeat removed from the fire chief telling all of them to get out, leave it to a smaller crew. And more time. And delay the boy couldn't survive.

She went. She kicked and squirmed forward, advanced shoulder and left ribs through as she held and protected the lamp—caver's maneuver. She'd learned a little of the art, in the way being a reporter mandated learning all sorts of odd things. One-handed, she stuffed the coat back to the side of the opening, out of the way of her ribs on the other side, then used her rib cage like a snake's, used elbows, and once she had them free, used knees, for as long as she had them free. The light silk blouse she wore offered no friction to the rock, and she slid more and more deeply into the hole.

She got all the way in—couldn't raise her head until she'd gotten further down the slope where Gene had lain facing the other direction. Then she propped the lantern in the rubble where it could throw light on the slope. In the cavity walled by fallen concrete and smashed cars she slithered down over the edges of rough concrete and jutting rebar in the rubble to the pool of water where Billy was.

"Ms. Lane?" she heard from behind her.

"I'm there, I've reached him." She held out a hand. Billy gripped it with chilled fingers and anxious strength. "Billy. I can get a rope. Can you get it with both hands? Can you get the loop down over your shoulders?"

"I can't," came the breathless, shaky answer. "I can't get my arm up."

"That's all right. Can I just take your hand and pull?"

"You can try."

She did try. It cost the kid pain. His upper body moved, stretched . . . but the lower body didn't. It hurt the kid. It hurt a lot. He dropped his head cheek-down in the rising water and then lifted it and looked her in the eyes with a dreadful, honest fear.

"I'm in a lot of trouble," he said. "Aren't I?"

"We'll get you out." She wasn't so sure of the promise, but she made it with everything she had. "There's ten firemen out there. There's police, there's ambulances. They're not going to go away until we get you out of here. All right?" Brisk and businesslike. Keep the kid cooperating and don't give him time to be afraid. "Where are you stuck? What's holding you?"

"I don't know. I can't feel my feet."

She reported the situation back, the water, the trap the kid was in. "I think one leg is pinned to the knee, probably the other. He's lively, strong—" She didn't know if her fingers could feel a pulse if they asked for it; they'd want to know whether that leg was crushed, and without scaring Billy, she gave them information that might tell them she didn't think so. "He's in water up to his chin, kind of standing, kind of lying down. I'm going to reach down under the surface and see if I can feel what's holding him."

They waited. She daren't soak the mike. She took it and the earpiece off—reached down along Billy's body, underwater, and found loose rubble, some of which she could move.

"Kind of a mess, isn't it?" Her face was inches from Billy's, upside down to him. The water was cold and smelled foul. She tried to make a joke of their plight. "But I think I can clear some of it." She came up with a piece to prove it to the boy, one as big as she could lift.

"Yay," Billy murmured, as enthusiastically as he could, but didn't lift his head.

It took a moment after that to pick up the microphone and earpiece and talk to the fire department about the situation.

"I'm trying to move my foot," Billy said when she'd relayed that. "I still can't move."

"We'll get you out."

"Yeah." He was brave, he was steady as a kid could be who was about to drown in muddy water. They were getting a mask and air hose. That was the next step.

But the medic out there, who didn't fit through the hole, was talking to her now about hypothermia. He didn't need to. The water was cold. Bitter cold, and she was in it and soaked, herself. Billy's skin was like ice. That might kill the kid as surely as the water would.

A pebble from overhead thunked down into the water.

She crawled back up to the opening. The rope she'd brought in had dragged her raincoat onto the rubble slope, and she retrieved it. She slithered back down to Billy, wrapped her raincoat into a tight bundle, and shoved it under Billy's head to keep it out of the water.

She started working, one arm braced on a rock above the water, one below it, feeling for anything she could move in the rubble, both fine grit and massive chunks, that had tumbled around him. Her fingers were already numb from the cold. They'd told her not to disturb rocks. But she had to. She brought up handfuls of gritty muck, fist-sized chunks, anything she could reach. The muck itself, compacted by the water, seemed set like concrete about the kid's leg.

"Ms. Lane?" That was a new voice. From the opening. "Jenny Whitmore, EMT. I don't know if I can make it in there. It's pretty tight."

There was a woman up by the lantern. She had help, Lois thought for a moment, and then saw the woman had made it in only as far as the waist and might not—a woman's shape—make it further.

"I'm trying to move rocks," Lois said to the EMT. "He's wedged in by stuff. I'm trying not to pull anything that's a prop, but I haven't got any place to put it, it's just so tight in here." Almost like a fish swimming, she worked small rock back past her body to a clear spot, a ledge, where she was setting rock and dumping muck.

"I can't make it through," Jenny said in distress. And a male voice, after, "That slab there is holding all this up. It's not one we can mess with."

"She's moving the rock out," Jenny said quietly. "I'll carry it out if you get full up down there. —Ma'am, can you take a pulse rate?"

"I can't feel anything in my hands. —Billy? Billy, stay awake, all right?"

The adrenaline had run out for him. Given the coat to rest his head on, he'd stopped struggling so hard, and he was pale as wax, eyes shut, resting with his chin just touching the muddy water. But his eyelids fluttered when she spoke his name. "I'm here," he said faintly. "I'm not so cold, now."

They couldn't get a pump in. She heard them talking about that. The only exit for the water was the same way they had to get in, and it was a choice between the outtake hose and her in the way, and now Jenny. She wasn't part of the consultation. She worked, and heard snatches of it. They could pump water or they could have someone in here trying to get the kid out, and that was the choice they had to make.

"His condition's deteriorating," she heard Jenny say, and she patted Billy's shoulder. "They're not talking about you. You're doing fine. Just hang on for me, all right? Don't let me down, Billy. I need you to tell me if you feel anything."

She found chunks of rock to pull, marble-sized, golf-ball-sized, anything she could get, and submerged her face and dug with both hands until her head felt as if it would explode. She used her midsection muscles to hold and lift, blew bubbles to keep the water out of her nose as she felt the edges of the next big one, and wondered whether it would bring collapse if she pulled it.

Jenny couldn't get her hips through the hole. A desk-sitting reporter who fought herself to a size-three couturier fashion, who *didn't* scale ladders or leap tall buildings at a single bound . . . *she* fit in a place where, she began to realize, even Superman couldn't reach. She had, with her small hands and sense of what would give and what wouldn't, to move the rubble delicately enough to prevent its collapse on a kid whose injuries she began to fear were more than broken bones.

And she wanted this kid, she wanted him not to fade away, she wanted to live to get out of this hole and she wanted Billy to live. *She* was going to get married. *She* had Clark. *She* had a life. She had a future. This kid had all his years in front of him. It wasn't fair. They were immortal, the odds were stacked for the young and the ones with a future . . . they couldn't die.

But they died, every day, on wedding days, on fifth birthdays, on school trips . . . it was her job to report such facts. She couldn't ignore them entirely, for herself or for this boy.

Move that rock. Keep talking to the kid, talking to Jenny, to the firemen . . . it didn't matter. Piece by piece, risk by risk. The rock shifted, she got one piece out and more rolled down and a slab grated and shifted, freezing her heart.

It stopped. She kept moving pieces.

The water had been below Billy's chin as his face lay against the pillow she'd made him. Now her coat as well as the top of the slab he was lying on were underwater. It was getting deeper, not rapidly, but steadily. She had to prop his head higher, wedge a rock in or something.

Had to get him out of here. Couldn't feel anything in her hands. But fingers still closed, joints still worked. The cold numbed the pain. Jenny talked to her, asked her questions.

She ducked her head and hauled, hard, on a rock wedged beside Billy's leg. It was that big rock, heavy, so heavy her fingers slipped on it, and she was going to drop it down in the water again and it would slosh other rocks out of place at the bottom and bring the whole underwater pile down that she'd just dug out, trapping Billy right back the way he'd been and maybe worse. She applied English to lifting the rock, she shifted its center of balance as she lifted, and as first her head and shoulders and then that rock reached the surface of the water where it suddenly weighed far more, she twisted her body and shoved it for the shallows, shoved it up and up the slope of the tilted slab and crawled until she could get it aimed toward Jenny. Didn't want to set it where she'd set the little stuff . . . little stuff if it got knocked back in could settle and grip like set concrete.

"Big one," she said, shoving to keep it braced, and Jenny, who'd worked herself around so everything but her hips came through: "I've got it. I've got it."

It was just one rock. All around them was rock. And she had to maneuver herself back to her vantage beside Billy, and reach down the slanted slab into the deep water where his legs were and try to move another, just as heavy.

"Come on, Billy, don't go to sleep on me."

She couldn't feel what she was doing. But her numb hand met stone, closed around it, and hauled that out, raked it into reach of her left hand and that hand set it aside in the shallows.

Another big one. Defeat trembled in her, welled up in her throat and stung her eyes and counseled quit; but that meant backing out, away from that sleeping face and letting the dark close around him.

That thought sent her hand questing down, down around that impossible rock, and then—then pull, pull, *pull!* and don't think of having fingers: the rock is all, and it moves, and the arm feels the weight and draws it up and up along Billy's leg, in the water . . . and the surface will come, where it weighs more . . .

Turn the wrist, aim and shove and no matter how it hurts, *shove* that rock aside to the shallows, make it go, keep it from falling back.

"Another big one, Jenny. You ready? It's trying to roll back in. I'm going to crawl up with it."

"I'm here." Jenny came and went in the opening. But she was there now, as Lois twisted to get the rock passed along her side and into Jenny's reach.

Lois squirmed back into position with Billy. And somehow the lantern near Jenny came dislodged, skidded down past her numb elbow and went underwater. Its unblinking yellow eye moved beneath the brown film of water, and moved, and moved as it slid down past Billy, and dropped away, winking out in the dark below the water.

Unthinking, she grabbed Billy, perceiving suddenly that there was deep water and deep dark and they were both in blackness. She held him in her arms in the grip of nightmare, and she pulled.

And this time his body moved as she pulled.

"Lois?" Jenny's voice was concerned. "Get me a light, somebody, get me a light, the lantern's gone."

There was light. There was shadow and light, illusory shifting about, wild flaring as Jenny moved the light someone gave her; but numb arms had their prize, weary body had its reward, a living boy, free, as Lois pulled him up the slanted slab that had been his resting place and backed inch by aching inch toward freedom.

"Ms. Lane?" she heard from Billy. He was so much weaker, but he held onto her, and she hurt him, she couldn't help it. He was trying not to cry out, but he was losing his breath, and she smoothed his hair with cold muddy hands and hugged him and dragged him back and back, herself hanging head down on the slope as she pulled him after.

"I've got him!" she cried, not quite believing it herself. "I've got him! I'm coming out!"

Hands grasped her feet, her calves, as she backed, gripped her lower legs and pulled, gently, caringly, providing her an easier exit than she would have had. She had to slip her grip to Billy's arms to get him through the eye of the needle gap that was the gateway to the living world, but he came through easily, so small a boy, so wonderful at the moment she could first lift her head from that narrow space and pull him to her.

"Easy, easy," voices said—one she thought was Jenny's. They pried her cold hands off his arms. They carefully lifted him away and laid him on a stretcher they'd brought down in hope of a rescue. They had the light. She glimpsed the glare of white sheet, of yellow inflatable splints, through a wall of dark, over-coated bodies. Light touched the firemen, the EMTs with their blue parkas.

There was no room there for her. She was ice cold. Her body felt as if she'd run ten miles. She was sitting still on the cold rubble and saw her purse. She dragged it to her, remembering the phone and the parents. She flipped it open and managed to hit redial.

"This is Lois Lane," she said, and heard the same voice she'd been hearing on that phone.

"*Yes*, Lois! What's happening?"

"We've got him out," she said, and it was fantastic to her as she said it. "I got a rock free, and I lifted it up out of the water . . ." She hadn't given them all the information about the rising water. She steadied her voice, regulated her breathing. "There was water coming up, almost to his face. I set a rock where it braced his head and I pulled the rocks free under the water and we got him out. The EMTs are with him, and the fire depart-ment. Jenny Whitmore is a fire department medic. She was passing the rocks back that I'd pass to her. We just couldn't get anybody into that crawl space . . . but he's awake. They're going to carry him up the slope . . ."

She could see them starting to do that. They'd gotten an IV started and Jenny Whitmore, covered in mud and coatless, was carrying that. They must have laid a lantern on the stretcher, because there was light coming from Billy's white sheets, like some painting of angels, a vignette in the dark.

She wasn't sure she could get up, but she got a knee under her and managed it, hugging her purse against her.

"Were you able to talk to Billy?" LNN wanted to know.

"During all of it. He'd do what I asked him . . ." Her voice shook. She was about to embarrass herself professionally and trained her misting eyes just on the dark and the figures ahead of her as she climbed. Distance. Distance. Distance. She wasn't going to go teary eyed. "He's a brave kid."

She reached the level floor, realizing it was the departure of the light and the object of her story that had drawn her like a moth, too exhausted, too witless to realize what instinct drove her. But the firemen were waiting for her at the steps, and one was behind her. One offered a hand under her elbow, and she needed it to climb. "Good job," the fireman said, and in one corner of her reeling mind she was immensely flattered by that, from these men, from these very brave men and women whose job it was to come into places like this—routinely, on city pay; and on another level she felt intensely sorry for herself, sorry because she hadn't gotten a chance to go with Billy, and sorry because they'd pushed her aside, as they'd had to, for Billy's sake. The kid was hurt, and she didn't want to speculate how badly, but she'd had to pull and drag at him and put stress on his insides, and that scared her.

He couldn't die. Not now. Not after all this.

She climbed to the top of the stairs and walked out into the shattered foyer, in the glare of what she supposed were emergency lights.

The darkness beyond those lights shocked her. She remembered the lobby in daylight, and here was dark beyond blinding floodlights, and the red and blue strobe of emergency vehicles.

Human figures moved in silhouette around those lights, but the dusty, mud-streaked floor was clear except for the cables snaking across the broken glass and the dust.

Sawhorse barriers and yellow police tape were outside. Emergency lights on tripods. The group of firemen with Billy reached the street. Pavement under their feet glistened in the strobing red of a waiting ambulance, and the rear doors opened, blazing with cleanliness and white light. They put Billy into that ambulance and she reported the fact on the cell phone as she tried to walk through the police barrier, following as close as she could get.

People surged toward her. Microphones and lights came into her face.

"Lois Lane!" one shouted at her. "Lois Lane!" the cry went out, and the microphones pressed closer in the hands of a living wall of reporters, cameras and their attendant lights turning the whole world to black and white.

She let the hand with the cell phone fall, and flipped it shut with the distraught feeling that somehow she'd known her reports were going out over the air.

But this . . . this overwhelmed her.

For about two beats. Until she'd gotten a breath and the habit of thinking in newsmode kicked in. It wasn't a keyboard in front of her, but it was the news, and it was her story, and she had the information to get out.

She tucked the phone into her purse, raked a sore and muddy hand through wet hair, and sorted a question out of the din of questions being shouted at her, and sorted the camera that belonged to that voice out of the dozen cameras focused on her.

"What was it like down there?"

What was it *like* down there? What was it like to have pulled life out of so much destruction? She was soaked from head to foot, covered in mud, and she knew that answer.

It was a challenge to a reporter to steady the voice down, arrange the images in a coherent way, and to *do* what she did as competently as she could.

"Nyet!" was the emphatic answer from the old woman with the formidable cane. "Nyet, nyet, *nyet!*" That was her answer, faced with the prospect of going down the mountain: one firm sylla-ble of the language they didn't have in common.

It was daylight. The scope of the disaster was evident in the abrupt ending of their hillside in a muddy gorge below, where the river that had fed the high lake now carved a new channel through mud and devastation.

And if the villagers had thought of going down to the town beyond the hydroelectric dam, of being ferried down by air as Superman would have to carry them, now they began to waver, and to look at each other and then to shake their heads and dis-miss any idea of deserting their mountainside, their woods. They stood in the dismal morning rain, having tied the little canvas they had to the trees to make shelters for the weakest and the smallest—a mother with a newborn, and the littlest girl with the cat and kittens.

But Granny didn't count herself among the weakest, and cer-tainly her opinion carried weight.

"Nyet," she said again and again. And something the young man translated into Russian as *ours, our land.* As the cane came down solidly on the earth.

Superman could stop a wall of water and turn back a flood. But deal with an old farm woman who didn't (he knew enough to muddle out the gist of her objection) intend to leave her cow, her hillside, her woods, or her neighbors? No.

What was more, he knew the old woman. Oh, not so much as her name, but he knew her in his own mother Martha, and his father Jonathan, and the things they'd taught him by personal example. He understood the source of her strength. She drew it out of the earth, out of the rocks of her mountain, a close-to-the-earth endurance that said that cattle got let out to pasture at sunup and milked at sunset and that *not* to do these simple things was a breach of faith with the sun and the moon and the planet itself.

Not that his mother, his father, or the granny in immediate defiance of him would put it quite that way. But a young man who'd lived by those rhythms, and by means of them learned about the planet to which he'd come as a stranger, couldn't argue with Granny that their lives and their health would be equally well served by transporting them away from their livestock and their land. It wouldn't be served by that at all, to impoverish them and set them in the hands of well-meaning strangers. And all of them on this hillside knew it.

The three villages above this one, whose houses had not been threatened by the flood but whose fields and pastures surrounded a lake which no longer existed—they knew it, he was well sure. Hard times were going to come here, hard times in which a local government cut loose from Moscow and already strapped for cash wasn't going to find it easy to rebuild the roads that had been completely wiped off the map, let alone deal with the ecological devastation and the distrust of the people.

It wasn't just that these people were cut off from the twentieth century. They'd never been quite *in* the twentieth century. And there was no longer reliable water, no longer electricity, no longer a bridge to enable them to cross to the lower valley road.

But maybe of all the people who could have been stranded in this remote valley, these people had the greatest chance of recovering the land.

The horse nickered softly. The chickens probably slept in the dark, in their crates. The pigs—he had no idea. But dumping these brave and steadfast people into the custody of agencies in town wasn't going to be the answer for them or for the land.

Getting their government to act and getting help and necessary supplies up here was a priority. And this wasn't the most politically stable area in the world. It was rife with ethnic troubles. Distrust? It was everywhere, on this side of the river, on the other, he was virtually certain.

"Tell them all," he said to the young man, Dimitri, who was his only translator, "I'm going to talk to the Red Cross. I'll get you tents. Food and water. A few days. It will be a few days. Can you live here? Will you be safe here?"

"Da," the young man said, and turning to the villagers, he said something far more extensive than that, a torrent of words that brought hope to the weary, desperate faces, hope and enthusiastic nods of heads.

He didn't think that it was an exact translation. He feared they expected miracles. But he'd do what he could.

Get to a phone. There weren't any here. The world had made itself a network of electronic nerves, but it operated most efficiently if one reached a nerve center. Tbilisi was on the other side of the mountains. Grozny—in Chechnya, to the north—was still reeling from war. He wasn't that fluent, and the lingering politics were a maze into which he was himself reluctant to deliver these people.

Istanbul, Geneva, Zurich, maybe, had an answer, and fewer language barriers. It depended on how fast he flew. "I'll be back," he said, and lifted into the air, faster and faster, until the rain was a river in the sky, a river from which he rose into mist and then into the cold clear presence of a sun trying to chase away the stars.

But it wasn't Superman trying to solve the problems of the village now, it was the Kents' son—it was Clark, thinking through his options, as a newsman charged with a responsibility to get the news out, and to get the news to those who most needed to know—

News to the organizations with the logistical capability to organize and move supply to a place so cut off and devastated: the Red Cross had already been working in the region since the earthquake. It already had, like an army, command and control set up and operating that would make communication far faster—it would know the availability of scarce supplies and it would have an idea of priorities already in place. It would have maps, and know it couldn't rely on the roads.

That was one thing. But without the news getting out to the general public, to the world at large, the best-run, most resourceful relief organization in the world couldn't help these people. The public had to know, had to have its conscience touched, had to respond with compassion and funds, or there would be no supplies to deliver.

Geneva was a patch of lights on a dark but dawning landscape as he streaked over: the Red Cross, based there, never slept.

But a newsman's sudden instinct kept him flying . . . for a city with a newspaper read around the world, for a city with contacts Superman had used before to get information out. He knew London phone numbers and the London phone system intimately, he knew various addresses; and since it was deeper night here, he even had a hope of finding the top end of that list of reporters at home, in bed—asleep, but he'd be forgiven.

He sped along the Thames with a rush that riffled the dark water, until he reached not a quiet street but a thoroughfare and a public phone where a card, among a scant few he carried, gave him access. A few cabs prowled the streets in the heart of London, black, blunt and efficient.

A handful of pedestrians moved on these streets of powerful institutions: neon glare was elsewhere, the traffic fading out in that brief sigh of breath between the neon beat of London nightlife and the gray hurry-and-bustle of a world capital waking to a new day. He held the cape gathered around him, tucked it close: in dim light, to an uncritical glance, it could trick the eye that it was only a coat. And he wanted no public notice.

"Hello?" came a sleepy British voice. "Hello?"

"Nigel? This is Superman. I apologize for the hour. I've just come from the Caucasus. A dam's gone. A village airlifted out." At times he found himself talking in headlines. "Are you free to listen?"

There was a scrabble for something. The light thump perhaps of a lamp, perhaps a water glass. A newsman for the venerable *Times* was focusing his wits, brain coming on-line. "Just a moment. Just a moment. I'm looking for a pen."

There were reporters on the sidewalk outside her apartment building, as there had been outside the hospital. That, coming home, Lois hadn't expected.

How is he? Did you speak to the parents? Have you spoken to the doctors?

Billy was in Intensive Care at Metropolis General, and yes, and yes, and what did they think? It wasn't a complete victory. People had died. Sixty people had died, and three hundred kids would have been in that building in the next four hours, for the soccer clinic.

But she hadn't told the waiting cameras that when they'd met her outside the hospital; and when another battery of them met her on the street outside the apartment she had only a few words, *thank you, no,* and *I'm not a hero: I'm a reporter.*

Lobby security of her apartment hadn't let the news services into the building, and no one had been clever enough or hard-nosed enough to get past it. She was grateful for that. Her coat was left behind in the muck of that basement, but a kindly nurse had lent her a windbreaker, and she'd scrubbed in a hospital shower.

The shoes were maybe salvageable. The clothes were a total loss. Dry clean only. That was a gruesome joke.

She left the reporters outside, crossed a deserted lobby, and took the elevator up to her apartment, half-expecting, half-dreading to find that somebody had gotten past the lobby and lay in wait for her.

The elevator let her out into a peaceful, otherwise deserted hallway. No reporters. No hassles. She was doing all right. The shoes still squished as she walked to her own safe door. Her hands were done up in enough Band-Aids to outfit a clinic. Band-Aids and yellow salve. They'd given her a tetanus shot at the hospital. A second shot of something else. They'd wanted to check her in for observation, but she'd wanted to go home, and she'd caught a cab when she could get free.

She was fine right down to the door of her apartment when she tried to get her key out and get it into the lock, familiar act, an *I'm home, I'm safe* act.

Then she began to tremble like a leaf in a gale. The key hit to left and right and all around the keyhole.

She said a word her mother would never have approved of and used both hands to get the first and the second and the third key in.

The door opened on home.

She shut it and threw the deadbolts.

Elroy was there to meet her. Elroy rubbed around her legs and she couldn't ignore him. He was fat and warm and furry and solid as she grabbed him up and went to check the answering system, hoping for word from Clark. She nuzzled her cheek against his fur and listened to a Why-haven't-you-fed-me? purr as she punched in the phone answering system. She hadn't dared access her answering system on the cell phone, with all the potential eavesdroppers in the world apparently keyed in to her. She saw blinking lights and punched in Play as Elroy buzzed with hope of tuna.

"Way to go, Lois." That was Perry. She was grateful he wasn't mad. "We're all proud of you."

The next was her sister, Lucy. "Lois, I'm so proud. I'm in LA. I saw the reports this evening."

Her mother: "Lois, I was worried sick. Call me when you get in."

There was no way she was going to call her mother and release a spate of maternal anxieties. It was one in the morning, and she was still shaking.

"That was your last message," the machine said. "Shall I erase your messages?"

Nothing from Clark. She'd told herself all the way back in the cab ride that he'd have been there. That he'd have left word.

That he'd phone from wherever in the world he'd gone. And he'd say, "Lois, I love you," and like Perry, he'd have been amazed. And she'd have deserved him being amazed.

But there was no Clark.

That was a vast disappointment. But there were times, he'd warned her, when there might not be a message. And she knew. You loved a man who could be—literally—out of this world, and you took your chances someday he might *be* there.

No sense waiting up for a call, either, not at 1:00 A.M Something had happened somewhere else. She just wished, selfishly speaking, she knew where that somewhere else was.

Meanwhile the hospital shower and the disinfectant soap hadn't done anything but put a disinfectant scent in her nostrils she couldn't sleep with. And the clothes she'd had to put back on were a mess. And her knees and her hands . . . her poor, bandaged hands . . .

She started undoing buttons on her way to the bathroom.

The phone rang.

Clark? She wondered and almost pounced on it.

But an instinct said not. She stood near it instead, shivering in the ambient temperature of the apartment, and listened while the answering machine cut in, while a reporter from a tabloid press said he wanted to talk to her and offered her five hundred dollars if she'd pick up the phone.

She had a strong desire to grab the receiver and batter it in lieu of the caller. She just lifted it and set it down, cutting the connection, and then set it on Leave a Message, which, operating with Call Waiting, was a short list of acceptable phone numbers.

Clark's and the *Planet*'s, for two.

She didn't fling the clothes onto the carpet. If your fiancé tended to come sailing in windows without notice, you didn't have that extra time to run about gathering up messes. She dropped everything into the hamper and stepped into a hot, steamy shower, soap with no cloying scent, just—clean. Just—her, again.

And her eyes shut even while she was standing there.

She'd slip down the shower wall and go to sleep there, but she was already going to be stiff. She got out, delved into the medicine cabinet for a couple of Advil, and chased them with a glass of water.

Clean, clear water. A miracle. She stood watching crystal liquid swirl down the drain and thought how she'd never asked herself how water got that clean.

She splashed it up in her face, dried her Band-Aids with a towel.

And went and turned on her computer.

Last thing. Last, defining thing—on any day.

They wouldn't expect her to turn anything in. But she would.

Had to. It was her story, and she wasn't giving it to any tabloid press.

Proud of you, Perry had said. She could run a little on that kind of octane. And on the reliance of those families, Billy's family, the others . . .

She started with what she knew: "A car pulled into the Maernik garage . . ."

She kept going, with fingers that hit wrong keys, and a mind that conjured that place, that smell, that fear.

She stored down to the comm directory and invoked the program that sent that particular file to the *Planet* first to disk and then to fax.

It shut itself down. Did everything but turn the computer off.

She sat staring at it. The keys blurred in front of her eyes. Wasn't sure she had the strength to move for the next three days.

Definitely time to get to bed.

She walked back across the carpet to the window which—yes— was unlatched. But on this floor only passing birds—or her fiancé—were likely burglars.

Miss you, she said to the dark and the wind. *Love you.*

The wind stirred the curtains, stirred her gown, ran cold fingers over fingers already too cold, as she shut the window.

She padded through the door to her bedroom, to her own safe bed. The bedspread weighed as she hauled it back and weighed twice that as she got into the cold sheets and pulled the covers over her.

She'd thought she'd fall asleep the minute her head hit the pillow. She'd feared desperately she wouldn't, and that she'd relive the hours in that basement.

It was neither. It was the questions that haunted her.

The *why*? The *how* of sixty dead.

Gas explosion was one theory that was going around the press corps, but she'd been a block away when it went, and in retrospect she wasn't sure she remembered a boom as much as a single, dull shock.

Collapse of the suspended roof was another theory. The Maernik Hotel had been a controversial design. There'd been a lawsuit. Hadn't there?

And now in its first year of operation . . . it *was* its first year, wasn't it? It fell down.

Death. Grief. Devastation. Twenty-three injured lying in three hospitals, six children in Metropolis General, and Billy Anderson in intensive care. One fireman with serious injuries. An EMT cut to the bone by falling glass.

A terrible day for Metropolis, a terrible, terrible day, and no one yet knew why. Her reporter's instincts wanted to lever her out of bed and send her searching fiercely after those answers, answers she was *due* right along with the innocent people caught in that collapsing rubble.

Rescue crews were still, by floodlights and using search dogs, combing through the debris. The hotel front desk and the computers had been shattered when the upper floors came down, and the day manager and three employees had died instantly. The Baltimore and Los Angeles Maernik Hotels, part of the worldwide Premier chain, were assembling data they had off the computers to find out who might have been registered in the building. At the same time, the Junior Indoor Soccer Association was checking its rosters and communicating with schools across the region, hoping that at that hour no other teams had checked in unknown to the boys they'd rescued.

Complicating matters, the hotel restaurant had been open. Businesspeople regularly used the newly opened luxury hotel, with its airy, glass restaurant, for meetings, for breakfasts, for appointments. There was just no knowing who had been inside that building at that dreadful moment. There were eighty-three independent tragedies, eighty-three lives either snuffed out without warning or wrenched out of their families and into pain and grief through no fault of their own . . . either through simply going to work that ordinary morning or having reason to be, at that critical moment, in that hotel.

She'd gotten a handful of boys to safety, and one of them, Billy Anderson, was hanging on against all odds.

The boy's parents had been grateful, had hugged her, kissed her, wept tears in the hallway where, in a borrowed robe and scrubbed with disinfectant, she'd finally been clean enough to come and meet them.

But by then the surgeons had said they were satisfied and it was up to Billy.

"Then he'll make it," she'd said to the parents, and believed it. "Anything up to him, he'll do. He did, for me."

The father and mother had cried and agreed with her, which made her feel . . .

As if it was a good family, a good pair of people who had every right to have Billy—which somehow dashed her hopes.

Wasn't that an odd thing to think? She'd no right to that kid. She'd no use for an eight-year-old from New Jersey.

But it had . . . hurt . . . so much . . . when the professionals in that muddy garage had shoved her aside, and taken Billy, and she'd never had a chance to say good-bye or good luck or anything.

Stupid thought.

Stupider yet, there was still a lump in her throat, a feeling she'd won Billy, *deserved* Billy.

And then been robbed.

Maybe it was impending marriage. Maybe that was why. Maybe some stupid instinct had cut in. But she could still feel the grip of small hands, the desperation, the trust the boy had placed in her, believing that she was the adult, she was the woman standing in for his mother, the one who'd pull him out somehow and save him from the unreasonable, unreasoning world.

For a moment back there in that dark, she *would* have fought tigers for that kid.

And almost—silly thought—she'd wanted to cry out and insist on her right to go with him to the hospital.

But then a hedge of microphones had stopped her and, in the subbasement of her mind, practicality had said another EMT in that ambulance was a lot more use to the boy than a muddy reporter.

She was glad to know he had good parents. But you'd kind of know, if they'd produced a kid that trusting and levelheaded, they were pretty special people.

He was probably the star of his soccer team. Or maybe not. He was a star in other ways.

Double deep breath.

She let one and the other breath go, lying in her safe bed, her eyes still seeing that dark place, that water, the boy's face in the light of that submerged lantern, while she fought the cold and the water for him.

Never had known that much time had passed. Longest and shortest day of her life.

Spiraling down, down, down to a satisfied, warm dark.

Chapter 4

The dawn in London gave rapid way to another twilight, stars shining in the sky ahead. Superman's many-time-zone day had now entered another dark, one of those days when even he had to remind himself that dawn traveled out of China toward the UK and the US while weather traveled *toward . . . opposite* to the traveling dawn, as this morning's deluge over Metropolis was a squall over the Atlantic and the downpour in the Caucasus was a mass of cloud headed for Iran, while the sun tagged after him on his westward route home.

He'd gotten an accurate time from Nigel in London and figured his approximate arrival time in Metropolis as about 3:00 A.M. He couldn't wear a watch . . . or he tried, but nothing so far survived. He bought cheap ones, and the one he'd tucked away in his departure this morning he'd bet was dead by now—for the same reason as the map was soaked and had been losing its print lines along the folds when he'd used it in a London phone booth to tell Nigel the locale and the precise metric details.

He trusted Nigel would break the news in Europe to get the international relief organizations moving. Nigel was a good journalist with a flair for expression, and Nigel knew him and would rely on his details regarding third parties being precisely right. Both those reasons were why he'd specifically picked Nigel out of all reporters in Europe to bounce out of bed at that hour in the morning.

But even at that hour Nigel couldn't have made the *Times's* morning deadline. A newspaper didn't appear like morning dew, out of thin air: the presses had been rolling through the night and by that hour the trucks must have been loading, at the very time Nigel was scribbling on his bedside table.

The *Daily Planet*, five hours later than London, wasn't through with that process yet. There was, if he judged it right, and he thought he did, a margin left for Clark Kent to make deadline. The front-page stories of a paper were subject to change down to the last minute. News meant *new*. You wrote any newspaper story from the top down, facts first, then the explanatory detail in increasing degree of complexity—because a story lost an unpredictable number of its endmost paragraphs at the hands of the editor, whose job it was to compose the page to fit however much space other stories hadn't taken. How much room was left depended on the competition for lead stories and on the page count; it depended on the room devoted to headline at one end and advertising on the other; it depended on how the editor decided to arrange stories and it depended on what came flying over the wires as they went down to deadline.

There was a little leeway in the process, but if he was right about his arrival time, he didn't need to call and ask for that leeway. He had time to do a good job. He'd been thinking ever since London, in the high, untrafficked night, just how he wanted to handle the story. He had his front-end paragraphs and his lead sentence, and the rest . . . he had an idea how he wanted to cover it.

His obligations beyond that could wait an hour. In exchange for benefits rendered, the US State Department didn't ask Superman for proof of citizenship and other governments of the world generally didn't create a fuss about his crossing borders—but when he had done it, and particularly when he'd done something that even marginally involved another government's citizens or property, the President of the United States preferred not to be surprised by a phone call asking *him* the details.

As a matter of courtesy, he'd taken time to call State from London and let them know, and probably tonight he should call the President . . .

Lois.

Oh . . . no. *Lois.*

Dinner.

His name . . . be it Clark Kent or Superman . . . was mud.

He came zipping in on see-and-avoid, taking a lower altitude than he liked to use on a daytime approach, as the steel-and-glass towers of Metropolis showed on the horizon. Simple anxiety and desire to be there faster increased his speed; but he had to hold himself in and get below the sound barrier before he reached the harbor where he might affect ships.

Patience, patience, patience, he told himself as he came in, gathered up his belongings off the *Planet* Building roof, and covered the twenty-minute cab ride in ten seconds—the one that brought him to Lois's apartment.

Not to the front step, however.

Her window was dark. And he didn't need to compound a bad evening by waking her out of a sound sleep—which moving that window might well do, if she hadn't locked it tonight.

As well she might have.

He *could* have phoned from London.

If the need to tell another person where he was weren't so totally new to him. Not since his early teens had he had to phone in . . . and he hadn't reset his mental processes. And here he was, outside a dark window.

He flew on, to another apartment where the window stayed unlatched. His own.

There he put on a pot of coffee, put his clothes on to wash—Clark's clothes could go to the laundry, but the others couldn't—and took a fast shower, scrubbing off with strong hospital soap. It was 3:05 in the morning.

He put on a heavy, worn old bathrobe, poured himself a cup of coffee, and flipped on the power switch to the computer that sat in a clutter of reference books on the bedroom table.

He put the clothes in the dryer and sat down, sipping his coffee and watching the computer boot.

He was, he thought with a heavy sigh, tired. He did get tired. He *did* like to sleep in a given twenty-four hours, and although he was as immune to caffeine as to poisons, the fact that his mind associated the caffeine intake with mornings was a little boost to his flagging spirits. He told his body, however, that there wasn't going to be sleep, even if it wanted it.

And that was like calling on his body to rise off the ground or to expect a couple tons of weight: it just had to know the rules. It answered, faithfully.

It wasn't particularly happy about the news, all the same, and said to the back of his mind that it would much prefer the mattress and nice comforting sheets, thank you, and that it had earned them. But the conscious mind answered that there was the story to write, and it wasn't going to get any decent sleep until it had that done.

Fingers flew. Clark Kent, unobserved, could type far faster than Clark Kent in the heart of the *Planet* offices; but the chip on the motherboard had limits, and so did the word processing program. So, most frustrating of all, did the keyboard. He had macros for everything he remotely found useful, and those bypassed keyboard speed, but he had consciously to hold himself to a rate the machine could stand—better than typewriters that took a certain time for the mechanical action of the keys, far better than the office computer (the *Planet* provided good equipment but didn't expect superspeed from its reporters). This laptop was the most extravagant item Clark Kent owned, but it still frustrated him.

He didn't see much difference between this pricey little machine and the tough older laptop he lugged about in public view, but intellectually he knew that difference was there—and it would help him now. He had one hour to write the best piece he could, to be sure the word got out while it was still news. He wrote his opening: *Superman raced to the rescue as a quake-damaged dam threatened a town of 20,000.* He had his subtopics.

Higher up, cut off by the quake, a village slumbered on the river's edge, below the dam, unaware of the fatal combination of wind direction and a crack below the floodgate . . .

Engineers downriver had opened floodgates and lowered the level of the water, which afforded a chance, Superman reported . . .

The woman everyone called Grandmother walked with a cane but refused to despair over the loss of so much of their labor and their worldly goods.

Superman reports her last standing above the floodwaters that had swept everything away . . .

"There was nothing more I could do without the relief agencies," Superman said, and made a personal appeal for international assistance to the area. "The Red Cross and other agencies are in urgent need of donations to meet the demand for medicines and emergency shelter after a year of famines and floods."

He arranged paragraphs, pushed, pulled, trimmed and refined, with one eye on the clock. At 3:45 he made the modem connection to the *Planet*, loaded his file to electronic storage and fax, and keyed Send.

Then he took a final sip of coffee, heard that the clothes dryer had cut off, and asked himself whether he wanted to get dressed and go across town to make that phone call to the President.

White House staff would receive it at this hour. But by now, warned by his call from London, the US Department of State would have been in contact with various embassies in the affected area, and the President would get the news from Superman in London with his morning briefing. There wasn't, at this hour, much constructive he could do in the United States.

He'd have to go back to the mountainous area and help with the relief supplies and help get that road open. He'd told State that he'd check back with them before he went. He wanted to help where he could, including taking requested aerial photographs for the engineers so educated eyes could figure out whether the pilings of the ruined bridge had survived and in what condition; and the engineers might also need specific items to tell them the condition of the lower dams.

For the upper one . . . they were not, from everything he knew, going to rebuild. The uppermost, the one that truly never should have been built in the first place, was by no means able to stand indefinitely against the quakes that rolled through the valley. He had a general policy against interfering in large government projects, and he wasn't a construction engineer nor wished to become one. But if, to recover that region from the policies of the past, given the political history of the area, he might volunteer to do further demolitions, if they wanted to reconsider the whole notion of those dams, he was willing.

Definitely a case in which Superman would be far happier if the government used its collective common sense and let the engineers and the geologists, not political considerations, make the decisions.

But right now he was going to go to bed and enjoy the . . . what?

Good Lord. Two hours of sleep? Two and a *half* hours. He could move a little faster about the apartment and still clear the door by six-thirty.

He could get thirty minutes more sleep if he flew to work. But, no, that was pushing it.

Not when he had to come up with something better than the flu to account for his ducking out yesterday.

You saved the best ones for when the excuses were hardest to come by.

An interview with Superman, that was the center of it.

Had to be.

He didn't live so far from the *Planet* . . . not as far as Lois. He often walked, and it was a clear, bright morning, just a little lingering chill in the air as he took his usual route, timed to a fare-thee-well on a good morning, and this was. Move on schedule in the city, and even the traffic on the street moved with you, the lights went on Walk with fair convenience. You saw the same vendors. You saw the same cars at the same lights as every morning, as if you were reliving the same day over and over again. You knew them by the dents, you knew them by the license plates, especially the creative ones.

And you dodged the familiar obstacles, the construction on Fourth, and the endless repairs at the manhole half a block down. He'd given way to temptation and looked into that one with a vision ordinary passersby didn't have, and he *still* didn't know what they were doing down there. A lifelong avocation, it seemed to be. They'd been at it since last spring and might have replaced half the phone cable in the city for all he could tell.

There was, on this route, the chance to use the phone—he'd make his call to the President—by stopping in at the 1930s vintage Fenwick Building, where there was a little-used public phone that faced the front doors.

He breezed in through the revolving walnut doors and headed for the phone, glancing at the newsstand in anticipation of the Planet's morning edition and his story somewhere on the front page if not running as the lead.

The headlines of every paper on the stand screamed pain in black type. CITY IN MOURNING: DEATHS MAY TOP 60 and MAERNIK SEARCH CONTINUES vied with the *Planet*'s SURVIVORS

PULLED FROM HOTEL and, in smaller type: LOIS LANE: "I COULDN'T LEAVE THEM"

His heart did an extra beat. He calmly put down the price of two papers, picked up the *Planet* and the *Baltimore Sun*, and did a speedread of the *Planet* article, in utter shock at what he was reading.

The Maernik, just down the street . . . *gone?* Lois . . . pulling kids out of the wreckage? He was appalled. The hotel was just around the corner and down the street. One part of him wanted to ask the newsstand attendant what he'd heard yesterday and the other part just wanted to *see* what his memory told him ought to be a normal, reassuringly ordinary street.

He didn't wait to read the *Sun*. He went outside, to the corner, and looked toward the *Planet,* where the whole street was ribboned off and blocked, where earthmoving equipment and firemen and police were working inside a cordon that stopped ordinary citizens.

It was unreal even to him, who'd just seen a dam dissolve and a village swept away. But it was true. It was very unhappily true. And Lois had been in the middle of it. He'd skimmed Lois's article enough to know she'd filed it last night, and she'd been well enough to write it. But—

The danger she'd been in appalled him. In the parking garage. Under tons of shifting rubble. Electric wires. He *knew* scenes like that, and it scared him just thinking about it. Those people down there, with the dogs . . . those were search dogs. They were still looking for survivors in that rubble.

He knew the alleys hereabouts as well as he knew the streets and ducked into one to do a blinding-fast change and launch into a flight so short it was a dive.

He landed. He didn't talk to the police or firemen in the first few seconds. He looked at that pile of concrete and tangled pipe and wire and shattered glass; he looked at that ravaged lobby

and down into the water-filled ruin of crushed cars and collapsed rebar, fearful there of what he *might* find.

And didn't. Then he felt he could draw breath.

The police captain and the fire chief had come quietly up to
him and waited for answers.

"I don't see anyone," he said. "I don't *hear* anyone."

"Are you sure?" the fire chief asked him, and Superman said,
knowing that it was a life-and-death answer, "Let me go closer.
Give me a little time. Pull everyone back, twenty or so feet."

He didn't like to waltz in, displace brave and tired workers, and
make easy pronouncements—but these weren't people to let
anything stand between potential survivors being found by any
means that would work. He felt their hopes settle on him, and he
became aware of reporters near the fence. One of them was a
stakeout from the *Planet*, and he made up his own headlines for
the article: SUPERMAN FINALLY ARRIVES, and RESCUERS
EXHAUSTED—far more painful headlines to him than any they'd
actually print. He hadn't been here, hadn't known what was going
on in his own city. In London he'd been giving out news, not getting it from Nigel. He'd been calling the Red Cross headquarters
about the dam collapse and the villagers, not asking them about
his own city.

The rescuers with search dogs drew back and called out for
quiet as he took his own feet off the ground, hovering into the
cavernous ruin in a silence the more eerie because the ordinary
sounds of Metropolitan traffic were a block removed. The
sounds of pedestrians were absent. Wind fluttered the yellow
warning ribbons, and the smell of earth and damp and stone
predominated the scents on the breeze.

He listened. He sharpened the senses he ordinarily dulled to
live with ordinary people and drifted near the standing pillars,
looking carefully at the surfaces.

He discovered . . . nothing.

Half the building was still standing. It was the north end that had collapsed, taking with it the glassed-in terraces, the ballrooms, the observation dome that had been all glass, a beautiful place—when he'd last seen it. He looked at the standing walls, and ventured into the basement and the shattered garage, moving with delicate slowness so as not to cause further collapse or disturb the air that held the scent of concrete and damp, looking deeply into the walls, seeking the evidence of what had happened.

He went down until he found standing water. There he gave a whistle that he was sorry for in consideration of the dogs upstairs, but the sounds that came back to him, echoing off the ruin, gave him an accurate picture in his mind of what the bottom was, and what lay beyond his line of sight.

His vision, linked with that auditory sense in some fashion in his brain, gave him an image none of the police or firemen's equipment could provide them. He even passed a quick scan over the microstructure of the concrete and the walls on the lowest level of the collapse—he'd had the unhappy job of going into many a chancy building, and he'd developed a routine that gained information on every front they'd want to know, information the investigators as well as the rescuers could use.

He went out then and met the searchers on the street. "No one's in there," he said, "dead or alive, to the best I can detect."

The two dogs with the searchers couldn't understand, they'd go in over broken glass and sharp concrete and search and search, faithful to their job and in such hope—magnificent dogs, who wanted to keep trying. He let them smell his hands, and he petted them in consolation.

"Good for that," a fireman said, and talked to his dog and told him—his name was Brandy—that he was *good dog* and *good Brandy*, and they were going to go home.

"I only wish I'd been here," Superman said. "What happened?"

"That's still up for grabs," a fireman said. "We just don't know. The investigators are already taking pieces to the lab."

"No explosion traces," he said, "not that I saw." But two tired firemen didn't constitute the official agency to receive his report to his city, and he had, himself, a lot of answers to give to Metropolis and to others, to questions that the firemen hadn't yet asked, that he urgently needed to deliver elsewhere. "Thank you," he said. "Thank you for being here."

"Our job," one said. It was what the good people always said. He rose out of the site and high, high above the scar the event had put on Metropolis, out of their view before he veered off and dived down to the alley he'd last entered as Clark Kent.

In a moment more, Clark Kent, with his two papers neatly folded under his arm, walked out, solemnly passed the rib-boned-off disaster site, and took the necessary detour down the block and around to the *Planet*'s main entrance.

He'd begun to ask himself, in the enormity of what he'd seen, what on Earth he could say to Perry that was going to cover this one.

"Morning, Mr. Kent." Carl the security guard was at his post, reassuringly ordinary.

"Morning," he echoed, and drew a calming breath. "Did Mr. White come by?"

"Nope. He sent down for breakfast. He didn't leave last night."

Not completely surprising, Clark thought as he got into the elevator. He'd taken that split second in the alley to scan the paper, to the limit air-resistant paper would let itself be handled with any speed, and by what he'd gathered out of the several pages he'd passed an eye over, the Maernik, a new building, had gone down without warning at 10:49 in the morning. The theories flying about were either a bomb . . . or a collapse in the parking garage, then the function rooms above that area, where nine people had been injured and seventeen killed, most at a business meeting. In the lobby a father and son had escaped due to the front desk holding up a piece of the ceiling, and others behind the desk had died. The restaurant and the terrace walk accounted for thirty-two dead.

At that hour, some few people had been in their rooms, cleaning staff had been at work all over the hotel, and the vanguard of the State Junior Indoor Soccer Clinic had been arriving at the hotel to set up their registration. Hence the boys trapped in the garage. Their coach had been up by the desk while they were getting equipment from the car. He was one of the ones that desk had protected. His son, another member of the team, had been the other.

And Lois, meanwhile . . .

He still had to figure whether for some reason she'd been in the building or had run down the street; but she'd had the cell phone in her purse, and a backup battery.

And for hours, *hours* in the ensuing chaos, she'd kept issuing her reports via LNN. By what he'd skimmed in other articles, not just the city but the whole nation, the whole English-speaking world, had been glued to those faint transmissions from the garage of the Maernik Hotel. Lois had kept talking, assuring the parents and a listening nation that two of the kids were alive, but trapped, and that rescue personnel were communicating with them.

In so much destruction, she'd held out *good* news, and the nation had latched onto it and refused to let go so long as she kept reporting.

Which led to those kids' rescue, one fairly unharmed, and the second boy, whose plight had seemed so hopeless, whose rescue—by Lois—the world called a miracle.

He wished he'd been there. But to have been there instead of where he'd been—he couldn't wish that. Thousands would have died if that second dam had failed. That these were his neighbors, in his own hometown—it hurt. And he had the same feeling anyone in the city must have this morning, reading the account, a question why such a thing had happened and a determination to know it wouldn't happen again.

He wanted to know why. It was his job to know. He wanted to walk out of the elevator and down the short corridor and see Lois at her desk, unscathed, and his city unchanged, the newsroom full of the usual tired jokes.

But Lois wasn't there this morning. Her computer wasn't on. Her coat wasn't on the coat-tree. His London Fog was there, from . . . was it only yesterday morning that things had changed so much in his city?

"Kent." It was Perry's distinctive voice with the inevitable question hanging just behind that summons. Perry was *not* pleased, and if what Perry believed were true, he wouldn't blame Perry.

Perry didn't say a thing, just went to his office, and Clark tagged behind and shut the door.

Perry took the desk, looked up at him with that under-the-brows stare he had when he was struggling not to blow. "*Where* were you, Kent?"

He hated this. He hated lying. And had to use his best and rarest: "I was on the line. I forgot to unhook the modem."

"Forgot to unhook the modem. I called your pager at least four times last night. Jimmy called. I'm sure Lois called."

"How is she?"

"You *are* out of touch."

"Is she all right?"

"All right enough to write the best story of her life."

"I read it. On the way to work." He didn't mention he'd walked. "It *is* good."

"I had to cut yours," Perry said. "Hadn't any choice. Metropolis *is* the news, it's the news clear to London and Paris. Moscow. Kuwait and Tokyo. Superman was off fixing dams and *you're* interviewing him. *Try answering your pager*, Kent, just for starters."

"Battery went down," he said. Second big-time excuse, a fabric of lies grown thinner and thinner. He hated interviews like this, and he didn't like his absence and Superman's brought up in the same sentence. "I'll get on it, Perry. I'm sorry, is all I can say. Is Lois coming in today?"

"Soon as she wakes up. She's got an excuse. A lot of us haven't been to bed yet, Kent. We've got every crackpot and every wanna-be extremist organization in the city calling in!" Perry picked up a fistful of While You Were Outs and shoved them across the desk. "The Committee for the Liberation of Whatever and all their cousins are ringing our phone off the wall claiming they bombed the hotel and it's to protest gene-spliced tomatoes or the trade talks with Japan, I don't know. At least ninety-nine point nine of them are liars. Maybe all of them. Find out which."

"Right." He took the fistful of notes and shut Perry's door behind him. He already knew what he thought, the way he knew what Superman had concluded. And meanwhile he had people on a hillside freezing to death and the President of the United States waiting for an explanation.

The President of the United States and Jimmy Olsen.

"Where *were* you?" Jimmy came up to him with a worried look. "What happened?"

"It's a long story." He crossed the newsroom with Jimmy close behind and picked his coat from the lot on the pegs.

"Have you talked to Lois?" Jimmy wanted to know.

"Not yet. If she's speaking to me." He put on the coat and started to stuff the messages into his pocket, then thought better of his sometimes windblown pockets as a security storage. He headed for his desk.

"She was great," Jimmy said, still tagging after him. "She was really great. I'll bet there wasn't a television in the whole country that wasn't tuned in to her in that basement."

He sorted rapidly through the messages in case one was significant and tucked the absolutely least likely in his pocket, the communiqué from the People's Committee on something-or-another. He put the rest in the desk drawer. In that pocketed, highly expendable message he had his excuse for leaving. Going to follow a lead, the pocketing of that message indicated silently to another newsroom eye. And leaving seemed a good idea right now. Jimmy wasn't the only one anxious to ask him questions or fill him in at great length—the filling-in part, he would have been vitally interested in, on a quieter day. "So I've read," he said to Jimmy's enthusiasm. "I didn't get the news till I woke up. An hour late and a dollar short. Was *Lois* all right?"

"She was a mess. Mud and everything. But she was great."

"If she gets in this morning tell her—" He saw Ron cruising in, likewise intent on questions, he was certain. If there was one place not to entertain a touchy secret, it was a nest of reporters. "I've got to check out this phone call. I'll be maybe an hour. —I'll be back," he said to Ron. "Got to make a phone call. If Lois comes in—tell her—tell her— Never mind. I'll talk to her when I see her."

He ducked out, detesting the deception that was the never-ending rule of city crises. Clark Kent was unreliable. Clark Kent was always elsewhere when the avalanche came down. Clark Kent always had an excuse.

Clark Kent was who he was, Martha and Jonathan Kent's son, Clark Kent was his real self—and he didn't like the impression he had to give, not now, not back all the way to his days at Smallville High. Here was a catastrophe to his city, and he was ducking out again, this time on Lois, with the whole world watching this time.

And now as soon as she did get into the office, *she* was going to have to defend his reputation against the people who cared about *her.*

It just didn't come out fair, sometimes.

Clark Kent used the elevator, not the stairwell, and hailed a taxi in front of the *Planet* Building.

He'd not seen, among his other concerns, whether his story on the Caucasus, the one that he'd labored over last night, had been picked up by the wire service, or whether Perry had killed it altogether. Not that his pride was riding on it. But the welfare of a village and a region was. The public concern that motivated politicians was riding on that information getting out to the hearts of people around the world, and it might impact the willingness of the State Department to commit resources to budge official positions in that area of the globe. That newly *oil-rich* area of the world: that might incline certain people in the State Department to take interest, because the oil supply to the industrial world affected trade balances, jobs, political alignments that oil-poor nations made in order to secure and maintain the flow of oil—but explaining to the American people how a situation in the remote mountains impacted the

Caspian shore, which most Americans knew less about than they needed to know in the first place—that took some deeper understanding of the situation: the conflicts that had racked the region reached the American people through photojournalism as a simple case of ethnicities run amuck, a question Americans did understand and latched onto as the truth. But it was far more complex than that.

He'd have liked to write an article on that complex region. He'd find a way to write that article. He'd talk Perry into it. That was his distracted thought as the cab wove through brisk midmorning traffic.

"It's worse with the street blocked off, you know?" The cabby was one of the chatty ones, and Clark muttered an agreement that traffic was bad, thinking to himself of the calls he had to make.

He had no idea whether Nigel's article had made the *Times* or whether the disaster in America had bumped Nigel's account as well to the second, third, or fourth page.

The Red Cross was on the site. Relief agencies were there, geared up for earthquake, but nothing was getting up the road to his stranded village—and the rest of the villages above that vanished lake, what with the blockage and then the bridge going out. He couldn't but think of the night his villagers were spending, clinging to what little they had. For a moment it was dark, and raining, and people were waving good-bye to him with hope on their faces as he took off into the sky . . .

And then the cabby was swearing at a pedestrian who'd almost caused an accident, and the world was sunlight and the yellow nose of the cab and a man with a boom box shouting at the cabby.

"Idiot!" The cabby turned to his passenger for support. "Would you look at this guy? Would you look at him? No sense, no sense at all!"

"Not a way to long life," Clark said, and fished in his pocket for funds as they rounded the corner to quieter traffic. He would just about bet that, given the hour, Lois was going to outflank him in another cab, going in to work while he was pulling up at the curbside of her apartment. But concern wouldn't let him wait, hoping she got there, hoping she was all right. He had to see for himself. And now her building was in sight ahead, past the cabby's shoulder.

So, to his dismay, was a clutch of reporters, TV news, cameramen, photographers, all looking for any sign of emergence from the building. He'd have known the mannerisms if he hadn't seen the gear and if he hadn't known the names of several of them. The cabby was slowing down.

"Drive past," he ordered the cabby. "Let me out around the corner."

"So what's goin' on here, do you think?" The cabby was one of life's curious minds. Alexander Ruis was his name. "Them's reporters. Is that what they are? Somebody kill themselves or something?"

Fine. A cabby with an inquiring curiosity, just what he didn't need; and Lois's doorstep under observation. That they were still there milling about indicated that she might still be in.

"I don't know," he said. Depend on it, the cabby was well aware he'd picked him up at the *Planet* and that those were reporters on a story. And depend on it, unless the cabby got a fare away from here, and maybe even then, he would circle the block to rubberneck after what might be going on.

Exactly what he didn't want the man doing. He got out and gave the man a five. "Listen. Do me a favor. Go around the block, pull up to the curb, and ask them what's going on. Just keep them busy."

"You a reporter?"

"Yes, I am." He made a fast retreat, toward the alley, which the man could weave into his other behavior, but at least now the man had a framework on which to hang his suspicions: a reporter trying to outfox the rest. Clark would bet the man (fear of adventure never drew a man to be a Metropolitan cabby) would do just what he'd said.

And common sense and prudence ought to tell him to take off down the alley and find a phone down the street at the drugstore so he could reach Lois that way. But the concern he had—and the thought that Lois might need a rescue—sent him to a quick change to a form that no one would be surprised to spot a number of floors in the air, if they chanced to spot him at all. But he doubted if the reporters on the front walk had gotten past building security to scout out the premises and discover which one was Lois's apartment. As it happened, Lois's apartment faced the other direction, and as long as the cabby kept them there talking, they wouldn't spot him at her window.

He whisked to the window in question and hoped that she hadn't locked him out.

Elroy was on the sill, ready to risk his nine lives if the window opened. He opened it and shoved Elroy off the inside sill before Elroy could get into mischief. Wind wafted the curtains as he whisked through—scanned the empty breakfast nook—and went to Lois's bedroom.

She was asleep. Safe. Her hair was mussed, and her hands . . . her poor hands . . . were cut and bruised and abraded, as ordinary hands would be, that had wrestled with concrete and steel in soaking water. He was reassured by her even breathing, her unmarred profile on the satin pillow, and his fear settled to a desire just to hold her, to hold her a long time. The hands looked so painful, and he wished he could take every bruise, every cut, onto his own hands—which he couldn't. She looked so beautiful, and so fine and fragile. It was a wonder to him how she'd done what accounts said she'd done. But there was nothing frail about the heart that had driven her to go after those kids.

She'd have tried to call him. She'd have expected him to come. The cursed pager, of course, had been with Clark's clothes, the cell phone likewise, and Superman couldn't have used it anyway, because it was a giveaway and it could lead to his secret identity. He wanted to gather her up right then and hold her and tell her how sorry he was and how very much he loved her. But he didn't know, sometimes, how exhausted a body like Lois's could be, or what she did need. She'd earned the right to sleep in today, that was certain, and if she had nightmares of that awful wreckage, he didn't want to bring them back into what looked now like tranquil sleep. He shooed Elroy away from a bounce onto the mattress and found a piece of paper and a pen on the bedside table.

Lois, he wrote, *I love you. I'm glad you're all right.*

And what else could a man say, when he wanted to sweep her into his arms and tell the world they couldn't come close to her until she was able to deal with it?

I'll explain when I see you. Be careful. There are reporters in front of your building. In the reporters waiting for her out there, he saw a threat as dangerous to her happiness and his as the physical danger of the pit she'd ventured into yesterday. He knew the danger she faced in the clamor for information: he'd kept his personal life in secrecy all his life, and, irony of ironies, chosen to work as an adult among those who gathered information, yes, to keep his ear close to the information flow. But maybe too he chose it because he perceived it as a threat to him and one he wanted to understand. He hoped she understood the types she'd meet out there—as if a reporter didn't understand what drove various elements of the news industry.

But in her moments of personal notoriety she'd never been the subject of so many *competing* organizations. There was the danger to her. Competition for information—*any* information, germane to the issue or otherwise—would drive the crowd out there to find any scrap they could. She'd always been in control of that search. She'd always, bottom line, been a reporter. But if he read what he saw building around her, to the reporters on this story she wasn't *just* Lois Lane, she wasn't *just* another reporter. Worse, there were things to find if they started digging. There were interesting aspects to her life that the less principled media, the real bottom-feeders, would pounce on. There were delicious bits of former associations, hints of former brushes with publicity—*anything*, fair or true or not. It would all interest their editors. In what she'd done, in the kind of figure she'd become in the news, in the keen national interest, she'd become not Lois Lane, reporter, but Lois Lane, public figure.

But what did a man who had his own secrets write about all that to the woman he wanted to marry? *You have associations you don't want the press to know?*

If you were a smart target, in a feeding-frenzy case like this one, you couldn't swear the tabloids wouldn't go dumpster-diving. A note like that, once written, might be found, providing hints to egg them on; that was one reason not to be explicit. And a wise man dealing with Lois Lane didn't ever imply she needed a keeper or a defender. There were times Lois listened with understanding and patience.

But given the adrenaline-rush events of yesterday, and what was besieging her curbside this morning, understanding and patience weren't in the immediate forecast.

So he left off the cautions and the caveats and the final draft read, *I love you more than I can say, I'm glad you're all right,* and *Be careful of the publicity, for your own sake.*

He leaned very close. He passed a hand just above her cheek. His skin could feel the warmth of her skin, even at that range. It was almost a touch. He could imagine the touch. He imagined the brush of his lips against her brow—and didn't, quite, touch. But the scent of her hair was there, the scent that was *her*, to him, that calmed his fears and touched all his hopes.

Maybe in her sleep and in her dreams she felt his presence. She stirred. He drew back, propped his note against the ginger-jar lamp on the bedside table, and stood there a moment, just reassuring himself of her well-being, waiting in case he had, after all, wakened her. Then he'd forego everything, presidents and schedules, for at least long enough to listen to her and hold her and be absolutely sure in his heart that she was all right.

It said something for Lois's depth of exhaustion that she settled again and didn't wake.

He left, careful not to shut the drapes in the window.

Chapter 5

A weight landed on the bed. It might have been rocks. Concrete. The world might have caved in. Lois was conscious of having just flailed a hand above the covers, but it made no difference to the weight, who walked calmly forward on her bruised chest and patted her cheek with a furry paw.

Elroy wanted breakfast. Now.

His human was sleeping past breakfast? Clearly something was wrong that wanted intervention.

Pat-pat.

Raise the ante. The Weight put a tentative foot on the pillow and licked her chin.

Lois waved an arm not quite aimed at dumping Elroy onto the floor. It was unlucky to do that. Cat owners for the last half century had been wary of starting the day by dumping the cat off. But it had been a good dream. Clark had been there. She'd felt his presence. She'd been so sure he was safe and all the world was right . . . for just an instant . . .

Then she'd been back in the parking garage, in the water and the terrible sounds and sights of the place.

Elroy tramped back across the covers. Undaunted.

"All right," she said. "All right." She stuck a foot out, and it hurt. Her knee felt raw and scarcely healed. Her arms hurt. Her ribs hurt. Careful assessment proved everything hurt and no little of it was skinned, not badly, just abraded, possibly infected from that awful muddy water—

Hadn't the doctors said that? That there'd probably been sewage in it? And shot her full of every antibiotic known to man, she supposed. But she moved. The body lived. She'd—

—gotten those kids out. She'd talked to the reporters. She'd gotten her story in. She was entitled to sleep into daylight. Perry would forgive that—grump and gripe, but he'd forgive it. If *she* forgave a certain—

Her eye met the note propped against the lamp on her bedside table and her heart went *thump!* He *had* been here. She *hadn't* dreamed it. He'd been here and he'd worried about her. She blinked her eyes into sharper focus and read it, not wholly surprised he hadn't committed on paper where he'd been and why, but—

But he could have been a bit more forthcoming with *I'm sorry.* The *I love you* part she could appreciate . . . that was sweet.

But *Be careful of the publicity?* Be careful of the *publicity?*

Maybe . . . maybe, she said to herself, drawing a calm breath, she was still just a little on edge. Maybe it just hit her wrong.

She read it again. Calmly. She did what she had to do and dealt with the cameras and the commotion as well as she could, she got her story in, and what was this, *Be careful of the publicity, for your own sake?*

She replayed that line in her head as she got out of bed, as she walked out of her bedroom, through the living room and into the kitchen.

She replayed it again while she was dumping Elroy's Kittyfeast into the bowl.

She stood there after, with an empty can in her red-knuckled and very sore hand, hearing Clark's voice saying it: *Be careful of the publicity, for your own sake* and it just—

Made her mad.

Where does he come in warning me about the public spotlight? I'll say the wrong thing? I'll put people onto *him*?

I can't be trusted?

No. That certainly wasn't how he meant it. He meant, bluntly, be careful. He meant once turned on, the publicity-machine was hard to turn off. He meant . . .

Maybe you can't deal with it?

She rinsed the can and put it in the bin. She washed her fingers, trying not to hurt her hands.

He meant the best for her. There was nothing malicious in his concern.

But it still gave her a nails-on-the-blackboard shiver along sensibilities quickened by another relationship. Luthor had wanted her to suit his image. Worse, he'd wanted her to suit *his* image of some fantasy *he* had. It still rankled. And she hadn't seen it. She didn't know why she hadn't seen it. She'd nearly married the man—the most up-and-coming businessman in Metropolis. And, blinded by the glamor, she hadn't seen what he was doing to her. It was things like that, that shook a woman's confidence in her own judgment.

Foolish even to think it: Clark certainly was no Luthor— Luthor was manipulative, domineering—ruthless, a trait she had misinterpreted as a positive trait: ambitious. But Clark, who spent his life doing things for strangers, Clark was the soul of kindness. Gentle—it was in his hands when, so powerful, he held her as he'd hold something precious and breakable, even to the point where she'd have to say, laughing, to the strongest man ever to walk the earth, "Clark, I don't break. Not that easily." And he'd laugh, and she'd laugh, and he'd float her right off the ground, just with a thought, so softly she didn't know her feet weren't on the floor.

He meant the best for her . . . as if . . .

But—was there just the least assumed seniority in that statement? The least hint of a *Stand back and let me?*

Probably she was reading it far too negatively this morning. She ached. She was sore and depressed after yesterday. She *loved* him. She loved him more than she'd ever loved anyone or anything in the world, that was how much she loved him, and wanted him—right now, she wanted him, to share mornings with, and to talk to. He hadn't wanted to wake her, and probably he'd wanted just as badly to talk to her.

That was it. And she couldn't let negativity creep in. It was in her attitude this morning. She was reading it wrong.

But there was the least little sour feeling at the stomach, the least little crack in the world, that maybe something was setting in that had set in with all the other relationships that had started with far fewer storms, far less rivalry . . . as if *now* he felt entitled to encroach, just a little *Don't* here, and a little *Let me do it,* and a little *Stand back, stand aside, you'll hurt yourself,* that overlay a Luthoresque: *I'll take care of you,* and *You don't have to work, You don't have to think, You just stand in the shadow and let things go past you.*

She felt a little sick at her stomach. A little terrified of the world, in a way she'd not been, even in that basement.

Doubting you'd get out alive, that wasn't a new experience. She'd been in danger before in her life.

Doubting the love you'd just begun really to believe in—again—was territory she'd been in, too, with every relationship that had unexpectedly gone away, as sane men suddenly turned completely crazy on you and started trying to run your life and wall you in to some prison they defined. In its way, it was far scarier than a concrete slab hanging over you. It made you—

—mad, and sick at your stomach at the same time. And a little unsure whether you were out of step with everyone else, breaking relationships because there was *none* that was right for you, or that you were right *for*.

If you'd been burned, badly, it took stupidity as well as courage to commit to not seeing the world through a filter of past experience. Yes, you were a fool not to learn from experience, but you were a greater one to assign the same set of behaviors to everyone you met for three or four months—and *then* go flying off the deep end for the first plausible, flattering liar you met. That had been the pattern she'd fallen into: she was a smart woman, but her ability to pick men?

Lex Luthor had been a prize, hadn't he?

But she hadn't *picked* Clark. She'd fought like cats and dogs with Clark. Wasn't that different? Didn't that say maybe that the rules of engagement had changed?

She shouldn't overreact. This *might* be the start of a fight. But it wasn't in Clark's character to try to control people. It was probably Clark trying to take on a role, that was what Clark had called it. Clark watched other people to know how to act, at times; she'd twigged to that. And if he'd gotten this protection shtick from some TV sitcom, she could deal with that.

She was sore, she was peevish, and she was sure that accounted for nine-tenths of her mood. She looked like death when she got the view in the bathroom mirror, and if she was going to have to answer questions and be photographed—and deal with Clark—she wanted at least not to have her hair standing on end.

And she wanted to follow this story to its finish. That, too. She wanted to know what had happened to the people she'd left last night. She wanted to know how things stood with Billy and his family, and with Gene, and with the other people they'd pulled out of the rubble. She wanted to know how many had lived and how many had died and she wanted to know what had brought that building down.

She phoned the hospital, as Lois Lane from the *Daily Planet*. She didn't ask to disturb the parents with a phone call, but they put her through to the Andersons all the same; and she couldn't hang up.

"This is Lois Lane," she began, and didn't get as far as, With the *Planet*. Tom Anderson said, immediately, "They're saying they might have to go in again. Another surgery. They're not sure."

"Tell Billy hang on," she said, shaken. She was seeing that place again. That frail hand holding on to hers. Billy, holding back the pain when she pulled on him. And there wasn't a thing she could do, now, as a reporter, but find out the truth. "I'm on my way to work, Mr. Anderson. I'll come by there as soon as I can get clear. Tell Billy I called. Tell him—I want him to get back to his team."

They'd talked about that, in the basement, she and Billy, in the intervals of her fishing after rocks. About soccer. About the other kids. She knew a lot of the other names, Andy and Ted and Tonio. She felt for Gene, an immensely brave little boy, and wanted to write his story, and his parents' story, in depth, for one of the world's great kids. But she'd fought the fight of her life for Billy Anderson, and they couldn't be telling her now that he wasn't going to make it. That wasn't *fair*. It hit her right in the stomach. "I'll check back," she promised Billy's father, and put the receiver back in the cradle, trying to recover her sense of perspective. Professional distance. She had a job to do.

She wasn't just going to work this morning. She was going to *work*. She went into the bathroom and put on the paint that hid the circles under the eyes and the scrapes that were going to be a nasty scab on her cheek and chin, and moussed and blew the hair until it showed signs of surrender.

She was down the elevator in fifteen more minutes, with the intention of walking down to the avenue where cabs existed in fair frequency.

She hadn't expected the barrage of cameras and microphones outside the glass doors. Her stomach turned over.

But there was nothing for it but to shove that door open and brave the barrage.

"On my way to work," she said, and to shouted questions, "I'm fine. Fine. Scratches. Just scratches. I wasn't *in* the building when it went. Have they fixed responsibility for it?"

They hadn't. The stakeouts didn't know, at least. She wasn't about to break news on her way to writing it, but die-hards unfettered by cameras pursued her with notebooks and pens clear to the avenue.

It got her a cab, at least. A driver was curious, and wanted to know what the hubbub was, and caught her signal.

Then, with her safely in the cab and the reporters in the rearview mirror, "Hey, I seen you on television. You're—"

"Lois Lane. Yes. On my way to work."

It was a running questionnaire on the way to the *Planet*. The cabby wanted to know every detail.

Down to the point where he remarked, "Looks like a bunch of 'em waiting for you," as they drew near the *Planet*.

Be careful of the publicity, Clark had said.

Maybe Clark had been to the *Planet* first—and seen what was waiting for her.

"Possibly," Superman said to the Secretary of State. But to any passerby it was Clark Kent at the antique phone booth in the Stillford Hotel, a couple of blocks from the *Planet.* He liked the venue. It had the old-fashioned green-vinyl padded seats and the comforting feeling of wood. And it had an aisle remote from the reception desk where no one in particular came.

That was a good thing, if your calling list included the White House, the International Red Cross, the FBI, and the State Department in a tightly laced sequence.

The FBI lab was glad to get his observation: it had samples, but there was a decided advantage to a moving, all-angles glance seamlessly interlaced with a mind and a memory. He was unfortunately widely experienced in what a bomb did to still-standing walls. And his visual observation was further backed by a sense of smell that could, if he consciously cleared the overload that ordinarily blocked his senses, identify a number of by-products from a recent explosion.

It was easy to say something existed—if it was clear to your microscope. It took a little longer to swear you hadn't missed something. Superman and the lab had come to the same conclusion—negative on the bomb theory—and that was helpful.

What wasn't helpful was what he learned from Geneva. Warehoused goods immediately adjacent to the quake zone were depleted; the International Red Cross and other relief agencies had moved in supplies two weeks ago to handle critical human needs following one disaster, and that had run certain other areas into need. A couple of hundred homeless villagers might find lodging in adjacent villages, but he understood their reluctance to give up their land, and one couldn't go shoving these refugees about in disregard of their property and their local traditions.

It was a region already badly done by, a patchwork of borders and ethnic divisions so chaotic he'd had to ask the State Department and they'd had to consult their maps in detail even to know what country he'd been in.

The old regime had dumped wastes, built factories, used resources, and moved populations with no regard to local needs or ecological concerns.

This generation reaped the harvest of bad decisions.

And Grandmother, who'd seen all of it in her lifetime, her wishes mattered, too—or should. Someone had to do these people the courtesy of asking them what they thought, and he'd left them with the impression that Superman, personally, was going to help them.

He wasn't going to abandon them.

That meant he had to go back. And he had to get the supplies they needed. The earthquake and the larger towns downriver might have depleted all the local delivery facilities, but there were other sources. Switzerland, while not the closest staging area, was a place where he knew names of individuals who knew how to move and expedite goods, and they had the equipment he needed.

It was also politically neutral, and they could talk to the governments involved. The State Department was looking into it.

Superman was their eyes, too. He'd seen the situation. The area needed that bridge restored, in order for those people to get their meager goods to market. Between the quake damage, poverty in the region, and the fact that the flood might have taken out the bridge pilings, there was the likelihood of a long delay in repairing that bridge and the road that went to it.

He wasn't an engineer. He reminded them of that; but he knew what he saw, and felt secure in reporting it.

He also knew the basics of brute force engineering, enough to know that what he set in place in an emergency was going to stand up at least for the short term, overbuilt in such a way he could trust it would stand; but if there was a chance to do better he wanted to have the advantage of that advice, and maybe some equipment and some help. He hadn't had a good look at the bridge pilings, those support columns that held up the surface of the iron bridge. In this case the pilings were probably of reinforced concrete. He hadn't stopped to look. They were set into rock below the water—and he knew the structure of the bridge was ripped out. But if those pilings had held fast in the rock and not been scoured out or knocked out, if even a certain number had survived the flood, putting a new deck across the bridge was a quick job. Replacing pilings was a difficult, time-consuming job. Replacing the whole structure with a suspension bridge, the kind that hung from the walls of the valley across the river— well, he wouldn't borrow trouble. If they were all lucky enough, the pilings had survived and they'd have the deck replaced in days, not months.

Meanwhile the State Department and the UN were going to get in contact with the Russian government—the area had turned out to be Russian and not Georgian, Ossetian, or Chechen. In one sense that was good: there were well-established diplomatic channels, individuals who knew each others' credentials and could walk critical information through the right official doors. In one sense it was bad: Moscow was a long way from the Caucasus and a government's natural, even responsible, tendency to want their own observers on the scene could slow decisions, because someone on the site didn't have the authority to move.

He had to trust, however, that the Russians would track down the records on the dams and the bridge, find and fax the information to the Russian Embassy in Washington, who would fax it to the Russian Consulate in Metropolis, where he could pick it up along with the information from the Red Cross and various other involved agencies. The State Department was experienced at doing exactly this sort of thing, and it was a profound relief to lay the details and his observations into the hands of Nancy Wills, whom he knew from personal experience let nothing slip between the cracks.

"Possibly," he said when she asked whether he would be going back immediately. "Depending on what you can find for me," was his conclusion to the matter. "Thank you. Thank you very much."

He wasn't going to get any sleep. He saw that coming.

He hung up the phone and walked past the gift shop, out through the elegantly appointed marble and paneled lobby, and onto the gray, busy street.

The *Planet* wasn't a long walk. And rival news services were still prominent on its doorstep, reporters and cameramen jostling one another for position. "Hey, Clark!" one shouted. Eddie, from the *Star.* "Clark, just a second!"

"Sorry," he said. "I'm on a deadline."

"On what?" the shout pursued him, and someone tried to delay him, but he made the doors and inside, where Carl and the receptionist held the lobby.

"Ms. Lane made it in," Carl advised him. "Mr. White's been asking did I see you leave and I said you went down by the site. I think he's looking for you."

"That's fine," he said. "Thanks." As he escaped into the elevator. Carl was an asset, a definite asset. A one-man message system. And *Lois* had arrived at work.

He was thinking about the bridge replacement: that was a surety. And he was thinking about what to do with the dam. The dam, Nancy Wills had said, had put his villagers off their original pasturages, and if he had a recommendation to voice among the engineers and the diplomats, *that* particular lake bed might go back to being meadow. It hadn't the pollution problems the lower river had, where industry had poured an unthinkable soup into the system. The high valley lake bed might still be viable as farmland . . .

But it was going to need a little help. It was a popular misconception that silt was automatically fertile, for one thing—Superman needed no research to know farmland—and while the edges of the lake bed were silt that might have a little value, when the water had moved in a rip down that valley, it would have taken with it all the useful topsoil washed down near the dam and left sterile deep earth and muddy gullies. Erosion would follow immediately, with all that barren mud flat, and the spring rains and snowmelt.

A series of shallow terraces, on the other hand, would hold the runoff. And hold in place the topsoil that might wash down from the slopes.

Terraces would fill with runoff and topsoil and a small series of ponds and riprap dams to get the water down to the newly expanded lower lake . . .

He could do that. *Yes!* He could do that.

He could turn that land back to productive use.

And prevent the ruining of the lower lake and the dam with silt.

He exited the elevator into the hall, hoping as he came into the offices to find Lois at her desk.

She wasn't.

"Clark!"

Perry was, however, in his office. It didn't take superhearing to detect the exasperation in that shout as he passed Perry's door. He stopped and put his head into the editorial office, where Perry sat keeping a hole in the next edition open, very probably, for the two ace reporters in his arsenal, against that information-seeking horde outside on the sidewalk. Reporters who *owed* him their attention and the decent exercise of their wits. The phone was blinking red, and Perry had the receiver in his hand, with somebody on hold.

Clark went to the desk, not willing to speak aloud in case that button wasn't pushed, and wrote three significant words on a memo pad: *not a bomb.*

Perry mouthed the words in implied question.

Clark nodded a deep affirmative and solemnly held up ten fingers. Ten minutes. And headed out to his desk as Perry recalled whoever it was on the line and got back to them.

Settling at his desk, he hit the red rocker switch that brought his computer up, dropped into his chair, and had his first line in mind before the program was up.

Fingers flew. Not too fast. Not showily fast.

Superman arrived this morning from overseas and visited the Maernik disaster site to assist authorities with the search and rescue. After thorough examination of the rubble of the hotel, he advised rescue crews that he detected no additional casualties or trapped survivors at any level of the structure. In an interview with this Planet *reporter near the site he expressed regret for his absence at the moment of crisis and said he had been engaged in another emergency in a remote mountainous area at the time. He praised the rescue workers and called them inspiring in their courage. "They aren't invulnerable," he said of the rescuers, "and they're working in areas of extreme danger. I can't say enough about the effort I see here."*

Superman also stated that he doubted a bomb was involved. "A bomb leaves chemical and debris traces I don't see here," he said, and declared his intention to report his observations to the FBI, which is currently investigating the case. He said regarding the phone calls from various organizations claiming responsibility, "Responsibility isn't in their comprehension. When the FBI labs have a statement, I'll listen to their conclusion. Right now the focus has to be on the innocent people who've been caught in this."

To the question of what ordinary citizens could do, Superman stated, "Support the people involved in this tragedy. Give your time and your money and your goodwill. The citizens of Metropolis have a deep love for this city, and they won't let this event overwhelm their spirit or their concern for those caught in this disaster. I couldn't be here. Thousands were. I'm very, very grateful to them for their courage and their refusal to give up anyone to this terrible disaster."

An FBI spokesman, contacted by phone, said, "We aren't ready to make a statement at this time," and said further that the FBI could neither confirm nor deny that they had received information from various sources, but that there would be a news conference at 10 A.M. eastern time to issue a progress report on the investigation.

He glanced over it. He ordered Save and he ordered Print, and he accessed Perry's desk and ordered Send.

But Perry's Electronic Desk being what it was, and the phone calls continuing to light up the available lines in, competing for

Perry's attention, he took the printout and crossed toward the physical office.

Lois was indeed in. Lois, in a gray, tailored suit, with the scratches and scrapes of the disaster evident on her chin and cheek, came down the hall by the conference rooms with Jimmy trying to keep up with her, a Jimmy with all his camera gear.

In that simple fact Clark had a clear notion where Lois had been, reporters at the *Planet*'s doors notwithstanding. Her adrenaline was running high, he could see that in the pace she set and in every line of her slim body.

Until she spotted him, and stopped in her tracks. He stood there with his story in hand, and she stood there with Jimmy and his cameras behind her, and the whole office seemed to be at a simultaneous dead stop, right down to the gathering at the water cooler.

"Lois," he said, with everything he wanted to say to her bottled up and impossible in front of an audience. That one word was all he had. "Lois? I've got to turn this in, and then I've got to talk to you."

She gave him one of those looks that said he had better talk, and talk volumes. And he reached Perry's door, and Perry's desk, with the intention of laying the paper within reach.

"Give it here," Perry said, and as he started for the door, "Wait a minute! I want you."

He wanted to talk to Lois. But he drew a quiet breath and waited while Perry scanned the page.

And looked happier. "Exclusive?" Perry asked.

"Exclusive. No question." His brain shifted from Lois outside to the muddy disaster site. And the rescuers. "I tried to word it so we don't end up backing any theories. He said he doesn't know for a hundred percent certain, and he doesn't want to miss something and create some controversy about their results. I couldn't get a statement out of the FBI lab—" That was the truth: he'd called once as Superman and once, last of his calls, as a reporter looking for information. "But Superman said that he's reasonably sure, and he was able to check areas for damage that they haven't reached yet. He says it looks a lot like the floors just folded downward, the way the layers are lying, but that's not something he wants quoted because he's not sure enough. I'm staying in contact with him."

"I need photos. I need photos of him standing there."

"I can't get that. I was there. He happened by." Lois and Jimmy had turned up in the doorway, and Jimmy edged in cautiously.

"I've got some shots of the site right now. Ms. Lane's got an interview with the fire chief."

"It's not written yet," Lois said.

"Ten column inches," Perry said. "Photos. *Photos,* boy. Great shades of Elvis, we're in motion here, we're going to rock and roll! LNN and WGBS and that whole alphabet soup on the front sidewalk are all going to have to read the *Planet*'s front page to know what's going on in this city!" Perry was on his feet, waving his cigar, and made a flourish of his hand toward the personally autographed portrait of Elvis that dominated the wall. "Go for it, that's what the King would say! If it wasn't those crazies on the phone, then *something* brought that building down, and it's a good thing there's TV cameras all over our sidewalk. The news is *here,* the news is what we do here, people, and if those guys on our doorstep want to know the latest, by golly, they'll read it in the *Planet!* We've got a twenty-four-percent increase in our print run, and we're selling off the stands. The world wants to know, the world's got a *right* to know, and we're the ones to tell 'em, boys and girls! We're the eyes and ears of the good citizens of this city, we're the conscience of the community, and we're wanting to know what happened down there that took the lives of sixty of our citizens. Superman says it wasn't a bomb. So? Well? What was it? Let's not chase the FBI's news conference tomorrow morning. Let's have a solid lead, here, Kent and Lane! Let's have *pictures,* Olsen! Let's not be running to play catch-up! Seize the moment! *Carpe diem,* people. It's Now or Never! Go out there and bring me something *ahead* of tomorrow!"

"Yes, Chief," Jimmy said faintly, and dived out before the cigar could clear Perry's lips.

"We're on it," Lois said fervently, and was out the door almost as fast. Clark followed, and seized her arms. Carefully.

Looked into her eyes. Lost his train of thought and his memory of the last twenty-four hours.

"Lane!" Perry said, and appeared in the doorway, commanding all attention. "Brilliant job, yesterday. Outstanding. A real outstanding job, wasn't it, Kent?"

"It was," Clark said. And was acutely aware he *hadn't* been there. "I was proud of her. I was very proud."

"It's all right, you doing interviews for other organizations. I'm not complaining. They say a good newspaperman never *becomes* the news, but you're a credit, Lane, you're a real credit to this newspaper, and you've got good sense, real good head on your shoulders. The *Planet* stands behind you. A hundred and ten percent!"

"Thank you," Lois said faintly.

"You give it the old try. Good for you, coming to work today. I knew you'd come in. Couldn't stay home. That's the old spirit, Lane, that's what I like in people! Don't you think so, Kent?"

"No question," Clark said.

"That's the spirit!" Perry said, and went after a ringing phone.

Lois let go her breath. Clark let go his, and seized her arm and steered her toward the back hall and the copy room.

"I was somewhere uphill of Chechnya," he said for openers. "I'm sorry, Lois. A dam broke."

"You could *tell* me where you're going!"

"I didn't think—I'm not *used* to telling anybody, Lois. I'm sorry, is all. I'm sorry I wasn't here. I feel awful, but there wasn't any way for me to know."

"I got your note."

"I didn't want to wake you up. I'd already been to work. That's when I heard the news. Well, the paper. On the way to work. But I didn't remotely think—except the dinner. I forgot about the dinner."

"I forgot, too." She put up her hand to wipe a strand of hair out of her eyes, and her Band-Aid-covered fingers looked terribly painful. The fingertips themselves were scabbed. "Except when I was lying there in the water. I thought—I'm supposed to go out tonight. I thought about my stupid hair." Her voice shook, and it wrenched his heart. "And I was trying to keep this kid from drowning."

"It was incredibly dangerous, what you did. You know that." He caught the wounded hand, ever so gently. "You were terribly brave."

"I was mostly cold," she said. "I didn't think I'd ever get warm again."

He couldn't stand to think of it. He pulled her into his arms—or halfway did, but Ron came down the hall and excused his way into the copy room.

"That was incredible, Lois," Ron stopped to say. "That was really incredible what you did."

"Somebody had to," she said. Ron was going to be working there, to judge by the folder he had, and Clark drew her a little further toward the rear conference room. And kissed her, tenderly, gently, when he wanted to hug her so hard; and then—

Then it wasn't a tender kiss. It was a lover's kiss. And her arms locked around his neck and his around her, and a man who didn't need to breathe on his way through a rainstorm found himself light-headed.

When he looked at her again her face was flushed and her breath came hard.

"I wished you were there," she said.

"I love you," he said. "Just—be careful."

"What was I going to do?" Her hands gripping his arms were hard and anxious. "There were kids coming out of that building! You'd have gone in there!"

"I'd have gone in there. But it's *different* for me." It sounded like a convincing argument when he said it. A second later, in the stormy vulnerability of her face, he knew he'd fallen into it. "Well, not that different. —Except my hands wouldn't look like yours. And if a piece of concrete fell on me I'd be in a lot better shape, wouldn't I?"

The temper had flared and fallen. But the sober, my-territory look chased it hard. "I'm not a china doll, Clark. I'm not your china doll. Don't ever think that."

"I know that. I know it very well. And I know you risked your life and it was your decision to do it. You were very brave. But now you need to keep a lid on what's going on out there. I don't care what Perry says, don't give them any more interviews. You're a reporter. You *want* to be a reporter, not a media personality."

"I can handle it."

"Nobody can handle what's out there on the sidewalk."

"You handle it! I can handle it!"

"No. I *don't* handle it. Lois, if I'm next to you, with the cameras—it's not a good idea. Tape's one thing. Black and white stills are another. From the right angle, I look like—" Even back here in isolation, even with voices at their lowest, he didn't say the word: *Superman*.

"I'm not going to hide in a closet, all right? I'm not a fool!" For a moment she sounded wobbly and exhausted, and the look on her face showed the strain she'd been under. But the set jaw followed, an expression he knew well. And believed in and trusted. Once Lois was thinking about something, she *would* deal with it.

He set his hands on her arms, wanting to take away the pain, helpless to do that, wanting to protect her from everything that might ever harm her, and knowing that she'd run far and fast from that, to save her own soul.

Justifiably.

"I know," he said gently. "I know. But you're a hero, Lois, and that's more than famous—no, listen to me. It's different *being* the news than being *in* the news, and you know that. It's different even than being a celebrity. In celebrities people expect flaws. Not in their heroes. If you let them, the news services will hype you onto every television in the country, and they'll shine light on every corner, including the ones you honestly don't want them into."

"The ones *you* don't want them into! *I've* nothing to hide!"

"*Everyone* does. Everyone in the world has things that don't play well in sound bites, Lois, you *know* that. It's like somebody going through your dresser drawers—through your garbage. And it's just that bad. *I* can disappear and they don't know. But *you* have an address. You'll *always* have an address."

He took his life in his hands—saying that, challenging the woman who meant everything to him. She wasn't ignorant of a thing he said. Believing that it applied to her was another matter. Having him bluntly remind her of past mistakes—including Luthor, now in prison—was a touchy area of her life. He didn't read her well on that score. But he saw the jaw set and he saw the brows knit and the hurt spring up anew.

"So you can *disappear,*" she said. "Is that what you're saying?"

He thought so. Then he re-heard it and was appalled. *"No, I'm not talking about leaving you! Ever! I'm trying to say*—be careful, that's all." There was deep hurt, just under the surface, and now he didn't know how she'd heard anything he'd just said. He seized her shoulders on impulse and was afraid then he'd hurt her sore arms. "If this blows up, Lois, I'll deal with it. Somehow. It might force everything—*everything*—public, and hurt us and give us no chance at a private life, that's what I'm trying to say. You can't walk away from the choice you make and you can't undo it once it's happened. I will *live* with whatever you do. But—"

His recital of specific events of her life muckrakers could find couldn't at all help the temper of an exhausted woman whose common sense he'd challenged with his warning. "I think you were very brave," he told her. "And I trust your judgment. Whatever comes, I *trust* you."

There was a sheen of unshed tears in her eyes. He didn't know for what. He'd hit her hard with his suggestion she retire to the background, and he'd advised her about things a professional in the business had surely already thought of.

And now he didn't know how to unravel the things he'd said and get his footsteps off that intimate, private territory before he trampled something else precious to her. She put her arms around him and rested against him a moment, and he held her. She wanted a kiss, then, a gesture, a little loving gesture, and he more than willingly gave it.

"I love you," he said. "Don't ever doubt it."

"Love's such a chancy thing," she said in a shaky voice and took a deep breath and kissed him, a parting kind of kiss.

"Don't doubt *me*," she said. "Whatever I do, don't doubt me. I'll work it out."

"I don't doubt you!" He wanted to shout it. He whispered it, between them alone in that hallway.

"I know," she said. "But it's *my* job, Clark." She traced his cheek with her hand and turned away. And left him bewildered as she walked away from him and down the hall.

Left standing there watching that slim, suited figure walk off to do her job, he wasn't sure things *were* completely right.

He'd encroached on her. And the penalty was—he had to believe her cryptic assurance at the doorway of that private territory, and he had to then offer her the assurance he would give her that personal room and just—let things alone.

Trusting her to handle her business—and a certain amount of his. That was what it was about when you thought about marrying, wasn't it?

He'd left Metropolis to an unguessed, unsuspected crisis, and she'd dived into the breach and gotten herself and others out.

Maybe—unprecedented thought—*he* had a partner. Maybe that was what they were hammering out between them. *He* had to go back to Russia and there was Lois Lane to handle things here in Metropolis, in the newsroom, in the lives of people he couldn't help.

Maybe—aside from being desperately, deeply in love with the woman—that was what it was like to have a partner.

Amazing thought. A thought which—from a boyhood as unique, alone, and in a personal sense, lonely—he'd never dared imagine for himself. He'd always expected he'd be alone and more so as he set Smallville in his past. That at least the essence of what he was would always be solitary.

And to discover the contrary after all these years? To have not a partner on the news scene, Clark's personal mainstay—but to have that slight, gray-suited form fielding some of the catches, at least the figurative ones, that Superman couldn't make? She'd know all the details, she'd get all the phone calls, she'd see things and do them if she could. He *knew* Lois. He should have seen it coming.

To have a partner so—fragile—so vulnerable to the chance and risk of the life he led?

His heart was no longer protected. He *cared.* He loved the woman. What did he *do?*

He somehow didn't think his parents back in Smallville had the easy solution to this one.

"Photos are right here," Jimmy said, brandishing a digital disk and computer printout. "Shall I take them in to Perry?"

"I'm nearly there," Lois said, and didn't look up from the keyboard. Her fingers hurt, and she'd typed nouns and verbs and adjectives with a lot of abbreviations. Clark picked them up on his terminal and cleaned up her typing.

Perry was five minutes from deadline on a noontime extra based on Clark's story. The presses were going to roll.

And nothing that wasn't in the computer was going to make it onto that page. The electronic age with a vengeance. And Perry was right: other news services saw Lois Lane's work with the *Planet* as a threat, the *Planet*'s old-fashioned reportage and solid writing as a standard they had to meet and beat—including finding out what angles the *Planet* was working on. They'd had one reporter from the downstairs pack try to get into the newsroom disguised as a janitor.

Far worse, the *Planet*'s stakeout at Met General said some tabloid reporter had tried to get into the patients' rooms. There were limits.

There were real ethical limits. Barging into injured kids' rooms. *Her* kid was lying in there in doubt of his life, and some lowlife was trying to get onto the upper floors.

She wanted to call the hospital. Wanted to know how Billy Anderson was. The world wasn't going to forget those kids. The world wouldn't forget Billy, or Gene, or any of those kids. She wouldn't let it happen.

"Two minutes!" Perry stuck his head out to say.

. . . the site will belong to the investigators, now. The rescuers are packing up to go. The mayor said, of the volunteers from so many surrounding cities, "They're the finest. There's nothing else to say."

She typed that last almost without corrections. Signed off on it.

"I've got it," Clark said, rattling a last few keys. The printer whined into action, and Clark reached up to close the disk drive. "That's good, Lois. That's real good."

NOT A BOMB: SUPERMAN VISITS SITE, and SEARCH ENDING were the two leads for the extra run, with photos, striking, heart-wrenching photographs, of a little girl at the police barrier. She didn't want to think about that until she'd gotten Perry what he wanted.

Jimmy was hovering, playing messenger pigeon. Clark gave him the disk. And the printout. "Tell Perry it's good stuff," Clark said.

"Right, CK!" The photographer who'd taken probably the outstanding image of his young career was off like a shot.

Lois felt as if *she'd* been shot and wanted to find a nice quiet couch in the restroom and lie down. There wasn't a bone in her body that didn't ache, and she couldn't remember if she'd turned off the coffeepot in her apartment. She was being neurotic about it and knew it. The coffeepot wasn't going to burn the building down. She *wasn't* going to ask Clark to fly over there—literally—and flip a switch she halfway remembered flipping before she turned out the kitchen light, anyway.

While all she could see in her mind was that basement. That rising water. Billy's hand.

"That's great!" Perry popped out of his office, and meant the praise. She heard it and brought her head up from her dull-witted focus on the keyboard like a long-distance swimmer in the home stretch, staring at shore.

"But we've got an evening edition to run in three hours, people. I want something on that front page. I know I'm asking the sun and the moon, but can you find me something worth that page? I *need* that page, people!"

The blood moved just a degree faster. The heart beat just a little harder. The brain knew where there was a story that needed telling.

"I'll get it for you," she said.

"Honey." Perry came over and patted her shoulder with Southern chivalry she'd learned wasn't in the least patronizing. "Lois, honey, you've done enough."

"It's *my* story. I'm going over to the hospital. I'm doing a write-up on Gene Pratt. And Billy. —Clark, do you have *any* idea how to find Superman? It'd mean a lot to those kids, if he could just show up over at Met General. Can you ask him to get over there? It'd be real nice if he did that."

"I'll give it a try," Clark said. "I've got his schedule, anyway."

He'd be there. Superman would be there.

And she'd be there, and she'd take Jimmy, and it would be a good story. One that would make sure those kids and those twenty-four injured and the dead stayed part of the picture no matter what the focus tried to be. That was important.

That it might not be emotionally easy for Clark occurred to her only after she'd asked it. She saw it, picked it up in the air, she didn't know, but it struck her how very much Superman would have wanted to have had the chance she'd had and fate hadn't worked out that way.

But he'd want to go over there, she knew that, too.

Chapter 6

Lois had made his excuse for him—or given him the beginnings of one. Clark punched in a phone number that he happened to know wouldn't be answered—it was a voice mail service Superman did in fact use, but he accessed the service, not the accumulated messages, and left another, in the hearing of Ron and Myerson, who were hovering near his desk.

"I know a place to look," he muttered to whoever might be interested, and shut down his computer and left his desk, remembering this time to take his raincoat.

Lois and Jimmy had already left. He took the elevator down to the lobby and took a cab to an address on Fourteenth Street.

It was an office building. It wasn't his destination. The immediate objective was a grim and fairly unused alley with a stream of questionable water running down the asphalted-over cobbles—his resorts were rarely to scenic and pristine places.

Superman rose straight out of that concrete pit and up the blind facades of two buildings without adjacent windows (another preference for his launch sites) and up, up, into a sunlit perspective of a busy city. He did a roll and redirection and dived, fairly leisurely, toward Met General, not wishing to get there too quickly, to anticipate Lois and Jimmy.

There was Met General, shining white and clean below. He flew over its parking garage, circled back above the elegant Japanese garden out front that matched the one behind glass that existed in its heart.

There was the cluster of newspaper reporter stakeouts, too, that camped around the canopied entry—stakeouts that gave a desultory glance to the arriving taxi and then scrambled for their feet, their cameras, their target beneath the canopy.

Lois, probably. With Jimmy. Lois was going to have to run that gauntlet, and it wasn't going to be reporter to reporter— what do you know, what are you following, hey, I saw your piece, that was good . . . .

He could give her an easier time getting in by putting in his own appearance. And did, landing on the sidewalk with a fair amount of speed and a last-nanosecond will to stop on the concrete, not a few inches below it.

He stood there watching the tide of lenses and microphones roll toward him—and seeing, beyond it, Lois and Jimmy passing the doors. She got in, the guards doing nothing to stop her. And she got Jimmy in.

The questions that came at Superman were blunt as only reporters could make them: *Where were you? How do you feel seeing this? What are you going to say to those people?*

And he answered them, in patient terms. "I was on the other side of the world. Russia. A dam failed." They didn't care about the danger of hundreds in Russia. It was this place they wanted to know about. Their papers had sent them here to get the story that was happening in Metropolis and they couldn't do otherwise. "I didn't find out about this until this morning." Cameras were clicking, whirring, snapping. Cameramen and photographers were jockeying for the right shot, and microphone booms swung around his head and over him by less than inches. It was hard to keep one's thoughts in a row. "I'm immensely impressed with the fire and police personnel. And with the citizen response. I'm doing what I can now, assisting with the investigation."

Shouted questions: *Do you hope to learn anything here? Was it a bomb?*

When he was Superman he wasn't the *Planet*'s employee. He'd worked that out in his conscience. And the *Planet* presses were already rolling, so the print journalists couldn't catch up. But the television cameras could get the word out immediately if he talked to these people.

What should he do? Take Perry's story and broadcast it? Lie to these people? At times he was between a rock and a hard place.

"I'm here to talk to the survivors," he said, and left, leaving the bomb question hanging, selectively deaf to it. He turned away to escape more interrogation and moved quickly. Police weren't letting the press past the glass doors—no reporter had gotten in, it seemed, except Lois and, by her fast talking, Jimmy and his cameras. Lois would have passed by the desk. He knew the hospital, too, and knew where she was going—but she had a start on him and already knew the room numbers.

He entered the lobby. The regulations required visitors to register, with very good reasons this week, and he went to the desk and received his card like any other visitor.

"Ms. Lane said you were here," the receptionist said. Her name was Lisa. He'd dealt with her before. And she knew he knew the necessary precautions for patients' protection. They'd let him go every place including the ER if he asked, but he had to stop at the warning signs and decontaminate like everyone else—more extensively than other people, considering some of the places he had to go. "Here's a list of the survivors' rooms. Ms. Lane's already up there."

The woman deserved a bouquet. He decided a rose was going to end up on that desk, out of his reporter's salary.

Up to the next floor—via the elevator: he made no disturbance he could avoid. Pratt was the patient first on the list. Gene Pratt—a young lad surrounded by teddy bears and flowers, and relatives in awe of their visitors, and Jimmy's camera.

"Is he well enough for a hug?" Lois asked, and receiving word from the nurse that a hug would be therapeutic, gave him a gentle one. Superman shook his hand and signed a soccer ball, and the boy was hugging it when they left the room.

There was an old woman next on the list. Her name was Mona, Mona Hartman. But she had no relatives. She'd gotten flowers and, confused by her medications, couldn't understand who would send them.

"All the world is sending them," Lois said softly, holding the old woman's hand. "All the world. They might be from Paris. Or London. A lot of people care. Is there anyone we should call? Is there a relative we could reach, no matter how distant?"

The old woman, who'd just stopped at the Maernik for a sweet roll, her routine every morning, said timidly there was sort of someone, and she was very worried.

It was room after room as they went down the hall. A young chambermaid. The building engineer. A businessman from Duluth who'd been preparing his slides for a meeting and who had no memory of the event.

Then Lois stopped by the desk and made a call inside the hospital, to the ICU. And put the receiver down with a pale face and a distraught expression.

Three minutes every two hours. Three minutes and three people was the rule in the Met General Intensive Care Unit—for the most fragile patients, those whose every heartbeat, every breath, was marked and watched by machines and devoted nurses. But it was close to the appointed time, and these visitors were—well, not available for long visits.

"Billy?" Lois said, and Superman waited, while the monitors beeped a steady thread of life. Even knowing, as Lois had explained to him, that they'd had to go back to surgery this morning, Lois might not have expected as grave a situation as the one they found, a boy in such desperate weakness. In all the skeins of tubes, with all the apparatus of monitors and IV stand, Billy Anderson lay very still in the scant sunlight that escaped the shut blinds. And there was such anxiousness on Lois's face, such a terrible fear—

Superman knew. *Clark* knew. He remembered Smallville, and a time he'd sat by a friend he'd saved—to no avail, as a human body simply couldn't heal. And you knew your strength was so great . . . but miracles weren't in your power. Somehow it wasn't fair, when you'd gotten a chance back for someone, and then it turned out there was nothing, *nothing* you could do, after all. Life was both incredibly tough—and so unexpectedly fragile.

Light and shadow. Light streaming past the shut blinds to touch the pillow with stripes of brightness. Lois's face—so tense, so concerned, and nothing he could do.

"Billy?" she said, demanding that second miracle. And with authority: "Billy, come on. Wake up."

What had seemed like a lifeless doll responded, an indefinable change of muscle tone and then—

Then eyes opened, and recognition was suddenly there: he saw it even from his vantage, as he saw Lois's face in that white, reflected glare, saw the soft, wonderful, wondering look she bestowed on the boy. She took his hand, hampered as it was by tubing.

"Billy. Got to get your head up, Billy. Got to hang on. Keep on keeping on."

As she must have said the same words in the depths of that basement. As he must have answered that voice and believed it and trusted it implicitly.

"Yeah," he said. Superhearing could hear it. It was so soft.

"You're in the hospital. Your mom and dad are here."

The beep of the cardiac monitor was steady and sure. And Billy turned his head and saw two parents who'd waited through the night—a father and mother who wanted to hug him tight, and who'd had to settle for watching and waiting a few moments each hour by his bedside.

Lois started to let go and leave. But Billy gave a lingering, slight tug on her fingers as she pulled free.

"You're all right now," Lois said. "You're safe."

"Is that *Superman?*"

"Sure is," he said, feeling he had no business intervening. But it made Lois's retreat easier, along the side of the bed, in the cramped quarters the machinery made. "I wish I'd been here sooner."

"That's okay," Billy said. "*Lois* was with me."

The parents captured the boy's hand, and his attention, and Lois went outside, past the nurse who'd arrived. It was time for Superman to leave, too.

"Lois?" Billy said. But the regulations were right: the boy was exhausted, and the nurse moved in, easing everyone out. The boy was back from the brink, and now the hospital staff and the doctors had things to do—things with hope of saving this patient.

Lois was in the hall, moist about the eyes and trying not to show it as she talked to the shaky-voiced parents. The parents were shaky, too; and they might, Superman judged as they exited the short restricted hallway into the ICU waiting area, *might* get some rest themselves, now.

Jimmy met them: there were no pictures allowed on this floor, again with very good reason, and Lois didn't ask. But in the leave-taking, the mother surrendered a treasured picture from her purse. "I thought till just now it might be all we'd ever have. Thank you, Ms. Lane. Thank you *so* much . . . ."

"I'll take good care of it. I'll bring it back to you," Lois said.

"We owe you," the father said, "everything."

Lois looked overwhelmed. And in the usual disorder of such moments the three of them passed the door of the ICU waiting area into the general corridor, an oddly assorted set, Jimmy with his cameras, Lois in her Band-Aids, and himself, red-caped, conspicuous in any company—but he might almost as well have been invisible, back there, to Billy Anderson.

Not to the people downstairs. Not to so many. Jimmy had gotten what should be a good photo—of young Gene holding his soccer ball. Lois planned a feature for tomorrow's morning edition. She had a tape full of personal stories that would make tonight's edition, too—while Jimmy had snapped photos where patients and families were willing, conscious they might go into the Metropolis archives, a lasting record of a city's heroism.

There were so many stories, so many lives tossed into chaos. Superman had personally promised the old woman whose name was Mona to get into her apartment and find someone to take care of her elderly Peke; and he'd promised another boy who'd broken both legs that, indeed, his teacher would let him make up his homework . . . not ridiculous concerns, *human* concerns, for people yanked all unplanned and unfairly into the headlines and away from the things that mattered.

And in such matters, Superman had a thousand hands, the volunteers who'd come in to feed pets, phone landlords and elderly uncles. It was a time when human attachments mattered most of all, and when other humans of like attachments understood, and stepped into the breach: *Clark* had a notion of a story he wanted to write about those nameless volunteers.

But the image that haunted him now was of the woman beside him, that expression, that moment with young Billy, the remembrance of which, in association with the talk they'd had in the *Planet* office hallway, wouldn't let him go. Walking beside him, Lois was quiet in a way that had nothing to do with the quiet rules on the floor.

Jimmy picked up the mood and looked worriedly at her, and at him. But what Superman had seen in Lois in that ICU wasn't anything Jimmy knew or had a right to know, unless Lois talked about it.

Clark and Lois had to talk. He didn't know when or where. She had a deadline. He had one, too.

And *his* deadline was overseas, half a world away, and had nothing to do with writing.

There were moments he felt the walls closing in on him, constraints of time and the life—the personal life—that always took second place.

Lois punched the elevator call button a second time. The ring on her finger was his ring, his promise to her, regarding a lifelong partnership human beings looked to have, the way that couple they'd just left had promised each other, and maintained that mutual promise in the young lad in that sunlit room.

He recognized that look Lois had had. He'd seen it shining in his adoptive mother's eyes.

And he had to ask himself—was it fair? Was it fair, that ring on Lois's hand, sparkling with promise that might not ever happen to them?

He didn't know whether he could safely have a child. He was the first, the only man of his kind on Earth. He and Lois hadn't talked . . . with enough frankness . . . about the chances and risks that attended children, for them; or maybe she made her guesses on the conservative side.

The elevator came. "I'll go down with you," he said as they stepped inside. "I'll give them an interview. There's usually a cab out front. Take it."

He halfway expected argument. But Lois was gazing wordlessly, somberly, at the elevator doors.

Maybe she didn't hear him. Maybe her mind was lost in that dark where hers had been the only voice a boy believed in, the dark out of which she'd brought that boy—and given him back to someone else.

The elevator reached the ground floor and let them out. There was a side door to the parking garage. Out front, through glass windows, he could see the cameras, the stakeouts.

"Jimmy," he said, "there's a cab in the drive. Go snag it."

Jimmy understood, and went by that side corridor toward the parking garage.

That gave him and Lois a few breaths alone, out of earshot of the desk, stared at by passing nurses and visitors.

"I have to leave," he said, as he'd said all too often in their lives. "I'm sorry, Lois. I've got to be back overseas. I'm very proud of you. I want you to know, I'm very proud of you."

They couldn't touch. Hands couldn't reach. They had to stand there next to the glass wall of the indoor lobby garden and be civilized and remote from each other when he wanted so much to have his arms around her after all she'd dealt with so well.

"Good kid, isn't he?" Lois said. "He's pretty special."

"I know," he said, and hadn't meant to convey all he meant, but maybe she read between the lines.

"Old hat for you," she said shakily. "How do you not get involved?"

"Tell me when you know," he said. She'd gotten to him. Right to the heart.

And he had to get away from her before the cameras' uncompromising eyes caught a moment they should never catch.

He couldn't say *I love you.* He gave her that little twitch and crinkle of the eye that meant, *We're being watched.* "I'm going back overseas," he said.

"Are you going to be able to get that lady's dog?" The ordinary things of promises and humanity were piled up and overwhelming the moments they had together. "I could do it."

He grinned at the thought of all the reporters outside chasing Lois to an old woman's apartment. "Run the lot on the front sidewalk a chase, you would. No, I'll do it. I'll call Bev." Bev was the head of Vets Anonymous, that did just one thing: take care of animals in a crisis. He had no doubt that Beverly already had a list. He'd see if Mona Hartman's elderly Peke, Sandy, was on Bev's list, and if not, he'd get into that apartment.

He'd get the other patients' requests to Lou, at Family Services, and doors would open and phones would ring until human needs were met as well as volunteers could meet them.

"You," he said to her, "get some rest. Get some sleep tonight. You hear me?"

"I'll try. You, too."

"No chance. *You* be careful." He was leaving her in reach of a story, and he knew she'd drive herself, and he knew she wouldn't get enough sleep, and he knew she'd take any chance to get to the bottom of the matter. "I know exactly what you're going to do."

"Wasn't there a controversy about the hotel?" she asked. "Wasn't there something about the roof, when they were starting construction?"

It had been a busy time in their lives for completely unrelated reasons when construction had been going on in that hotel. The *Planet* itself had been changing hands, and changing hands again. Not to mention Lois nearly making a disastrous marriage with Luthor—Luthor who had become more and more unbalanced . . . threatening all the world with his inventive, obsessive malice. Clark—and Lois—had had a lot on their minds when the Maernik was being built.

But it was in Clark's memory that she was right.

A cab was pulling up at the curb, reporters trailing it, probably from the parking garage, where they'd have intercepted Jimmy. Others were waiting out front. Lois was going to have to walk a gauntlet of reporters who weren't so closely connected to the disaster as to be on some family's visitor's list, and who were, bluntly, jealous—if they were human.

But Lois was also news, in and of herself, and he didn't, personally, want his picture in every newspaper in the world in close association with her. "The cab's here. Jimmy's got it."

Love you, her lips said, risking it. And she turned and walked briskly across the terrazzo to the police guarding the doors from the reporters.

He didn't wait. He went the way Jimmy had gone, careful of the breakable door—but once it was shut and secure at his back, once he was in the concrete garage, with parked cars on one side and the gaping doorway of the garage on his right, he launched himself for the blue, blue sky.

But thoughts chased him, even into that refuge.

Did Lois want a child? She wanted her work, she'd made that clear. She wanted what she'd built her life around. And he knew—he knew this wasn't a woman who'd readily seal herself indoors and abandon all her dreams, her love of the chase, of the city, of the whole world. Lose your momentum and you lost everything at the pinnacle of the journalist's trade. They'd say—whatever became of . . . and then forget her name.

If he were an ordinary man, he'd say to her . . . go for everything, career, kids, and the chances any married couple took. He'd help. He and she would bring up a dozen kids, with two hard-working, kid-loving model parents of the sort he'd had.

Kids who'd run and play in the pastures, clamber over the retired tractor, climb into the mysteries of the hayloft and look for the screech owl that startled the evenings.

But that wouldn't happen. They lived in the city that was life and breath to Lois. And even if they didn't live in the city— there was no place to hide from gossip, if there came to be children who weren't . . . ordinary.

Maybe she was thinking of such things. Maybe she was growing scared.

He was. Both thinking of such things. And growing scared.

But—if *he* could have a son—

He'd had two fathers. Two extraordinary fathers, both models of courage, and love. And had he nowhere to pass that legacy?

What would a child mean to him? What would it really mean . . . if he really, really thought it were possible to see that look on Lois's face—for a little boy or girl of their own?

And what if they ever found out absolutely to the contrary? What would it do to their relationship? Or to him and to her individually?

They had to talk. They really did.

And the world just wouldn't give them time.

The evening edition reached the late watch in the newsroom. "Great," was Perry's judgment. And Lois tried to spark an interest in the printed result of her day's labors. But there wasn't anything left. She'd finished the piece on young Gene. Fingers ached, back ached, ribs ached—she didn't want to look in the mirror, let alone at the imperfections she'd known she let get past her aching fingers, on the schedule they were keeping.

"You get home," Perry said, finding her slumped at her desk, head on hand, poking with a relatively undamaged forefinger at the touchpad. She hated mice. She really truly hated mice.

And she was hunting back through files, saving down what she found with clicks of a relatively unbruised thumb.

The *Planet's* morgue—the record of old issues—had gone over to computer record a year or so back. Certainly before the Maernik Hotel was built. What she wanted should be in there.

Perry had failed to get her full attention. He laid the current issue of the *Planet* down on the side of her desk, the issue that had her lead story on the survivors, and Jimmy's photo of the lady, Mona Hartman, the one with the elderly Peke. When Jimmy'd taken that photo, the light from the window had been on the woman, and the old lady, her face a map of choices made and lived with, looked like everyone's grandmother, good and kind.

Jimmy's photo, which she had to compliment him on. He'd done beautiful work, if you could call any part of the recent days beautiful—

But you could. That was the point Jimmy captured on film. That beauty was in the solemn little girl by the police barrier at the disaster site, so sober, so concerned. It was in the face of Mona Hartman, in the hospital, whose whole family was a little Peke dog that she didn't even dare to rate as important with all the grief around her . . . until someone really asked.

And it was in the somber, black-clad circle and linked hands of the family down at the cemetery, where the first funeral of many, many funerals scheduled was being held. Ron had had that assignment, and he'd done a wonderful piece of writing. She looked at the photos, and the faces, and Jimmy's photos, and knew that what the photographers had captured was beautiful: the love, the human caring, the bewilderment of people who'd led their lives never expecting to be the center of anything so dire. But dignity. That was the thing. From the little girl to the old lady to the grieving man at the cemetery: resiliency, and endurance, and tradition. Human dignity.

That was what she wanted to deal with, that was the story she wanted to tell; dignity—and justice. And for Billy—and for that beautiful old man Ron wrote about, burying his wife, she wanted to know why.

That was the burning question now, *why.* Amid all the feelings of helplessness and outrage, there was *why.*

"Lois." She was aware of Perry's hand on her shoulder, gently shaking her, while she stared hypnotized by the images of the living and the grieving. "I'm going to get you downstairs, hear? I don't know where Clark's got himself to, but I'm going to take you downstairs and get a cab, hear? You get your coat."

It was a rescue. She didn't know how she'd get home, without someone to guide her. She'd stayed too long at work, she'd extended too far, and right now she felt bruised in more than her body. There'd just been too much, and Clark, her Clark, her Clark whose arms she wanted around her, was somewhere in Russia.

She saved her working file down to a stiffy disk and put it in her purse. She shut down. When the light of the monitor screen went, she realized that most of the lights in the newsroom were out. Jimmy was still there. Perry was. Ron was. That was about all.

Perry helped her with her coat. She was so sore she could hardly put her arms in the sleeves. She tucked it around her, took her purse, and looked at Jimmy and Ron.

"Good work," she said, "really good work." There was something infectious about the spirit in the *Planet* in the last twenty-four hours. And she had to pass on what was welling up and brimming over in her, but she came close to getting soppy about it. Real close.

But Perry took her arm with the compassion of an honest-to-God Southern gentleman and led her to the elevators and down to the lobby.

"You youngsters just move aside," the editor of the *Planet* said to the junior reporters staking out the *Planet's* doorstep at this tired, twilight hour. "You just move over. This is one tired lady."

"Ms. Lane," one persisted, and Perry fixed that one with a snarling stare.

"Boy," Perry said, "you be polite to this lady or I'll call old Saul Abrams and see what *he* thinks."

That was still a potent name at the *Daily*, even in this brash generation: a name out of Perry's generation, mostly out of the picture at the *Daily* these days, but a man with standards attached. That name won a retreat, and Perry signaled a cab prowling the street.

He swept the door open when the cab arrived at the curb. "I'm seeing you home," he said, and she was grateful for that.

She'd bet her street was still staked out. She wanted her apartment, and her Elroy, and her shower and her bed.

She was walking wounded, and she'd held the pain back all this time. But she was feeling at least as if she'd caught her breath by the time the cab pulled up to her apartment, with—depend on it—stakeouts.

"I'll get you to your door," Perry said, as the sharks closed in.

But the cabby exited *his* door. Suarez, his license had read: she always noticed. Emilio Suarez. And Suarez opened their door wide, shoved back the importunate reporters with a grand gesture as if he were Cinderella's footman, and defended both of them until she'd reached the locked doors.

She was safe, beyond that. The LNN dish was parked on *her* block, and she'd rather it wasn't; but they were a good crew and she wouldn't mind giving them an interview in the morning.

"Not tonight," she called out to the waiting reporters, even rising to sympathy for the stakeouts. "I can't, guys. In the morning—in the morning, I'll talk. I'm so tired."

It was the promise of an interview. It was something won of their patience, which let them off the hook; and Perry had gotten her home, matter-of-factly, simple courtesy, Perry would insist, and maybe it was, to him; but the quality of the man who saw that as a simple matter—she treasured.

"Thanks," she said. She saw a tired face and wondered how long since Perry had seen his own home. But no one was there for him. Alice was gone. Their son Jerry was gone. Perry went on, working too-long hours, throwing himself into the making of a newspaper—creating something, working, because it was the right thing to do. But his generation didn't understand friendship with a woman. He'd be her knight, her boss, he'd understand a joke about romance and seeing her to her door, but everything came to him through that filter. She couldn't crack that gruff shell without, truth be told, cracking her own and risking the whole working relationship.

"Thanks," was all she could say, again, at the glass doors of her apartment. "Perry, you're the best. Get some rest, yourself."

Hero was a role he understood, maybe, in his heart of hearts. Maybe she gave him something he could take home with him, to a dark and empty apartment.

The doors locked automatically. The building manager, the policy was quite clear, wouldn't let the news services into the lobby. She had about enough button pushing left in her fingers to push the elevator buttons and to get home to her floor. She had her key out. You always had your key out.

She got the door opened, and Elroy was there, rubbing around her legs as she shed a coat that weighed more than it had in the morning; as she realized that the flowers on the coffee table weren't part of the ordinary scene.

A bouquet of lilies and daisies. She knew, with a little lift of her spirits, who could have set them there.

He'd left a card. It had the logo of a florist from the other side of town. It said, "Check the fridge."

Oh, you wonderful man, she said to herself, and went and opened up the fridge, Elroy doing a loving dance of anticipation about her ankles.

There was a plastic container of breakfast rolls from Broadway's. There was Chinese, not the way he *could* go out for Chinese. But there was Mongolian Pork and egg rolls. She was suddenly so hungry she could have eaten it *without* benefit of the microwave.

"I love you," she said to the empty air. She understood. She had her job and he had his and they each did what they had to. But this was like a warm blanket around tired shoulders. And she didn't know how to get him back, in their war of kind gestures, for something so practical and so thoughtful.

The smells of her favorite Chinese restaurant mingled with the perfume of lilies as she microwaved dinner and as, fresh from the shower and with a new set of Band-Aids, she served herself and sat down. Elroy parked himself in front of her feet, at attention, with a purr probably audible downstairs—clearly reminding her only an ingrate would eat *all* of it.

Chapter 7

Flying was no cure for want of sleep. The brain wanted time to recycle: when it became all one long, uninterrupted day, the ability to keep going and keep thinking was no warrant it was healthy, even for Superman.

But he could do it, and *could* under the circumstances meant *had to,* with lives and promises riding on his conscience; he hurtled through the high, cold air with the sun at his heels and the sky shadowing ahead of him.

The Atlantic, in those rare patches free of clouds, was a finely wrinkled gray sheet fading rapidly to night. A traveler from space would have thought the planet uninhabited. All traces of humanity disappeared at this altitude, and if he chose not to look more closely or on a finer scale, he could imagine himself alone, solitary, in a sky where not even planes intruded.

Planes tracked the jet stream and the prevailing winds to reach Europe. He knifed through them. *They* conserved whenever they could and relied on lift. He drew energy as he needed it—in fact could survive without food or water—but matter was a headier fare, and one of Big Belly Burgers' unrepentant hamburgers, with fries, would have come very, very welcome if he'd thought of it in the flurry of phone calls that he'd made—on his card—from a service station in Park Ridge, or if he'd thought to order *two* Chinese dinners when he phoned the order.

Then, he hadn't been that hungry. But he was burning it up, drinking in the energy around him, turning the air colder than surrounding air and creating microweather as he went, an effect that could generate a sparkle of ice as moisture froze in midair.

Now his keen vision saw the lights on the shores of France, not so many lights as there might have been a little earlier in the local night.

He wished he knew what Lois was up to. He trusted her heart, but he didn't trust the forces of information seekers moving around her. She'd met publicity before; but even if she did nothing to provoke it, the sensation mongers would rake up every piece of file footage, every incident, every scrap of her life.

Tell Lois that she had the kind of photographic past that yellow journalism could make into news? He'd tried.

And it just wasn't that easy to reason with her when Lois was as tired as she was, when she was in pain. He thought she'd understood his warning: he hoped they'd agreed. He wasn't sure he could imagine the cost it was to her to keep going, physically, after what she'd spent of herself in that basement, but he knew what the cost would be for her to duck down and stay out of the search after answers for those people in the hospital.

Her feature story was written by now. The evening edition was on the trucks, on the stands, headed for the hands of regular subscribers as he crossed the coast of Europe.

And as if he were the moving second hand of a clock and the rolling Earth and the day-night terminator were the clockwork, he sent the sun below the horizon behind him and entered the traveling shadow of night.

Lois was on the trail of a story he wished he could cover, and he was here. Around the planet, between earthquakes, fire, and flood, he could only hope to jump from disaster to disaster: a quake in Turkey, a forest fire threatening Russia's oldest nature reserve—like a man in a burning house, he saved what he could, sometimes a logical, reasoned choice, sometimes just a choice to act because he could act.

And then to discover he might have committed himself on one thing when he was needed elsewhere . . . that happened. It did happen.

Hard choices. Always hard choices. Did he value one life over another, American lives over Russian or Fijian? Now there was Lois, now there was a partner—to help on the one hand, to worry him on the other—because putting out fires sometimes meant going head to head with those culpable through negligence, who might want to duck responsibility, or those who had no human compassion. It meant going up against authorities, and those who'd kill for money, and worst of all, the self-obsessed who saw nothing but their own goal, and who'd kill and maim for nothing but a demonstration of their imagined power.

It wasn't a bomb that had taken down the Maernik. The more he reviewed the images he'd kept in his mind, the more he was sure of that.

But the vultures gathered, all the same.

Killers, potential killers, all of them, wanting the limelight for their cause, deaf to any requirement of logic that the target be related to the problem. Lois might represent—something they could use.

Predators like that included even the media: Morgan Edge, and his ilk, using the power of the small screen for his own gain, and increasingly willing to show anything, images more powerful than reason while, like subliminal conditioning, voices droned in the background, telling the viewer in what nook of the momentarily unreasoning mind to store the image.

Lois was the darling of the nation now. But positive news about the *Planet* wouldn't sell Edge's sponsors. *What have you done for us lately?* would be the operative words, and they had to outreport her or be more sensational—and how did you get more sensational than the *Planet's* last two issues? Answer: you *found* something, and if you were Morgan Edge, you found something sensational that damaged your opposition.

High, cold air was around him, and the glimmer of stars ahead of him, the thin atmosphere streaming past as he hurtled across the light-dotted European coast. He entered the airspace of France and streaked on to the white sentinels of the Alps. Mont Blanc was his signpost, and Lake Geneva his beacon as he dived Earthward—scanning for the staging area he'd used before, the same that he'd agreed on with the International Red Cross.

Down and down, to a warehouse on the outskirts of Geneva, where a van with the red cross on its side sat in the light of a pole.

He dropped lightly onto his feet in front of the van and wasn't surprised when the door opened and a man hopped out with a clipboard and a flashlight in hand to assist ordinary reading, in the blue-white light of the argon lamps overhead.

"Superman," the young man said. Jean-Baptiste was his name, Jean-Baptiste Delaplace, a friend from other missions, a man wearing the Red Cross insignia on his sleeve.

Superman took the offered hand.

Immediately, then, Jean-Baptiste, the expediter of anything a relief effort needed, offered his clipboard. "I have everything, if you will sign, Superman. I have maps where—if you can possibly do something about the bridge—your impression of the condition of the pilings will tell us a great deal, and save an immense effort."

"I received the fax." He had gotten it, at a mail service, during his last-minute foray after telephones and Chinese dinner. "I'll do what I can." He signed the receipt. "The State Department is handling the paperwork, so it's clear at the other end. All right?"

"*Bien, bien, merci.*" Jean-Baptiste's English was excellent, but he slipped, perhaps trying to think of a last-moment item. "No change. No difference."

"*Oui.*" Superman bridged the language gap without thinking. "*Merci bien.*" He'd scanned the manifest, or whatever one called it when the vessel involved was rectangular, canvas-covered corrugated steel with a blunt cone bolted to the nose. "Good job."

"*Tout va,*" Jean-Baptiste said and waved a farewell as he lifted into the air. "*Bon soir,* Superman! *Bon voyage!*"

"*Merci, merci,* Jean-Baptiste!" The container was rigged for lifting—the easiest way for him to get it airborne, and he hauled it aloft, confident in the Red Cross, who knew what forces of acceleration and what wind and cold it had to withstand, and who would have packed it to stand anything.

Geneva fell away behind him. He climbed above the lake, past the air traffic lanes, seeing the blink of aircraft running lights, confident, too, that Jean-Baptiste was on the car phone telling the airport that the blip on their radar was a large shipping container being airlifted to Russia.

On a notable run, airlifting such a portable unit to Ethiopia, the harness had snapped. But he'd caught it long before it hit the lake.

Relief agencies were on the ground in that remote part of Russia right now, and dawn should be starting there, but the loss of the bridge had made it next to impossible to get supplies to the village refugees or, the State Department had said, the villages on the missing lake. The long way around, along the shores of what had been a high mountain lake, was a route of many kilometers at a crawl, on a road equally affected by the quake—and beset with the political troubles that had taken hold in this remote little area. This container, the size of a truck itself, was a medical station and feeding station when it unfolded, so at least there would be something available to assist the villagers before and after they could get medical personnel to the area.

And he had a laundry list of other necessities he had to provide, those that weren't packed tight in the interior of the portable: secure shelter, secure pure water supply, good drainage, adequate food and means to cook it—all the things that supported health.

The items he hadn't brought, he was going to have to lift up from the town below the dam.

Long night, he said to himself, looking at the stars above the Carpathians.

But he trusted that, country folk that they were, his villagers weren't helpless on that hillside where he'd left them last night. Rain and all, they'd had the tools to obtain shelter, and no group of farmers was going to sit moaning and helpless in the rain as long as they had the supplies he'd given them. Drinkable water wouldn't be a problem where they were situated: beyond catching rainwater, the mountains would surely offer springs the villagers would use if they had the nutrition and the physical strength to climb to get to them.

Getting rid of water was another matter.

And food—beyond what he'd left them: food, too, for the higher, undamaged villages who were now cut off from civilization. Again, farmers and fishermen weren't helpless, and they could live for a while, but there were elderly folk with them, and sooner or later they were going to need that road desperately.

Helicopters had no landing area on that steep hill. The Red Cross had gotten, so they said, a few loads in this afternoon after the weather improved. But they had to hover and drop supplies, and that was risky both to the supplies and to people on the ground. There were power lines in the area from which the choppers had to fly, and those were risky in the dark and the bad weather.

Let him see what he could do, he'd concluded in the calls back and forth with the State Department.

Meanwhile they'd gotten ten large tents in this morning—if things had gone well, if the supplies discharged from the copter hadn't rolled down and off a cliff, or lodged in a tree.

And there was going to be a bog where their lake had been, a lot of land with a serious drainage problem, dead fish—a smelly mess and a health hazard, even at that latitude, that altitude, and in the cold air. That lake bed, still a stream course, was feeding water and human and agricultural waste down into the lake lower down. Now the ecological problem that might have been postponed had become acute.

It was no good, to take these people away from the land that defined what they were, to cast them into an urban environment and onto the charity of others. That wasn't rescue.

He had plans. The farm kid from Smallville had a very good grasp of what these people needed most, and experts from agricultural programs and universities all over the world had been channeling information into what had come down to a message from the State Department: *We're talking to their government to get the plan approved.*

And one, confidential, from the embassy in Moscow: "It's a rebel region. The government is concerned about the rebels in the area. They don't want supplies brought in. They're dragging their feet on permissions."

Granny might have been a Bolshevik or a nationalist rebel in her youth, but there hadn't been any secret weapons in the houses he'd stripped in desperate haste. Superman didn't set himself up to judge, but he knew noncombatants when he saw them. Likely it was deep, deep politics involving the whole district and its relationship to the central government; ethnic groups, no knowing what sort. The mountains were a patchwork quilt of languages and ethnicities.

He had to ask himself whether a copter landing pad, if he established one, was going to be used primarily for doctors and supplies—or for other purposes; and what he was getting into. A career of crossing international boundaries into the lives of people in crisis hadn't left him ignorant of such possibilities.

If you were going to help people, it was a good idea to find out what was help and what wasn't. That, for starters.

The body wanted to sleep. The mind wasn't having much luck, Lois decided, and wouldn't, not with that computer disk lying over on the table in her purse.

The body wanted the wonderful smooth sheets—but the mind had been on a track when Perry had interrupted her quest through the archive, a question that it couldn't let go, ignore, forget, or otherwise dismiss.

And, much as Lois hated herself for certain personality traits, a shower, a satin gown, a cup of microwaved milk (disgusting) did nothing to put her curiosity to bed, even when the knees wanted to cave in and the eyes were overwhelmed with the urge to rest.

One look, one short look. She'd been so close. She thought she'd nabbed the right files out of archive.

They were holding more funerals tomorrow. A lot of them. There were a lot of people not getting any sleep tonight. There were people in the hospital who weren't that comfortable, either. Including Billy Anderson. His parents weren't getting all that much sleep.

She might have the *why* of it all right over there in her bag.

It wouldn't take too long to flip on the computer and take a look. She got the disk, sore fingers and all. She took herself and her Band-Aids over to the chair and sat down, powered up, shoved the disk in.

Files. Titles of files. A quick scan for dates: the hotel had been under construction last year. And the hotel opening. That had been—what? December?

But before then, there'd been controversy about the design.

There'd been a lawsuit. It hadn't been her story. She'd been otherwise occupied. And the *Planet* had been in turmoil at the time, too, with prospective buyers and everyone worrying about the fate of the paper.

They'd just not quite had their minds collectively on the Maernik controversy. She'd been working—briefly—at the television station, a period of her life she didn't like to remember.

But the *Planet* had covered the lawsuit; and if, digging into those back files, she should discover that some good investigative reporting could have blown the whistle, stopped the construction, saved all those lives—she *really* wasn't going to sleep tonight.

There it was. Right around the time she'd nearly made the mistake of her life. A woman *didn't* forget the date of her almost-wedding . . . to the man whose company, Lexcorp, was the one doing the suing in said lawsuit.

She also didn't forget the date at which her job had been threatened.

The date at which everyone's jobs had been threatened. She'd been so focused on a conniving scoundrel—believing Lex, believing in his glittering, glamorous promises.

But Lexcorp had been going to build the hotel, that was the way it had been; and when the scandal broke that had stopped her marriage—the truth about Lex Luthor's activities, his extortion and his plots against the city—the scandal had also stopped the hotel construction. The Premier Hotel chain, which owned the flagship Maernik Hotels and two other less luxurious, less avant-garde chains, had changed contractors on the Maernik Metropole Hotel after the site had been cleared for construction and the machines were in place to excavate the foundations. It was, to the average citizen, she was sure, a nothing story, one of those things from the second page of the Business pages, swept off the front pages of the paper into secondary importance by the more widespread troubles of Lexcorp and Lex Luthor's reputation around that time. The Maernik had changed architects and abrogated the former contract.

Lexcorp, amid the near collapse of its financial empire, and the apparent death of its CEO, had sued, fighting back against the breaking of dozens of such contracts throughout the region. All the while Lex Luthor's reputation went down, down, and down, and news stories, breaking at the rate of one a day, were bringing out daily examples of his dealings.

Lexcorp hadn't folded: it had scrambled to distance itself from Luthor and Luthor's illegal actions. And sued everyone who tried to get out of contracts with them.

There it was. PREMIER HOTEL CONSTRUCTION DELAY.

Her eyes were blurring with exhaustion. Elroy had seated himself on the table beside the computer and purred at her, a soporific sound that had her eyes all but crossing with desire for sleep. Elroy was disabused of the notion he could tread on the keyboard. But he edged close.

She'd asked Art Hampton, at the Business and Financial desk, who'd told her the approximate dates.

But it wasn't Art's piece. It was Monique's. Monique had quit the big-city pressure and gotten a job in a financial magazine during the whole *Planet* buyout fracas. *Monique Simms,* her name was.

Monique had once had a job with Galaxy Communications.

What time was it? Nine-thirty.

Nine-thirty-eight.

She keyed up her card file. Monique hadn't been at the *Planet* long. Had blazed into the *Planet* after Morgan Edge, over at Galaxy, had fired her. She'd been there during the time Lexcorp had owned the *Planet,* and gone out again, quit, not at the *Planet* long enough to build much of a network.

But she had Monique's phone number.

The warm milk had worn off. Her nerves were like piano wire. She dialed the number she had, fighting Elroy for access to the phone, and got an answering system.

"Monique. Monique, this is Lois Lane. You wrote an article on the Maernik Hotel. I need to know the lowdown. Anything you know that didn't make it into the article."

It was curious. Someone had picked up the phone. She'd bet on it. And then, just as she gave her number, a male voice said, "Monique's dead. Six months ago."

Her heart jolted. *That* was unexpected news. "I'm very sorry. I'm from the *Planet*. I—hadn't heard. No one had—"

The man hung up the phone and left her sitting there, rubbing Elroy's head as Elroy butted her hand for attention.

Monique was dead. That was a shock.

Art hadn't known. Monique had quit the paper and hadn't been there long enough to develop ties to anybody, she supposed. So no one had known.

But *dead*. How? When? Why? A reporter's chain of questions came quite naturally to this case. From Galaxy Communications to the *Planet*, from the *Planet* to . . . where had she gone?

She dialed another number from her file. Art's.

"Art?" Art was an older man. Classical music was in the background as Art Hampton picked up. "Art, it's Lois. Sorry to bother you, but it *was* Monique who did that piece on the hotel. Did you know she'd died?"

"Died? No. No, I didn't know. She was a kid, for God's sake."

Anybody under forty was a kid to Art.

"A man answered. I guess a boyfriend, maybe a husband. Said she'd been dead six months and hung up."

She waited for reaction from the other end.

"I had absolutely no idea."

"I've got an article here, on the construction delay. You said you didn't remember anything. But is there *anything*, Art, any scrap of a thing?"

Art was a good, solid business editor. Death didn't often figure in the stories he handled. There was a moment of silence. "There was a whistle-blower. Testified *for* Lexcorp and said that Cross & Associates—they're the company that Premier had picked to do the Maernik job instead of Lexcorp—was cheating on contracts all over the city."

"Fill me in, Art. Please."

She hadn't been at the *Planet* during the time Lex's company had been involved in the original contract with Premier Hotels, the time Art was referring to. Lex had been courting her during those days, had bought the *Planet* and nearly run it into the ground. Had put her on staff at LNN, she'd had her head in the sand, and she'd not realized the *Planet*'s financial troubles were Lex's doing. It was a hard time to refer to, with *Planet* staffers who'd been there when the old *Planet* offices had literally blown up, when Lex, at her wedding, had supposedly committed suicide.

They'd thought Lex was out of the picture for good, until the rat turned up again and the police laid hands on him for a string of crimes that were then coming to light. She'd been mortally embarrassed—humiliated, not only about the personal foolishness of almost marrying a snake like Lex, but the professional shame of not having stood with her friends and colleagues. Something had gotten into her head about that time, and good friends and Clark might have straightened her out and gotten her thinking straight, for which she owed them everything; but going back into those days and referencing that particular stretch of time with someone who'd been suffering with the *Planet*—was excruciating.

"About that time," Art said, "we got our angel." Meaning Franklin Stern, who'd bought the *Planet*. "Lexcorp needed liquidity to pay off some short calls as well as for legal fees; and then the Premier chain found a loophole in the Maernik contract. It nearly killed them."

Freely translated, Lex had spent too much, Lexcorp needed cash in the worst way.

"So Lexcorp did the design for the Maernik!"

"No, no, they had done a design, but the Premier chain claimed the contract was void and awarded a contract to Cross Construction. Who did their own design. Then Lexcorp sued. The Premier chain didn't want even the suspicion of a connection to Lexcorp, not even so far as using the design. And—" A small clearing of the throat. "—scandal involving the Lexcorp CEO enabled them to void the contract. There was a Reputation and Goodwill clause. The Premier chain won."

"So what's this about a whistle-blower?"

"A Cross Construction engineer contacted us saying the Cross design was flawed. I assigned Monique Simms to interview the man. Galaxy ran the piece. We didn't." There was a small pause, as perhaps Art dealt with the terrible question— what he'd had a chance to report about that hotel, and hadn't.

But others had reported it. The information, true or false, had gotten to the public. Art had nothing to be ashamed of. He'd been on the job making decisions. She'd been in the throes of emotional crisis. *She* hadn't been on the job.

"You didn't believe it?" she asked Art.

"Howard Cross is a reputable architect. Galaxy ran the piece." It was the second time Art had said so in as many minutes, pounding that point home, that the information hadn't been secret. "We didn't go with the story because we waited while Premier had another firm check it out. And while city engineers went over it. It wasn't so. It just wasn't so."

Art said it wasn't so. The hotel design was sound. While people lay in the hospital. And in caskets.

"So," she began slowly, "what do you think? What's this whistle-blower's name?"

"Smalley."

"Do you have any idea of his whereabouts?"

"Right now? The cemetery."

"When?"

"The day the article came out. Suicide. Cross denied firing him. But he committed suicide."

"Was it suicide?"

"Maybe. Maybe it wasn't. Smalley said Cross had ignored his advice. He said the design wouldn't hold up under snow load. He'd sent that in a letter to the chairman of the Premier Hotel chain, and died."

Monique . . . was dead. A man named Smalley . . . was dead. Sixty people . . . were dead.

Maybe she should adjust the air-conditioning. Maybe it was exhaustion. She felt chilled through as she made a courteous end to the conversation with Art and hung up.

But she had an agenda for tomorrow, something to fight for, something to win.

No bomb, Superman said so.

Clark said. Clark said. She had to keep the trail of information accurate in her mind and never mix up the sources, if she was going to keep Superman's secret.

She shut her eyes and she saw hospital beds. Tubing. Jagged lines of light on a scope, lines that defined a life. And Billy's hand, closing on hers, because the voice that had spoken to him out of the dark for so many hours said, firmly, *Wake up, Billy.*

He came back for her when even his parents hadn't roused him.

That was the faith he had in her. And she had a lead on what had put him in that bed. If there'd been fault covered up, she'd uncover it. If there'd been fools, she'd find them. An engineering investigation into a structural failure was going to take time: weeks and months of measurement taking and wrangling, maybe, for the engineers to do their jobs, but the families of those people deserved the right answer, not just an answer that protected companies from lawsuit.

Monique, dead. That had been a shock. She wondered who the man answering the phone had been.

What Monique's short life had been.

Lord, this was one of those stories with threads going under so many doors, and a reporter sat and shivered with exhaustion and the desire to be following those leads.

And Luthor. God, Luthor. Was there no burying the corpse of that old association?

He, Luthor, was in prison on Stryker's Island. Safe . . . in prison . . . where she hoped he stayed for the rest of his life.

Creepy thought to take to bed. She gathered up Elroy's buzzing warmth and carried him, stroking his well-stuffed self as she went.

No need to go in to the office in the morning. She'd call in from the field. Tell Perry she was on a lead.

She didn't want to set the harpies out front to flapping about her trail, alerting every carrion crow in town.

She dumped Elroy onto the bed and crawled beneath the satin sheets, under the weight and safety of the blanket.

Superman, she thought, on a sigh, as her head hit the pillow—and Elroy trod the pillows, creating hills and valleys.

Wasn't it in mountains, where Clark had gone?

Clark. Superman. She loved two men. It was extraordinary how alike and how different they were.

Clark just had no business in Russia. Superman definitely did.

Tents were up, a little spider's nest of tents pitched crazily among the trees in the sunlight, ropes stretched to tree trunks, supporting canvas. The wagon was part of it all. The pony, startled out of sleep, was picketed by the tents along with Granny's cow. The pigs and chickens set off an alarm, as a truck-sized module arrived out of the clear blue sky.

"Superman!" a child's voice cried, and the villagers, huddled together around the warmth of a modest fire, rose and came to see this wonderful item in his hands . . . which was no easy matter to set down. Superman hovered with his load while villagers lent a hand, moving a pile of rocks and brush up to brace one side.

He eased it down, let go gingerly, ready to dive to stop it sliding down. A one-man construction agency couldn't simultaneously brace and rig a platform and hold the thing in the air; but with it off his hands—literally—he could scurry about doing a little rearrangement of the hillside, smashing up rock into rubble and fill and then into finer gravel that settled in and held the larger rocks. It was an essentially noisy process. The dogs barked and chased something they couldn't see. He had a lot to do, and he didn't do it for show, but the villagers, who'd probably seen movies but never television, and had certainly never seen him in action, applauded and cheered whenever he stood still to consider his next move.

"What is he doing?" figured in the questions. He knew that much. But he just couldn't explain the details.

"Ohh," came the knowing exhalation when he moved the truck-sized module firmly onto the foundation he'd made. "Ahhh," as he began to adjust and level it.

Even Granny was impressed when the aerodynamic cone came off and extended legs to become a sheltering pavilion, on legs that Superman's hands didn't need a wrench to adjust.

Then he dropped the hatch beneath the cone and revealed supplies packed to the walls of the mobile medical unit. The first thing he set out was a generator, to run the lights, and the fuel to power it.

Then he set up, to the side of it, a portable shower and a sanitary unit, which the villagers, muddy and bedraggled, thought was the funniest thing they'd seen.

"They send us toilets and electrical generators!" The villagers laughed. "Perhaps next we get a commissar!"

"We *need* the toilet," an old man said. "No use for the commissar!"

Laughter followed that sally.

And Granny and the notables had to have a tour.

"There are electric lights," Superman said to his translator, Dimitri, the same young villager who'd flown with him to save Granny. "But not much petrol for the generator. Doctors will come. But they send medicines everybody should take, to prevent getting sick."

He was the first candidate for hand washing, with the sterile water and disinfectant the unit provided. He cleaned spots on various villager arms and delivered injections that, he was sorry, did hurt. But less than fever would. If you were the only outsider who could get there, you had to be a medic at need—you had to give the shots, patch the wounds, and you had to explain, through the translator, the necessity of keeping nonsterile hands off the equipment that real medics would use, once he was able to get the road open.

But much as he had to take on himself in the emergency, the decision of what to do next wasn't his. These people deserved a voice in their own destiny, and through the young man who translated, he laid out the possibilities to the village. He spread out his map and discussed where the lake was now, and where the other villages where, where the road went, all those things.

The road. That was what they understood: that was what located them conceptually within his map—when it was possible this remote village had never seen a printed map. He wasn't sure that they had. They understood what he was demonstrating once they realized that, and they were glad to know that the other villages, those that had ringed the missing lake, were still there.

"There," Granny said through the translator, jabbing the map with a newly scrubbed finger. "There was our village. That is *our land*."

"Before the dam?" It was the lake bed she pointed to.

"Before the dam," Granny said, and lamely, through the medium of the young translator and the occasional contribution of others leaning close about the map, he heard the story, how the government had built the dam and moved them off their land at gunpoint. The place where the lake was had been their pasturage. And the government had taken it. What he'd heard from the State Department indicated the lower dam might have been for electrical power; but the upper one had very likely been simply to break up a troublesome unity of villages.

"Maybe," he said, knowing that he was stepping where not only angels but diplomats feared to tread. But these were farmers. He knew what they felt about that land. "Maybe it can be your pasture again. The earthquake will happen. It's a bad place for a dam."

"Good place for sheep," Granny said decisively, and rested her hands on the head of her stick. "Very good place for sheep."

It was a mudflat, soon to be rank with its dead fish and dead weeds, a mudflat eroded into a chasm with the rip that had taken out the dam. But clearly there had been in the original pasturage a stream that channeled the water from the mountain heights down the valley, ultimately to the lowlands. That stream was flowing now, he was well sure, in his personal memory of a broad, dark scar shining with isolated pools of water as he came in by air.

"The old river ran here?" he asked Granny, and traced what he thought would be the line.

Granny's arthritic finger traced a truer line, and through the young man's translations he learned the particulars, the valley of Granny's youth, a green and beautiful valley.

The old regime had cared nothing for that. Ill-conceived engineering, industry let loose to smoke up the sky and the land—the valley had been part of some plan to electrify the region, or simply a promise to try to impress the locals, or a boondoggle for an official hell-bent on power. Whatever it was, no dam ought ever to have stood there.

And a face hardened by difficult years grew softer, gentler, just in the telling of it. And angry when she talked about the corruption and the failures.

He didn't want to raise hopes that he could do anything. Too much land might have washed away. Dirt wasn't just dirt. Topsoil was different from sterile, far-under-the-surface earth. There was life in the one, not in the other, and you couldn't just dump dirt from just anywhere onto the place and expect it to grow good weeds, let alone be good pasture.

A botched job was what this district had already gotten, rural traditions run over and trampled, farmers' common sense ignored in favor of some party-line executive with industrial and political dreams that wouldn't work.

Botch the recovery, however, and not only wouldn't weeds grow, it would become a maze of eroded gullies, silting up the dam below.

It was with the least little hope that the old woman looked at him.

"I'll try," he said.

The harpies on the doorstep doubtless told the harpies at the *Planet's* door that she was on her way to work.

But the cab hadn't gone there.

She hadn't gone there.

She went instead to a donut shop out by the state office complex and bought a sack of jelly-filled and cream custard Bismarcks.

Then she took the same cab to one of those thoroughly workaday venues a reporter had sometimes to search. She went to the third floor of City Hall (a mere wrong turn away from the court and the orange-clad principals of the docket) and shared a cup of morning coffee with the woman who used to work at the motor license bureau and who now worked for the Records Bureau. She *never* gave up a contact.

And Beeb never gave up a fondness for donuts from the Hole in One, six miles away by cab, across from the motor license bureau and as good as on the moon from Beeb's present job location. Lois knew the way to Beeb's heart, and enjoyed a gloriously sinful raspberry Bismarck herself while Beeb, in a more somber way and with the implication Beeb ached to do something to find answers about the Maernik, said she'd be glad to hit the computer in answer to a question.

"But I can tell you Cross is big," Beeb said. "A lot of big jobs. That's who the city had build the Arts Center. And there's the telephone building. And the hotel. This is about the hotel, isn't it? I saw you on television. I read your paper. How's that little boy?"

"Improving. Thank God."

"Just a minute." Beeb stuffed the last of a cream custard Bismarck into her mouth, dusted her hands, and headed for the outer office like a fighter heading for the ring. She set herself in front of a terminal in that office, at which she labored with enviable speed. Lois sat and sipped the good donut-shop coffee and watched through the glass panels as Beeb retrieved something.

Beeb came back with a printout and sat down, offering it to her.

It was Cross Construction's entire list of building permits and executed contracts over the last ten years.

The brand new Arts Center.

The new Sun Tower Retirement Center.

The new parking facility and Children's Wing of Metropolis General Hospital.

She didn't say a word, although her heart had just gone thump, and still beat harder.

"Those so-and-so's did the hospital," Beeb said, with indignation in her eyes.

"I don't know what the story is. I tell you, I *promise* you, Beeb, a phone call when I know what the truth is. The minute my editor knows, you'll know. Don't talk about it, don't tell anyone."

"It's public record," Beeb said. "And you aren't the first to mention Cross, I hate to tell you."

"Who?"

"LNN."

Lois gulped coffee gone tepid and objectionable. "This morning?"

"About an hour ago. They weren't here, but they were running stuff on Cross Construction. I don't think they had the list. But it was on the air about Cross. I saw it at breakfast."

Beeb had seen it at breakfast. *She,* Lois Lane, ace reporter, prize-winning *fool,* hadn't had the television on and had counted on the donuts for breakfast.

Of *course,* reporters who'd run the story on the Premier Hotel–Lexcorp lawsuit were going to remember there'd been a charge that the Cross design was flawed. Everything was an *of course* to reporters at LNN, whose parent company, Lexcorp itself, couldn't be ignorant of what had become one of the key points in the contract dispute with Premier Hotels.

Of course LNN had the story. What LNN had access to was limited only by what Lex Luthor and his lawyers *and* his architects had been willing to commit to file folders or computer records.

Ask what an LNN reporter could lay hands on, metaphorically speaking, with a simple phone call, while she was chasing across town trying to get things the hard way.

Lois Lane, ace reporter, was playing catch-up with every media news organization in the country by now. Playing catch-up with the *world,* for that matter. If she wanted to know what was going on in that department, she might as well go back to the Hole in One and watch the news over her second cup of morning coffee.

That wasn't an option.

"Can I use the phone?" she asked Beeb, treading near the brink of Beeb's rules about reporters, she was sure; but Beeb was willing. She used the phone book, looked up Cross Construction, and tried the number.

Busy. Busy. Busy.

Ask how many *other* reporters were trying to interview Howard Cross. Phone, fax, or E-mail, there was going to be a human wall of reporters at Number 5, Industrial Park Plaza.

"No luck?" Beeb asked.

"No," she said. Lois Lane, wonder child, was being outmaneuvered, outclassed, outgunned. She ached in every muscle, the letdown after the euphoria of the success was arriving with a vengeance, and she momentarily asked herself if maybe a day off wouldn't be a good idea at this point. She'd lost half a day to sleep after she'd written her initial article, she'd written a good story yesterday afternoon, but she was just running out of leads. Score one for LNN.

But there was someone she knew who could speak with a special knowledge on the Cross-Lexcorp controversy. Someone she'd rather not deal with. Someone she'd as soon not see again as long as she lived.

Her former fiancé.

Lex.

Lex Luthor.

Chapter 8

Night, after a day of surveying and moving supplies.

And a military camp, the other side of the river, the staging point for the Red Cross and the other relief agencies.

Night didn't stop consultations. A lantern hung from a tent pole of the staff tent illumined a table of maps and charts and a circle of tired faces. They were civil authorities, Russian military and technical personnel, a Red Cross administrator from Uganda, and Superman, a single brightness in among so much khaki and so many mud-stained uniforms. The engineers had been working since the quake. So had the army.

Now the army, laboring nonstop, was prepared to move in old pontoon sections as a stopgap, but with the water level sunk, the whole approach to the river a chasm leading to a mud terrace, leading to another mud terrace, it was going to be difficult to restore the road. The earnest hope was that the bridge pilings were going to be viable.

Superman watched as the senior engineer, an elderly Russian with thickened knuckles, drew a sketch based on the more obscure printouts, charts, and sound-ings—which the engineer didn't expect a layman to grasp.

The sketches made certain things clear, however, and the printouts of subsurface features, so complex they looked as much like weavings as printout, made sense in ways Superman didn't admit or explain. He'd met the like of such soundings many times, and his layman's eye made sense of the readouts in ways that had very much to do with the way his supersenses integrated in his brain.

There'd been a time before he was thirteen he'd been sure he was going blind—the supersenses had started sharpening, giv-ing him ways of seeing and hearing that had really started before that but, one week at about thirteen, had begun to accel-erate to a point of approaching chaos.

He'd had his moment of teenage rebellion against a set of senses making less and less order of the world. He'd taken off walking down the road and walked clear to Bernham village and back again on the edge of his thirteenth winter, because the visions were coming to him so strongly and hammering at him and blurring and revising the world he knew, until he couldn't be sure he wasn't going blind or mad. He'd wanted to lose him-self until he could be sure, worst thought of all, that he wasn't going to hurt his parents, his friends, the whole town. He hadn't known what was happening to him. There'd been no one to ask. He'd feared to upset his parents.

Lois in her articles called it X-ray vision. But it was more like sensing *through* things by what echoed and what didn't and let-ting the visual sense interpret it: the conflicting images made ripples if you looked at it without spreading it out in your mind; and you did that with a kind of depth perception that didn't depend on binocular vision but on actually *getting* infor-mation from *inside* an object. It hadn't been until he saw that printout in a science magazine that he'd known ordinary people built machines to get a look at what his naked eyes were trying to show him: the whole world *was* those wavy lines if you looked too hard, until the brain found ways to put 3-D in that image and integrate it with echoes and hearing and all the other things the brain picked up. The machines couldn't do what his senses did when he focused down on an object. Not without a whole array of computers assembling the images the way his brain assembled what his senses took in naturally and on the move.

"I see it very clearly," he murmured to the senior engineer, who was from Moscow. "I see it, no problem." He wasn't quite as sure of his vocabulary when they were talking in precise engineering and mathematical terms, but he was sure that he understood the lay of the rock and the set of the pilings that sustained the critical bridge. *"Spaciba."*

"The lights—" one of the juniors began. There'd been worry about getting lights down to the bottom of the muddy water, where there was no visibility.

"I don't need them the way a camera does," Superman said. "It's all right. I'll be back."

He was tired. He had no right, he told himself, to compare his exhaustion with theirs, but after nights of no sleep and no dreamtime and a steady diet of crises both theirs and his own, he was tired. A hot drink and a meal had come welcome at the aid station. A fifteen-minute nap would have come more welcome than that.

But he was glad the army had flown in the engineer and his charts, and he was glad to talk to the man from Moscow. The printouts made a lot of things clearer because they were a historical record of what the bottom had looked like before the flood. The man, insisting the foreigners know that *his* administration had had nothing to do with building the dam, had the authority to get them from a government office in Pyatigorsk; they'd been expedited thanks to a request from the White House to the Russian government, and they were invaluable.

If he could find the present state of affairs, in this night of cold drizzle, and compare the result to these charts, it would make the military engineers' jobs easier. It was volcanic rock down there beneath the flood. The bridge pilings had been sunk into it.

The question was whether the swirling, particulate-laden floodwaters had changed that bottom profile, scouring the bottom very much like a water-borne sandblasting, and how deeply those pilings were still set.

He excused himself to men who might now get a little sleep. He stepped out of the tent and launched himself into the air, above the tent and surrounding camp.

The previous night—the region being ridden with bandits and revolutionaries sometimes indistinguishable from each other—the army had lost a vehicle to a mine.

A rebel group had claimed *they* had blown up the dam. And at another time, in other events, it wouldn't have made him angry; but he'd seen enough in the last couple of days, and here it was the same thing. Anything, anyone's grief for publicity. Pounce on the phone and try to coattail other humans' suffering to grab a bottom-paragraph notice in the news. From a reporter's point of view—these useless hyenas jammed the phone lines in a disaster, right along with the crackpots wanting to complain about brain waves being beamed at them by microwave towers.

Then there were the ones who'd actually carry out such acts, who were somewhere beneath honest hyenas.

No bomb in this case, either, unless one counted a prior regime that had scanted its geological studies in advance of, of all things, a succession of dams holding back acres of water, rather than hear any single engineer stand up and say, *It's not safe.*

A failing of courage on this one, for certain. The old regime had moved Granny and the peasants of the village off their land to build that monstrosity, and now their meadow was a gullied mudflat. He'd seen it by day and it wasn't a pretty sight—a mudflat ringed by beautiful snowy mountains and high-country villages just melting out from under winter.

The land was badly damaged. Topsoil had gone right down the river and settled on the bottom of the lake, to choke the fish in that lake before it piled up against the next dam and caused problems there.

What made a body of water or air drop a load of particles? Change in energy. The water had to give up energy . . . and it precipitated silt suspended in it. It had dropped most of it when the flood had hit the lake.

It had also dropped logs, boulders, rocks of every size. Building materials.

An idea occurred to him as he hovered over the night-shrouded river, in the dismally cold outpouring of a precipitating heaven. *He* was a heat sink when he stoked up for a major effort, and he didn't draw on an environment that contained living things, because he could do them damage. But in this desolation, he wasn't near things that could be harmed.

To wield power such as he had, one had to think, think hard of consequences, of a chain reaction of events that would follow a chill-down of the river water: fish and shellfish and algae would be the first to be harmed in terms of how fast they processed and reacted to the change in their environment. But fish, vulnerable to sudden changes in temperature, could flee an advancing line of ice water into the warmer, cleaner waters of the lake. The water had undergone chemical change: the thermocline had vanished, as top layers and bottom layers of the lake had mixed. But that was a fait accompli. And the fish were alive. Bearing cuts and with irritated gills and stressed by the temperature change, but alive.

That lake, with all it held, was a resource. It was going to survive, barring the upper flat dumping silt wholesale into it as the water continued to flow from the mountains.

A dredge, which he could manage, could lift the mess back up to the ravaged pastureland. That still wouldn't fix matters: the first rain would bring it right down again. But he could get topsoil from somewhere. He could move in trees to provide stable windbreaks, and use whatever rock he scooped up for terracing to prevent the soil from sluicing down the gradient.

He was positively cheerful as he hit the water, and the hungry feeling began to vanish as his energy rose and that in the water around him slowed. He drew in a deep breath and *looked* at the bottom mud and the stone. He banged a rock against one of the columnlike bridge pilings beneath the water, a noise that echoed back to him in a picture of the bottom.

There was erosion and there was damage. The pilings nearest the shore had held very well. The bottom had a deep depression in the center that had undercut another, and here was a touchy operation. Heating the area, which might melt and repair the rock, could damage the concrete.

But he could chill down the concrete with a rapid intake and blowing of watery breath and a heavy draw of energy while heat vision concentrated the energy into the igneous rock. He concentrated his heat vision on the rock. Water tried to boil around it and he sucked in and blew it out. Rock glowed in the murk like a sullen red sun, extinguished itself against the pillar, and gripped it fast as what had been magma supercooled around it under the gust of his lungs.

That piling wouldn't budge. And the metal reinforcement of the concrete piling, like the concrete itself, hadn't appreciably felt the heat.

It was a transaction he didn't explain to his enemies, or to the curious.

But high school physics had landed on his juvenile ears with the same dawning of personal revelation, personal freedom, in the same measure as the revelations of his biology course had begun to offer him a frightening litany of what he wasn't.

Physics—he loved with a passion. And he studied biology as a list of damage he could do, unthought, if he didn't memorize the stress limits and life requirements of things he dealt with.

Death was a biological problem. And you couldn't undo it once you'd caused it. In nature, things chain-reacted with a vengeance. He knew now that the cold and heat he'd balanced, underwater in a flowing river, was still traveling down river. It was a condition that the fish and algae and the villages that depended on them might survive. The shellfish, in that settling silt, were potentially in trouble, however, and racing along underwater and into the lake down by the hydroelectric dam, he searched the depths for a shellfish bed he blasted clean with his breath.

You couldn't save all of them. Like nature, you saw that enough would survive to reproduce. And that bed would, if it lived, reproduce and replenish life in the lake, natural filters, every one of those little creatures.

Was there a biologist in reach of the army, to tell him the life requirements of the shellfish and the lake fish and the food chain from minnows up? That would be as helpful as the engineers at the next stage. But people in various regions of the world hadn't grown up as he had, learning to consider that both answers to a situation were as vitally important.

He surfaced and streaked back to the tent, only slightly damp—and scared the drowsy soldiers, who didn't see him coming. Tent walls billowed. Maps flew. But the stakes held. He'd judged that at the very last second, to a nicety.

"I have your information," he began.

"About what?" was their instant question, as military aides holstered guns nervously pulled.

"The pilings are sound," he said. "Will you call the engineers?"

Chapter 9

Stryker's Island wasn't open to tourists. It was, from the heaving deck of the once-daily visitor center boat, a gray, windowless fortress with nothing but a dock for the visitor and supply boats, a maximum security prison in midriver, next to the biggest thicket into which an escapee could vanish: Metropolis itself. And Stryker's Island in the face it turned to Metropolis took no pains to present a comfortable image to the city, only to do its job: confining, limiting, walling in its population.

It was a small company on the visitor boat, all women, most looking tired, some hard, a few who seemed to know each other. Standing by the door of the little cabin or seated on the hard plastic benches, the women talked in voices that seldom rose above the sound of the engines, the slap of waves against the hull.

It had taken moving heaven and earth for her to get a pass and an interview. She'd had to negotiate with the governor to get this cleared.

Billy had gotten through a crisis. Another one. They'd gotten him out of intensive care. She wanted to get there, but couldn't. She'd fought all day for this appointment at the prison.

In such things she measured time . . . between phone calls to the governor.

The boat reached the wind-shadow of the high walls and chugged up to the concrete dock and the little security post. The engines backed and eased the boat in with hardly a bump. The gangway went out, the women got up and formed a line at the cabin door, and Lois joined the queue, uneasy in the company of women whose lives and motives were further outside her imagining than those of the criminals incarcerated here.

There might be a story in them. She told herself so. She didn't willfully cut herself off from questions like motivation and loyalty, or desperation—she didn't know. She didn't empathize. She didn't see them as like herself, but the eyes of the guards who passed them ashore might not see the difference, except her suit and her pinstripe wool coat came from Bothwell's, and her face, showing scratches and scrapes, didn't have the deadly stamp of weariness and hard times.

Her papers, which she'd gotten at the security station on the city shore, didn't say the same as the rest. She laid down her *Planet* ID and the signed permit that was different from the ones relatives carried. The officer's tone changed immediately, dealing with her, became charged with respect.

They gave her a red Press tag and not a white Visitor badge. They drew her out of the line, and ahead of the rest, and gave her priority over them; more, the officer in charge knew her name. "I saw you on television," was the approach, as the officer walked her past the barred, modern gate, past other guards and an electronic lock.

It was that notoriety that had gotten her to Stryker's Island—
that and the fact that every reporter in the city was engaged in
either following her or following the other leads on the case.

She was the first one to follow *this* end of the story, and
she'd bet that no LNN reporter showed up here even if they'd
thought of doing it: LNN as well as Lexcorp was trying to
live down its origin and its former connection to Lex Luthor.
Lex was *not* LNN, and had no influence on its policies or its
corporate structure: that was the position LNN's corporate
heads took, as other CEOs and new boards of directors came
in to reassure anxious stockholders after Lex's—presumed—
suicide and disgrace. LNN hadn't been eager to cover the
subsequent investigation or to reach deep into its archives to
provide background during trial coverage when Lex had
proved to be very much alive, and culpable for looting trea-
sury funds as well as for murder, attempted murder, and a
dozen other crimes. The grand jury had been in session
longer than any grand jury in Metropolis history just racking
up the charges. And LNN at that time had largely ignored
the story.

But she very well understood LNN's reluctance to confront
the man who'd once been one of the most respected corporate
heads in the country, who'd moved in the glittering high altitude of Metropolis society, who'd been ready with his pocket-
book wherever it would secure influence. Lex Luthor had had
the ear of senators and committee heads in Washington and
he'd truly contributed so much innovation and growth to
Metropolis that covering his downfall was a little—particularly
for LNN—like reporting a family scandal.

Every closet had a painful secret. Every nook one could investigate held painful remembrances of times when association

with a glittering, meteoric force in Metropolitan life had been exciting, full of brilliant conversation and wonderful whimsy.

But that whimsy had gone inexplicably to the darker side and left his former associates both bereaved and ashamed.

She knew it better than any corporate executive. She, Lois Lane, who'd been at the altar with the man *she* thought she'd known so well.

She didn't like to think about that nightmare—the absolute classic nightmare of reversal of fortunes. And then she'd had to duck the cameras—the tabloids wanting to interview her and get Luthor's "bride's" reaction to his suicide; the phones ringing months later to get Luthor's "bride's" reaction to his reappearance.

She hadn't wanted any of it. She'd been excruciatingly embarrassed.

And it was no great joy she had coming here now, and standing with these gray, sad women and reflecting that there, but for the grace of God and Clark's steadfastness, she would have stood, her reputation tied to a felon and even her capability to sign her name affected by a marriage that would have ruined her career.

It took a lot to board the boat to come here.

It took a lot to walk down this hallway, not to the interview room the other women used, but to a special high-security area: that was what they'd said.

A special area because Lex Luthor wasn't an ordinary prisoner. And because no ordinary security was adequate to hold him.

Electronic locks thumped open as the guard used keys, two in number, one supplied by the guard outside. A solid door opened onto a grim, small room with a grid of thin wire, five inches to a square, suspended like a web between a safe railing, on her side of the room, and safe bars, on the other. A plain white wall was behind those bars. It held a door. There was no furniture. There was no furniture on her side. One stood waiting, at the bar, with the wire web just out of reach.

An electric charge thumped and hummed. The web was alive. And deadly.

"That's fifty thousand volts, Ms. Lane," the guard said. "Stay behind the railing. That's safe."

"I understand."

This level of security attended the man she'd been willing to marry. It was surreal.

So was it as the door opened behind the bars, and a figure walked in, in those flimsy prison slippers, in a white uniform that—this much was so incongruously like Lex—was fresh and pressed, though with no regard to whether a seam was straight.

And his hair—it had been so thick, dark, a wonderful, masculine thickness she'd liked to touch; but he was entirely, strangely bald. Not shaved. It was just . . . gone, so she understood, from one of the medical treatments he'd undergone.

The bars cast a strange shadow over him. He stopped a little back of them as she stopped a little short of the wooden railing.

Doors shut. The guards had drawn back.

And left her with this silent, this strange figure barred with shadows.

"Hello, Lex," she said into that silence.

He moved forward then, so that light fell on his eyes, and a diagonal bar of shadow went across his face. The eyes hadn't changed at all. They could look so soulful. And so mocking.

"I wondered," he said, "how long it would take you to come here. You do need me, so it seems. How *is* the outside world? Day and night? Rain and sun? Do those things still go on?"

She couldn't imagine an existence so deprived. She thought she'd go mad.

Then she realized in that one sentence he had her thinking about his agenda and not the other way around.

"I trust you hear what goes on," she said with all the coldness she could muster. Which wasn't enough to convince anyone, least of all herself. He stared at her. Just stared, with those remarkable eyes that were still the Lex she'd known, that still carried humor, and wit, and made you believe in him. "About the hotel."

"What about the hotel? What hotel?" A calm, a reasoning voice. "Don't be nervous, Lois. Nothing's changed. Nothing's different. What can I do for you?"

Why had she come here? Why had she thought she'd get any truth?

"I thought," she said, "you might know something about the hotel. I thought, after all you've done, you might still care—"
—about this city, she'd started to say.

"Of course I care, Lois. When you ask, of course I care." He moved closer to the bars. He had such beautiful hands. One entered the light, curled itself around the bar, stark white on gray steel. "What hotel? What are you trying to say?"

She hadn't been nervous. But he treated her as if she were and she was becoming what he wanted. And he'd go on, making her spiel it out, all. She drew a breath and gathered up the essentials as if she were talking to a child. "The Maernik Hotel collapsed. People were killed."

Was that genuine astonishment, that lift of the brows, rounding of the lips into silent surprise, the drawing back of the whole body into barred shadow? The hand stayed. "So the hotel came down."

"And Lexcorp said the design was flawed. They sued."

"Who sued?"

"You know that Lexcorp sued the hotel chain!" He was stonewalling. It was part of the act. She knew it was.

"Lois, I had a good deal else on my mind after the two of us
. . . separated." Fingers flexed on the bars. The voice was imper-
turbable, caressing. "But, yes, they should have sued. Did Cross
build it?"

Holding out just the tiniest promise of cooperation to prevent her breaking the mood.

"Yes. Lexcorp maintained the design was flawed. *What* flaw?
What's your take on it?"

"Why don't you ask Harold Cross?" The voice was low, and
the ghost of a smile danced in the dark eyes.

"I'm going to ask him. But I'm asking you."

"*No one* asks me." So, so soft, that voice. "No newspaper. No
television. Only books. Only books, Lois. I've read yours . . . ."

"The hotel." She was adamant. Anger warmed the chill from
the air. The hum of the charged wires underlay everything. "If
you're going to stonewall me, Lex, I'll be out of here."

"What do you want to know?"

"Lexcorp had the bid for the hotel construction. When you
disappeared—"

"Yes?" He was staring at her. The light-and-shadow face held
anticipation. Both hands held the bars, and he leaned his forehead against the steel. "When I disappeared?"

"You were disgraced." She enjoyed saying that. It was the
only way to get to him, that terrible, terrible pride. "Cross
offered his design and the Premier chain invoked the Loss of
Goodwill clause in the contract to break the agreement with
Lexcorp. Lexcorp sued to maintain the contract. Or to collect
funds. How *did* they settle it?"

"I'm sure I don't know." Lex hung against the bars, as close,
as intimate as he could get. "Tell me."

"Premier won. Or maybe there was a settlement. I'll look it up.
It's not important. Probably you don't know my answer anyway."

"It's so good to see you, Lois."

He wasn't going to rise to the lure. And she'd seen enough, heard enough, endured enough.

"Have a good day, Lex."

"Tell Cross he was a fool."

She'd glanced away. She glanced back sharply at the figure lounging lazily against the steel.

"In what respect?"

"Just tell him."

"I'll know not to come back." Ants were crawling over her skin. A prison had a smell to it. It had gotten into her nostrils and settled on her skin, her clothes. She knew that Lex was obsessed with her, that whatever he was in cold blood, that blood didn't run cold where she was concerned, and that she'd never be absent from his thoughts, not in this place—and not if he reached the sunlight. It was the one weapon she owned with him—so long as he was locked behind bars.

"You can't help it," Lex said softly. "You won't forget me, tonight, when you go to sleep. Will you, Lois?" Slender fingers uncurled from the bar and emerged into the light, a white, beautiful hand. "You're such a tactile creature. You love satin. I remember. You should always sleep on satin."

"You're really out of touch." She was safe, while the bars were there, while the current flowed. And two could play his game. "I don't think you have what I need."

"What you *need*, Lois, is a man. All your artistic brilliance, wasted, *toiling* away in the sordid day-to-day of White's little paper empire. Reporting on traffic mishaps. Domestic trifles. Wondering if you can afford a pair of shoes. *Knowing* you can't afford the really good wines, the really exquisite things. That suit, for instance. Nice, but *not* the standard you're used to."

"We're not here to discuss my wardrobe."

"Or your writing career? How much have you gotten done, I mean, really done, Lois? Still looking for an evening you aren't exhausted? When will that *be*, Lois?"

"The hotel. Or I'm out of here."

"Pyramids."

"Pyramids?" She wasn't sure it wasn't some new game. Or Lex was going around the bend with her.

The hands left the bars to shape a triangle. To invert it, two long forefingers touching, two thumbs making the top. "A single pillar beneath it all, upholding the whole design. And if that goes—" The hands clenched and curled. Concrete shattered, rebar bent, glass broke, and fourteen floors of a fifty-story hotel pancaked down into the garage . . . was that how it had happened?

Her breath was stopped in her throat.

"Cross said it would stand the strain. Heating and cooling, summer and winter. . . ." Lex's voice was soft but animated. "Expansion and contraction. All that motion above it. A pyramid distributes weight, do you see. It focuses weight—here." The hands reshaped the design. "Upside down, the weight is here. The Lexcorp design distributed the weight in buttresses . . . the points of a square base, with footings running out from the base into the bedrock that underlies the city. The oldest rock in the world lies under the city, the oldest, the densest, the most solid. But Cross and his design turn everything upside down, bring all the weight down to one pillar. Architectural arrogance. Because he *can* do it is not a proof he *should* do it."

"And that gave way. That would collapse the hotel."

"If that one pillar gave way, *yes.*" This was the Lex she'd known, an enthusiasm almost boyish in its vitality. "Yes, it would have. The difference in the two designs—the reason there'd been no high-rise building on that particular site—is the cost of sinking deep enough at that particular point to set pillars against the bedrock. The south side of the building, yes: the bedrock is solid. But there's a depression to the north. We said, sink three deep pilings to reach it. Cross said he could sink one—*one,* to hold up fourteen floors of the south tower."

"Saving construction cost?"

"Not that much. That's the point. His construction techniques, to take advantage of that single support, cost just as much. Lexcorp design—" A pause for breath. "—My design— didn't require any special manufacture. Everything was in warehouse, off-the-shelf items—"

"From a Lexcorp subsidiary."

Both hands returned to the bars. "Lois, you wound me."

"But it would have been."

"Lois, my dear, *Cross* would have bought his standard supplies from our subsidiaries. It wasn't the loss of revenue from *that* quarter. It was simply unwise to go with that design. Engineering says it was unwise. Am I not *right?* Can you say now that my design wasn't *right?*" Lex pulled back from the bars and gave a dismissive wave of the hand. "But that was my successor's concern. I was by then no longer concerned with the day-to-day operations of the corporation. The hotel chain wanted out of a Lexcorp contract and here we are. —How many died?"

"Sixty. Hundreds injured." There was no way to fix responsibility on Lex. As things sounded, *Lexcorp* had been giving good advice. "Did you do the design yourself?" Lex was a genius— literally. He'd built Lexcorp around the rare combination of financial and engineering ability. His slide into madness was a tragedy of lost promise, not only for his company but for the city which could have benefited so much from his creative side.

Unfortunately, there was that other side. She'd met it.

"Of course I did it myself." Lex hadn't done the college study in architecture, in law, in business, in engineering, that would have given him the degrees and licenses, the requisite letters after his name. He'd built an empire and *hired* those who had them only so they could vet his ideas. "Going against my design was their choice. They'll have to live with it. Won't they? Your face is scratched. Your hands are cut. Who did that, Lois?"

"I did it, hauling a little boy out of the hotel."

"You weren't in it!"

"No," she said calmly. "But hundreds were." There'd been such genuine concern in Lex's voice. And such relief on his face when she'd said she'd not been inside. *Why* did she feel he'd cared about that answer?

"And where was Superman?" he asked. "Where was your friend when hundreds of people were in harm's way? Why were *you* pulling boys out of basements? I wouldn't have let you do it."

"Superman was overseas."

"Overseas. Where's a good man when you need him, eh? Overseas. And your poor hands, your poor face. I'll think about you. I'll dream about you tonight. Will you dream about me?"

"I don't think so."

"Oh, yes, you will." The solemn face flashed that lazy-eyed, boyish grin that she'd once thought so engaging. "You will."

"Smalley. An engineer named Smalley. How did he die?"

There wasn't a flicker. "I have no idea who you're talking about."

"Monique Simms."

"Who?"

"I've got to go now."

"Go ask Cross his side of things. But come back when you like. And you *will* come back, Lois. You'll know when I'm thinking about you. You'll know when the breeze blows through your apartment at night—that I've been there, in my dreams."

"I'll change the locks, then."

"That won't keep me out." He tapped the side of his head. "I'll be *here,* Lois. I'll always be *here.* And someday—" He drew back into the slanted shadows. "Someday you'll look in the mirror and I'll be there in the flesh, standing right behind you. Change your locks, change your phone, change your address, go anywhere you like: I always know. I'm always there. You're *mine* and no other man will ever take my place."

"I'm my own, and you've gotten boring, Lex. That's the ultimate sin. You've grown boring, and I'm leaving." It was incredibly dangerous to bait him. He *was* clever, and though the ties to Lexcorp were officially severed, he had had an immense organization behind him. But with her, to torment her, he'd delegate nothing, and she knew it, and rode the wave of a giddy defiance of the bugbear he tried to be. "—Guard, I'm ready to leave."

"Scared you, have I?" He was grinning. "Lois Lane in full retreat."

"You'd better keep it all in your dreams, Lex. You're in here for the *rest* of your life."

"Don't count on it."

The grin stayed, challenging her. She'd have gone back to that wooden railing and taken him on for another round, but she'd gotten what she'd come for and the guard had opened the door behind her, expecting the interview was done.

"Boring," she said, and walked out.

The guard shut the door, a noise that thundered up and down the hall. "Nasty customer," the guard said. "I'd take anything he said with a grain of salt."

"I do," she said.

But she couldn't shake the last sight of him, a white, pajama-clad figure in slantwise bars of shadow, faceless to her.

Saying, *Don't count on it.*

There was *nobody* more dangerous.

And she couldn't get Lex Luthor out of her mind as she made the ferry crossing back to the Metropolis shoreline, her hour done, the same as the hours of all the other women, sitting, as all the other women sat, on a cheap hard bench in a heaving boat bound back for the city.

Her hands knew what Luthor's hands felt like. Her mouth remembered his kiss. Her heart remembered the glittering world he'd held out to her, wife of one of the most brilliant, most powerful men in the world.

Mrs. Lex Luthor. Heads would have turned at the theater, as the two of them came in. The limousine would be waiting at the curb as they went out. Mrs. Lex Luthor, they'd have said.

They'd have locked the front doors of Blessingdale's jewelry store and given Mrs. Lex Luthor a private showing of the neck-lace . . . *the* necklace they'd displayed for five years in a special case, inside.

Mrs. Lex Luthor, they'd have said, and she'd have had that reservation at The Twelve Tables for the asking.

That was the life she'd enjoyed for a few giddy weeks. That was the shining future she'd mapped out for herself.

But where would Lois Lane have lived, when Mrs. Lex Luthor enjoyed the penthouse view, high above the world?

Where would her life have been when the rich and the pow-erful and the heads of state came to call on the Lexcorp CEO? She'd have been on Lex's arm, in the receiving line, smiling until her teeth dried out, and the only questions she could have asked all those important guests would be, *How are you?* And *How do you do?*

She'd have been with the cook and the staff, arranging the dinners, that was where she'd have been.

While Lex had his cigars and his brandy she'd have taken the wives to the parlor to talk, in a charade of female fellowship, a society of rivalrous small-grade sharks, circling outside the current of real power and looking for floating morsels from the bigger sharks. It was too outré. Too strange. Right out of some romance.

She'd almost had that. The beautiful view. Life at the top of the world, all of Metropolis spread out at her feet.

She sometimes thought about that view—whenever the mundane world closed in: she could have had servants; but she struggled at her own front door in a dim hall with a half gallon of milk trying to come out of a defective grocery sack and her keys tangled in a knot; and she asked herself (at such times) whether maybe there hadn't been some attraction to being an arm ornament to the world's richest man. Whether maybe she couldn't have made something of the job.

She thought about that view on days when she tried to make an appointment to get the kitchen disposal fixed and agonized over whether to shut Elroy in the bathroom or worry all day that the repairman might not like cats. On days like that and in moments of weakness even yet she asked herself whether hostessing a clutch of women oh-woeing their offsprings' private schools would be that deadly grim.

She could get writing done, her logic in those glitzy days of engagement to Luthor had told her. If she married Lex Luthor she'd never have to stand in the rain in a sudden shortage of cabs.

That she still looked wistfully toward that life rather like a woman looking off a high building and wondering what the wind felt like on the way down—that worried her. *That* was stupidity.

She didn't miss Lex. That was a curious thing. She'd wondered how she'd react, seeing him again, and in such circumstances, and now she knew. He could still disturb her; but she didn't have any personal feelings for him—nothing left but regret, she decided, as the waves thumped and whispered along the hull.

Nothing but a sensual trip, the whole episode of her infatuation with Lex, and who *wouldn't* want to be rich—until they counted the cost to their soul?

All in the past, that chance was. She wouldn't ever be rich, not on a reporter's salary. Not on two reporters' salaries. Clark was her future—at some moment they could get it together, in what had become a commedia of calamities, of mismatched intentions, missed communications, mangled declarations of love, devotion, and schedules.

And she loved him. She *loved* him despite the moments they fought and the moments they disagreed. He did care about things outside himself and it wasn't just to flatter her.

How could she have ever imagined herself in love with Lex? How could she have failed to see the bitter truth in the man?

Failing to see the good qualities in Clark? That was another matter. Clark worked very hard not to be caught being competent, or any of those things calculated to win a woman's heart . . . except that delightful shy twinkle that, even when they'd met, had said: *I know a secret.*

He certainly had; and the secret was a man as brilliant, as capable as Lex—a man who, when he swept you off your feet, did it just about as high as you could go without oxygen.

And who hadn't a greedy, malicious bone in his Kryptonian body.

Talk about contrast in men.

And similarity.

Curious thought.

Both of them . . . quite, quite brilliant. There *was* that. Creative. Clark was, unexpectedly, that.

Both of them . . . superlatives. Walking superlatives. Was *that* the key?

She had no patience with second fiddle, not personally. She didn't wait, as she hadn't waited the morning the hotel came down, for someone to get in front and lead. It wasn't in her nature and that wasn't what she expected in a man, either.

That sort of led to a jam-up in the doorway, didn't it? He and she, diving for the same story?

But she didn't take being second to anyone.

Alpha type, that was her. She'd watched other women, including her mother, *take* the order to go to the parlor and get out of the way. Her mother was brash, and a lot of other adjectives, but for her father, in male venues, her mother tucked down and went to feminine purgatory while her father and his military veteran cronies smoked up the den and reminisced. And she'd thought—

She'd thought it was a soldier thing. Her mother wasn't a veteran so her mother didn't have a right to sit there, and her mother was the hostess and she had to find something to do with the other wives, who . . .

. . . didn't have anything to do with that room, either.

While she, as a little girl, used to contrive excuses to get away from the gatherings that discussed curtains and recipes, the feminine equivalent of baseball statistics. There'd been a bookcase just outside the door to the den and she'd used to take as long as possible choosing a book because *she* wanted to hear the adventures from the men in the den, not the recipes.

She hated that banishment. She hated it with every fiber of her being, and she'd had rocks in her head if she'd for two minutes believed she'd take that role for Lex or any man. She was a partner to her partner, not a mannequin, not an arm ornament. It was outright greed that had led her to Lex; it must have been.

Or it was the misled hope of an adventure. And power of her own.

Not almost good, to Lex's excellent.

She wouldn't take second-best to anyone. It was the challenge of the best that had drawn her to him, subconsciously knowing they'd fight to the death.

And Clark—*Superman*—

Scary thought, that was. It was quite a territory she'd consistently carved out for herself. She stood in the glassed-in cabin of the visitor boat on its return trip, among these women who weren't at the high point of their lives and, watching Metropolis's dockside grow nearer across the heaving water, she asked herself how many chances a woman got.

Her mother was going to worry about her until she married. To whom and what then had always been immaterial. Her father, lacking a son, had pushed her toward personal excellence. The one was her mother's definition of safety. The other was a psychological imperative. And after she'd gotten to look like a woman her father just . . . lost interest in her. And left her outside the magical room where the men told stories.

The relationship with Lex wasn't the first zero-score she'd managed. Romance soared and fizzled. Bliss was just around the corner and then it was an . . .

What had Jack Norden said back in college? An incompatibility of goals.

She was doing all right with her goals, thank you.

She'd done all right for herself in her life.

Until Clark walked into her life and challenged her professionally and until Superman blazed across the horizon and threw her entire life into chaos. The business with Lex? That had been everything her mother valued. Wealth. Money. Fashion.

And she'd run from tweed-coat, solid-citizen Clark straight into Lex's arms.

Doing what? Looking for her mother's brand of success? The colonel's wife? The civic hero's wife?

Not with the drive to succeed her father had drilled into his son-surrogate. Her mother had wanted her daughters without blemish. And her sister Lucy took to the sky, as far from Mama as an airline could take her, with the excuse of a tight schedule, while Papa's favorite son-ette had gone into the life of a reporter.

Why don't you try television? Her mother had seen television as a chance to wear designer clothes.

Lex had bought out the *Planet* to get her on the air, and her mother had been ecstatic.

She'd lost her mind, was what.

And she'd gone into the washroom and cried tears when she'd gotten her old job back, and the gang back, and Clark back, in the refurbished, repurchased *Planet*. Perry had forgiven her for things Perry didn't even know she was responsible for.

Clark did know. Clark still loved her. And something in her was so scared sometimes. A love that started as a friendship and just . . . grew. A love without recriminations or fault or you-should've's was territory she'd never been in.

To this very hour, she kept looking for the drop-off point, the edge of the universe. She kept feeling, in everything with

Clark, a kid-in-wonderland excitement and a fear that behind her the birds were eating up the bread crumbs that marked her trail back.

Far, far different than she'd been with Lex. Stunned, bedazzled, maybe.

Incapable of distinguishing stalking from love, control from caring, obsession from adoration.

He gave her the willies, now. If he was domineering and obsessive then, ask what he was like now.

And ask why for two heartbeats in there she'd fallen right back into that time, that mind-set, that habit, when if there'd ever been any magic, it was all sorcerous, not a fairy tale.

The boat bumped up against the dock. Engines backed water and churned as the boat rubbed against the buffers. The women got up, and Lois moved from her standing vantage, out the door of the cabin and toward the gangway as they ran it out. She was first off the boat, feeling the icy wind off the river bite through her coat with particular chill.

Lex had always been . . . she knew it now as she'd known it for months . . . mean-hearted.

Now she had the dire feeling that his mind was walking the edge of downright crazy, and that if she'd ever left his mind, she'd just done something very dangerous in providing this man another contact with her, another focus for his madness.

Cross, of Cross & Associates, had likewise bumped up against Lex's empire. Cross had stood up against a lawsuit and won.

It was worth asking . . . what kind of man Howard Cross was. He was refusing interviews, so she'd heard. Reporters had besieged him all day long, in vain.

But she might have—it was a feeling she had all of a sudden— a key to open that door.

Chapter 10

The army was breaking out the bridge-building equipment, on vehicles that growled and struggled with the mud. Superman delayed his own work to deliver stacks of huge sections to the area closer to the river, which, visible to him in spite of the darkness, was flowing between bare banks of tumbled boulders, logs, and chunks of the failed dam.

The army was going to cross the river that flowed high and free after the dam break and bring both ends of an already-established road back into operation, a road that maintained ties between the whole high country region and the district capital. The alternate route to the lake villages on the north shore of the present mudflat was a precarious track: he'd seen it, and there was no way without literally moving mountains and creating more devastation to bring a decent road through to the high mountain communities.

So the route had to be across the river: a ravaged mess of a river, and one that would be responsive to seasonal changes. The snowmelt which was now running highest gave a good forecast of the future size of that river.

And the bridgehead was being reestablished. Give the army a chance to get those floating sections in operation, and the villages that survived on the former lake might have groceries in a week or so.

He, meanwhile, had a road to clear and repair. And along with it, a truly major job.

The river was a brown thread in a muddy course. The water from the heights and the former lake bed was still coming down dirty—in a steady rain.

That could only get worse, if it went unchecked.

But he began his road repair with the borrowing of an army truck he didn't intend to use in the ordinary manner, a truck for which there'd been fierce argument. He needed it. He was not going to carry rocks one at a time from the mountains to the mudflat of a lake bed. If he damaged the truck, he'd come up with a replacement. Somehow. He promised the head of the motor pool and tracked a permission to the head of the division down in Pyetigorsk.

Clearly the officer who'd posed him that requirement hadn't expected him to attempt it, let alone comply inside half an hour.

He signed the requisition proffered in the uncertain hands of a private. The army *insisted* on the signature . . . or the harried motor pool officer demanded it, because someone was going to ask *him* what happened to the truck. And after a trip to Pyetigorsk, it was a small favor.

They were then willing to clear the gate back and let him move the truck. But he didn't take it out in the conventional way, and only requested the fuel be drained.

Then he moved it. Straight up.

It was a convenient flatbed, the way the wagon in the village had been, and more convenient than ferrying an equally available truck from Pyetigorsk. He took it to the remnant of the road and gathered up rocks from the quake, at the same time eyeing others that might have spent fifty years falling off the mountain and piling up onto the talus heap the road building had left.

He carried the truck up to the start of the mudflat, parked it, improbably, in the middle of the devastation, and plunked those rocks down for a foundation.

With them, he began building a channel, a disgusting business that involved shoving a lot of mud and holding one's breath all the while, until he'd rearranged the water flow into a controllable deep channel. He'd spotted, with his thermal vision, the natural flow that reached the lake, and with that load and uncounted others, at speed limited only by the aerodynamics of the truck, he built channels and terraces.

He might, he supposed, have taken time to introduce himself to the villages up there and explain to them the source of the miracle that, involving a flying truck and the construction of stone channels, proceeded so rapidly the growth of those channels would look to them like a rapid-motion film, in between the slower, more stately flights of a Russian army truck through the area—bringing in the loads of rock he needed.

But it took longer to work his way through the maze of local dialect than it did to build a stone bank, and he opted for the building, not the explaining. What he did had to be done, and he didn't distract his attention from his masonwork, which had to be accurate, and substantial.

Like building a wall. Pa Kent had taught him the knack. Pa Kent's rubble walls, stones garnered out of the plowed fields, had stood and were still standing; and every time he was tempted to say of a bad fit, *Good enough,* there was a remembered, *Fix it now or fix it later,* in his father's voice, to remind him there wouldn't *be* a "later" in this remote valley. What he did was what these honest farmers and shepherds would have for as long as sheep grazed and crops grew, and Pa Kent's son wasn't going to leave a group of farmers and shepherds to look at his stonework and say, What a sloppy job that American did.

No. Do it right the first time. This masonry would hold the banks firm and let grass grow where grass needed to grow, without the gullying and erosion. Sheep and fields would exist here, not the same as they'd been because the land had changed. But he arranged vast areas where he'd dump the silt he'd recover, to provide a firm, level base that wouldn't puddle water to drown seedlings or give sheep foot rot.

And he'd meanwhile try to figure where he could get topsoil that wouldn't be missed elsewhere. Some construction site was the best bet, soil of a type and consistency that these farmers' traditional methods would best deal with.

That meant black dirt with a remnant of compost from high pine forest. He'd made intimate acquaintance of it, in its soggy form.

It was a full day's work, with all the power he could muster, to do the delicate shaping of the canals and channels with borrowed stone; and having located a dredge downriver (another exchange of signatures and promises, this time through a handshake with the town mayor, not a trip to Pyetigorsk), a succession of sloppy trips upstream to the disaster site. He scooped up silt near the dam, and in dripping, messy loads that streamed a nasty mess down near (but not on) the army engineers, he cycled back and forth from a lake he was trying not to roil up too much to a mudflat he was trying to level.

He dumped mud in between the webworks of his canals and channels, mud that he dried to a crust, at least, with a baking of heat vision and gusts of breath. Like flesh between veins, the land began to fill out, as water, still muddy but a mere seepage through the stones, was squeezed out into the appointed channels.

A ruined land was coming back. A ravaged Mother Earth was healing an unsightly wound.

And it was with vast relief when, by a setting sun and a clearing in the clouds, he plunged into the chill, clearing water of the lake. He'd been so coated with mud the villagers would have taken him for some strange, compost-covered lunatic.

He came out clean, filled his lungs with mountain air, and shook the water out of his hair in a showering of drops that caught the sun.

The sunset over the mountains was gold and pink, casting the snow in illusory blues and whites in the shadowed parts. It was a wonderful evening.

He wished he could show Lois. He wished he could hang here in the sky enjoying the view.

But he still had work to do.

Twilight was deep as he whisked up to the mountainside, from which, in the very far distance, Granny and her village might have seen very odd things proceeding, at least in the army advancing across the river. He doubted any of them would have seen what he'd done up where the lake had been, the forest being between them and the view of their old home.

But he'd tell them.

So Superman expected.

But the moment he came in sight of the villagers' camp, he had a sense of something wrong; and when he canceled out the daylight to get a thermal picture of the camp, he *knew* something was wrong. The livestock wasn't in sight. A small campfire was going, and people were there, gathered about its warmth and light, black figures next to the emergency module he'd left the village.

But it was a very small fire, with fewer people than he'd have expected.

He landed close by them, and people reacted with intakes of breath and a flinching from surprise that hadn't been their reaction before.

"Chto eta?" he asked, and Granny, sitting with the group, made an effort to rise. Someone had been very rough and careless in the open-ended medical module. The place looked, in fact, stripped.

There were women, children, a handful of old men. No young ones. No livestock.

Granny tried to tell him. But the young man who'd done the translating wasn't there to mediate.

He didn't know the words. But he caught a few in Russian. The little girl, the one with the kittens, mimed shooting a rifle.

"Soldiers?" he asked in Russian. The army was across the river. "Bandits?"

Granny had a lot to say to that. Leaning on her stick, she gestured toward the mountain and said something about the horse, the wagon, the chickens, and the young men.

And fools and rebels.

He had the picture, then. "Where?" he asked, and everyone talked at once. Some cried, dabbing at eyes surreptitiously. A few maintained a thin-lipped and fearful silence. And a young woman mimed a gun at the head, a shot.

He got that picture, too. Rebels had taken every resource, robbed the survivors, forced the young men to go with them. The sight by day of the Russian Army advancing on the place had either alarmed rebels existing in the hills and convinced them that they, and not rescue, were the target; or the rebels had seen first the quake and then this flood-caused severance of the road as an opportunity to take this territory and fight a guerrilla war with an army unable to extend a firm supply line to the region.

Bring a large force in, and they might shoot, possibly starting with the uncertainly loyal men they'd taken.

"I need clothes," he said, and took off the cape. He bent down and muddied a hand on the trampled ground, wiped mud on his face and through his hair, mussing it and assuring it stayed mussed.

"Clothes!" Granny exclaimed, and waved her stick. There was protest, and confusion, and he gathered that the rebels had made off with the spare clothing, too.

But out of the tangled mess of their baggage, the women found a pair of aged, muddied trousers and an arthritic old man of considerable girth contributed a plaid flannel shirt and a hat. "Son" was one word Superman could understand out of the old man's dialect: the old man wanted his son back alive, and would have stripped to the skin in a snowbank to accomplish that.

There was distress among the women because there were no guns. A woman offered a kitchen knife from among the folds of her skirts.

"*Nyet,*" he said, "*spaciba.*" Shoes were a problem. But the old man provided those, too, heavy boots that had seen a lot of walking.

Then he had the most complicated matter to explain, and rendered it down to, "Granny, please come—" and a gesture to the mountain above them.

She pointed aloft and up toward the hills, nothing daunted, a figure as old as the mountains, with her kerchief and her thick skirts and her walking stick; and she was light as a feather when he swept her up in his arms and took to the skies, Granny and a young man flying through the night air in a scene that (it occurred to him) might have come from fairy tales.

He flew low and slowly, partly not to burn Granny's skin and partly because it wasn't easy to shift from a lifetime of seeing the mountain from one perspective and, instantly and in the dark, locate something from the air.

Granny followed trails by starlight, followed them, for her experience, probably very fast indeed.

"There, there, there!" she said, as their winding course around the shoulder of the mountain revealed a wooded nook and the faint gleam of fire.

It was a camp, and a fairly permanent one. He didn't know when the raid might have happened, but he'd bet the rebels had been lurking about, perhaps even known to the villagers, until they saw the army advancing faster than they could explain.

Then they'd grown alarmed, seized everything they could, and made their way back to this camp, half a day away, he figured, using the horse and wagon to get the pigs and chickens to their camp.

The chickens, clearly, had met an unhappy fate: they were roasting on spits in the midst of men dressed not much differently than he was, except they had coats.

He set Granny down very gently on the trail where she could feel she knew her way; and he set himself much closer to the camp before he began to walk at a sedate pace toward the firelight.

He could see the horse, the wagon, the pigs. Piles of medical supplies. And some of the men at the fire had guns and some didn't. The ones who didn't—he recognized. Including his translator.

Two men, standing, had guns in their hands. Sentries, he thought, and just kept walking.

Suddenly the majority had guns in their hands as one man saw him and jumped up, some pointing guns at him, others at the villagers in their midst, and clearly inclined to use them.

He shambled toward that bristling cluster of men by the fire, gave a deprecatory wave of his hand, and didn't resist when two came and grabbed him.

They shook him, they yelled into his face, they clearly wanted to know who he was and whether he was an army spy. They spoke to him in Russian, which wasn't their language, but which they thought was his.

They shoved guns into his face and they threatened him and he made himself loose-jointed and stumbled when they shoved him. "Speak up," they said to him, clearly imagining they had a spy from the army, and meanwhile his greatest concern was the couple of men who prudently had weapons leveled at their new recruits, prepared to blow them to eternity if they made a move.

The leader, so he seemed to be, grabbed him by his shirt and shook him, shouting into his face with bad breath.

A gun barrel hit his head. He took his cue and fell down. And was kicked several times.

Meantime he was waiting for a little moment of distraction. Blow up the ammunition? He could do that. But they were primed to shoot the local lads and might do so if frightened.

He suffered a few more kicks, and assumed a listlessness that he hoped would put them a little off their guard.

He saw his translator's face and knew, then, that lad at least realized keenly who he was.

The bandits *didn't* expect a man to move laterally from dead rest on the ground; they didn't expect the move, too fast for human eyes, that grabbed the two rifles aimed at the recruits and sent them off into the trees at such high velocity they probably imbedded. They *didn't* expect a presence fast enough to stop automatic weapons fire aimed at him and the recruited villagers.

He collected a wad of bullets and in grim humor dropped a baseball-sized lump of metal on the ground in front of him, the result of his collection.

Then it dawned on the rebels that they were in serious trouble. They let off a concentrated burst from several guns as the erstwhile recruits, finally having some notion of what they were dealing with and who had come into the fray, dived for cover behind the nearest rocks.

Relieved of concern for them, he neatly fielded all the shots, gathered himself another baseball, and flung it at the mountain. It boomed from the impact alone, showered down rock chips as if a cannonball had hit—it had—and the rebels broke and ran.

He wasn't through. He streaked after them, ripped guns out of hands, out of holsters, and sent every firearm flying. The forest resounded to splintering impacts and screams of men who thought their unprotected bodies would go next.

He didn't need to do more than that. They'd fled opposite to Granny's position, past the horse, who'd tried to bolt, and a lot of startled pigs who were still squealing in their crate as he whisked back to Granny.

He found her plodding her slow way toward the fracas, doubtless with a notion of bringing her cane into the fray.

No explanations: seeing was easier. He swept her up and deposited her at the fire, where she and he were instantly the focus of a rush of grateful and anxious ex-recruits. They hugged Granny. And him.

They'd regained the horse, the wagon, a crateful of pigs, and the roasting chickens looked done. If they were to lose the source of eggs, there was no sense wasting the sacrifice.

The rebels, Dimitri judged, wouldn't try another recruitment. Not in *this* area of the mountains.

He'd gotten the livestock back before they were revolutionary rations. They all, as soon as they got the horse hitched to the primitive shafts with its makeshift bandit harness, were going back down the mountain to the camp.

And in the remote chance the rebels might be lured back by the ammunition they'd abandoned . . . he got the wagon and the young men headed back to the villagers' camp, saw them around the shoulder of the mountain and out of the way, and set the ammo dump off.

It was a satisfactory explosion. It was particularly satisfying to know it made a nice beacon, it started no fires in the damp woods, and it *wouldn't* find its way against and into vulnerable human bodies. Lives wouldn't be wrecked. Children wouldn't be orphaned. People wouldn't be killed or maimed.

And he met the little party for a good-bye. He wasn't through with the reclamation of the land, but the army had the bridge making in hand, which would at least stabilize the region. He'd just scared the rebels out of the district, so there was no chance of an army operation turning up anything that was going to start a shooting war on top of people's other problems.

Stealing relief supplies—not just enough for their survival, but making people destitute and recruiting them at gunpoint—didn't recommend their cause to him, not even for the neutrality he tended to observe in a nation's differences of opinion. Banditry was banditry. He knew that when he saw it in operation and had no qualms about sending the perpetrators off into a damp night without their supplies or weapons.

He'd told Granny, through his young interpreter, that he'd begun restoration of the land where the lake had been. And that he'd be back. He trusted them to get down the road the bandits had taken up to this camp, with all that they'd lost plus the bandits' leavings.

But meanwhile, he had a city of his own in crisis.

He had a woman who loved him—still a strange and giddy thought—and he wanted to be home for a day, where his own city needed him, and where he trusted the woman he'd chosen for a partner—he *liked* that notion—expected *her* partner to check in and answer roll call.

Chapter 11

He was still a very, very hurt little boy, Billy was.

But he noted her presence. He made a little wave of his hand.

"He's getting well now," Billy's mother said, in dogged disregard of the lack of response. "He's a lot better today." And Lois hoped so, and that there really was improvement since the phone call from Billy's parents. But Billy looked so glum, and it was in its way less response than she'd seen before.

Come, his parents had asked her. He needs cheering up.

So she'd brought, among other things, a soccer magazine from the newsstand down the street from the *Planet,* but Billy didn't have the strength to open it. He scarcely could look at the pictures, though he tried to. White light came through the window. Billy always wanted the shades open. He had that much restored interest in the world. But he was so weak.

She turned the page for him. There was an open letter in the seam of the magazine. With the letter-head of the Metropolis Meteors, and the signature of Esteban Santos, the man who'd led the hitherto struggling Meteors to the top of the National League.

The venture of a small, pale hand, as scabbed over as hers, toward that letter with the shining gold emblem was worth every penny she'd almost spent—but it wasn't her gift. Sammy, at the Sports desk, had made a phone call, and a world-class soccer player had responded and made another phone call. In a chain of phone calls from very good, very generous people, Billy was going to the whole next Meteors season as the guest of the team captain.

Billy and every survivor of the disaster.

Fingers caressed the embossed letterhead.

"What's it say?"

"It says, thanks to a really neat guy in the *Planet* Sports desk, that you and your mom and dad have a season pass to the Meteors games. You and your whole team."

"Cool." There was a quaver in the voice. "Way cool."

"And a coaching session for the whole team. How's that?"

The face fell.

Trouble. Maybe the trouble that had set in and turned Billy so listless and unresponsive his parents called in a stranger for help.

Her kid. *Her* kid, on loan again, from two pretty generous parents.

She'd hoped this would cheer him up.

"What's the problem?"

Billy tried not to cry. He hadn't, down in the pit, in danger of his life. Things had just piled up on him, and the chin shook and the eyes leaked despite his best efforts.

It was more than his father and mother could stand. "Billy?" his mother said, trying to take his other hand. But Billy snatched it away.

It didn't take a degree in rocket science.

"You don't want to play again?" Lois asked.

"I can't."

"Who says you can't?"

"I'm in *here!* I got stitches all over—"

"They'll come out pretty soon. You'll *be* good as new, Billy."

"No, I won't." Billy thought he was being conned and he was mad, Lois judged that. He was also eight years old.

"What does the doctor say?" Lois asked. *She'd* talked to the doctor and the parents before she talked to Sammy at the Sports desk, and Billy's sudden, unexplained despondency was the central question in the extent and rate of his recovery. "The doctor told us you'd be back on the field this summer. Did he tell you something different?"

"I'll be sick."

"No, you won't."

"I've got stitches."

"When those come out, you'll be strong as before. Athletes have stitches all the time. Fix a knee, the stitches come out, they're back on the field."

"Not in their middle. They had to take out stuff."

"Nothing you need."

"So why's it *in* there?"

A young kid's questions were sometimes silent, the speculations far ranging and much grimmer than adults knew.

"Spare parts," she said. "You ask your science teacher when you get back to school. But scars can be strong as natural skin, and you won't miss anything they took out. The doctor says so."

"Yeah?" *Don't con me* was the unspoken plea. The jaw was trying to steady down.

"Promise." He'd stopped listening to her voice as the voice in the dark. That time was over. He'd come back to face the world and he'd feared the terms of his existence were going to be nar-rowed. It *wasn't* the case for him. "You're lucky," she said. "You're real lucky."

"Is Lenny alive?"

"Everybody in your team made it. I swear. That's the truth."

He moved enough to cock his head and look up at his par-ents, on the other side of the bed. For the first time, he looked to his parents, and thought his voice from the dark might be lying to him. "Is that true?"

"Yes," his dad said. "A lot of people died, Billy. And Tom Elliot's got two broken legs. But none of you kids died. You're just real lucky. A lot of people didn't get the chance you got. So you have to use it. You have to walk out of here."

"Yeah," Billy said.

"You're going to be on the field this summer," his mother said.

"Yeah," Billy said to that, too. And passed his fingers over the Meteors logo. "This is cool. Thanks."

It was about time for a reporter to remember he wasn't her kid. That it was a story, just one more story, of lives she brushed past. The kid had come out of the dark. He'd remember her for the rest of his life. He'd be grateful. His *kids* would be grateful when they heard the story. That was a kind of posterity.

But it was time for her to leave.

"I'd better go," she said.

The parents came outside the room to thank her. The mother hugged her. The father did too. She walked away down the ster-ile white hall and took the elevator, empty-handed, down the now-familiar path to the front gate.

She'd *like* to go to the parking garage and have a look at the deep basement. But she wasn't ready for that, and she wasn't ready to lead other reporters to the pieces of a story she wanted to write. She'd not met morning deadline. Perry wasn't upset. He didn't blame her for a shaky couple of days.

"I'm working on something," she'd told him.

It happened to be the truth. But the pieces of it hadn't been easy to get.

Records on one William Smalley. Suicide, alone in his apartment.

Records on one Monique Simms. Suicide. Found floating in the river.

She'd run the gauntlet of reporters getting into the hospital. She ran it getting out . . . but they were few in number now.

"Lois!" one said, and slipped her a note as she was getting into the taxi.

Carmen Alverado would like you to do a studio interview for Nightscape, it said. *Please call.*

She didn't know what she had to say to a television interviewer. She wasn't the news. She reported it. Clark had said it, and he was absolutely right.

There wasn't much to report right now except that the investigation into the cause was continuing and that a bomb had been ruled out, that the survivors were improving and the dead had been buried.

It was that shocky just-after week for the event that had shaken the city and the nation. The fervor for more information was seething out there, a city, a nation, the world still stirred up and still clamoring for information; but information wasn't forthcoming and it couldn't, by reputable newsmen, be manufactured.

So the tabloids ran riot on the stands. So she'd heard from Perry when she'd called in. She hadn't seen them, but several of the scandal sheets were represented in the stakeout at the hospital, and they'd snapped a lot of pictures of her that she'd rather not have given them.

But she didn't know what else she could do. She couldn't hide.

The taxi wove through traffic, and the driver complained about a bus pulling out in front of him—just the luck of the traffic. They were going slower, now, with no view but a huge silver bus end.

"You're that reporter," the driver said.

"I am," she said. It embarrassed her. But she was That Reporter to every taxi driver, every shopper in the city.

"Pretty neat thing you did."

"Thank you," she said.

"Pretty horrible, that place." The taxi driver wanted to talk about it. She was a prisoner in the cab. She listened to his theories on bombs and terrorists while they rode in the wake of the bus. She knew an equally troubling thing that she didn't tell him.

And she'd asked to go, not to the *Planet,* but to an office plaza that was a long cab ride away from the hospital, a long, long run to the expressway, the cabby asking her questions all the way. She had the surly feeling, watching the numbers tick away on the meter, that she should charge him instead of the other way around.

She'd had a phone call from the mayor this morning. They wanted to give her the Civic Medal, and they wanted her to attend the awards to all the firemen and policemen, and there was going to be a fund-raiser for the expenses of the people caught in the disaster.

She couldn't say no to the fund-raiser. But she'd begun to flinch from her personal notoriety. The aftershocks were settling into her nerves now. Maybe it was dreaming about it at night. Maybe it was still seeing that pool of muddy water and the hanging cables, and fighting the cold and the pain to move those chunks of concrete every time her head hit the pillow.

They wanted to give her a medal. She wasn't sure how she was going to get through a speech about what she—*she,* the reporter—couldn't articulate. They said she'd written a brilliant article. They said Pulitzer.

In her mind, she hadn't done nearly enough to express the things she'd seen and heard.

If she got up in front of a lot of people, she didn't know what she was going to say.

Or maybe she felt she hadn't done her job until she had an answer for the city that wanted to honor her for doing what a human being would do.

Honor the firemen and the police, yes. They'd done their jobs, they'd done them magnificently, the way they were trained to do. She'd been lucky, was all, lucky she hadn't met an electric wire, lucky to have been in the right place at the right time, but without the firemen behind her, without the EMT who'd come as far as she could, she didn't want to think about her chances— or Billy's. She and Billy had become a symbol, a portrait of a disaster that had exacted a cruel, real cost on hundreds of affected people who *mustn't* be forgotten, and who deserved recognition for their stories, for their courage in that crisis.

That was the speech she'd make. That was what she'd say.

When she got enough sleep. When she wasn't running on adrenaline.

But the mayor's event was tomorrow night. She didn't know where she'd find the strength.

And Clark—

She really, really needed him. Clark, she'd say right now, here's a lead for you. Here's who to talk to. Here's where to go.

Clark would have had a fit, knowing where she was yesterday. He'd have had words to say to her.

She'd dreamed about Lex last night, too. Lex had said she would. And he was right.

She saw him behind her eyelids today, as often as she saw that watery pit.

She saw him smile at her, Lex the way he had been, dark haired, handsome, full of mischief.

Mischief. Malice. She knew now what she'd seen and not recognized.

Madness . . . since his recovery. But the malice had always been there.

The cabby exited the expressway. And she knew when she saw the office park—and the LNN dish—that it was going to be a scene. She had her cell phone. She had the number of Cross & Associates. And dialed it.

"This is Lois Lane," she said to the woman who asked her business.

"Mr. Cross isn't available. I'm sorry."

"Will you *ask* Mr. Cross? Tell him my name. I'd like to speak to him just for a moment."

"If this is about an interview, Mr. Cross isn't giving interviews."

"Please tell him I'm from the *Planet*. I'd like to talk to him just for a moment."

In the windshield of the cab the building and the gathering out front were dead center.

"What *is* your name? I'm sorry."

"Lane. Lois Lane." She had a card and she played it. "Tell him I was the reporter *in* the Maernik."

"One moment." Clearly the receptionist was stressed. And this might be a wasted trip. But she hadn't yet played all her cards. She didn't want to play them—on the phone—being aware that there might be an illegal interception of the phone call. There were sharks in the waters. Clearly. They could track where she'd come from. But they couldn't get out to Stryker's Island in time for the next edition and they couldn't duplicate the interview she'd had out there. She was, this time, *ahead* of them. And if there was one name that might open Cross' door—

"Ms. Lane?"

"Yes?"

"Mr. Cross will see you. But no one else."

"I agree," she said, and earnestly wished she had Jimmy with her. But she didn't think they could get him in, anyway. And she wouldn't blame Cross for not wanting to have his face identified.

She'd given the cabby the address. The cab entered the driveway and pulled up into the army of reporters, negotiating it slowly, with frequent complaints and swearing from the driver.

"Look at them," he said. "Hey! You!" He rolled down the window and made gestures at reporters crowding his path. "We got a lady wants through, you bums!"

She paid the bill and a good tip, with a dismissal, before she stepped out of the cab into a mass of her colleagues, at least half of whom she recognized. Prominent among them was LNN's Frank Borden.

"Hello," he said.

"Hi," she said, and had microphones shoved at her, so thick she couldn't brush past them.

"What's the story on Cross?" vied with, "What's your reaction to the Galaxy reports on Cross and the mayor?"

Her answer had to be, "*What* reports on Cross? —Excuse me!" A microphone bumped her ear. Reporters were shoving at each other, jostling her, worse than usual with an interview; *she* was usually one of the pack, and they gave her not an inch.

"Back up," Frank shouted, trying to get her some room. She was glad and grateful for that, and Frank said, "I'd like to do an interview on our mobile link, if you don't mind."

Cameras were a little in abeyance, and microphones were to the side, seeing that she hadn't broken a story for them on the spot. She didn't want to do an interview. That question on Cross troubled her. Yes, Cross had done contracts for the city and the *Metropolis Daily Star* was a newspaper that favored the mayor's often-agitated opposition. The whole business smelled of dirty politics getting into the act.

And coming from the hospital and the personal side of the story, as she had just done, she was mad.

"Not now," she said. "I'm not the news, for God's sake. Go interview the fire department. Go interview the guys who were with me down there."

"Is it true," another reporter asked, "that you're still involved with Lex Luthor?"

Her heart stopped. And restarted. Temper almost choked her.

"What *about* that story?" Frank asked. "Is it true you were out at Stryker's Island yesterday?"

What did she say? Her face, seen on a dozen cameras, probably registered far too much. Cameras clicked. The red eyes of news cameras were all around her.

"I was following your lead, Frank. It was your lead, wasn't it? LNN had the story."

"But the prison authorities let *you* in," Frank said. "They didn't let us in. Why do you suppose that was? Luthor *agreed* to see you?"

"What did Luthor say?" someone shouted.

"Excuse me." She gave a shove at Frank, the traitor, and headed for the doors, experienced in the journalistic crush and expecting no help from the security guards she could see beyond the glass doors of the office building. They weren't about to open that door and risk a human wave sweeping through the lobby.

She reached the doors and showed her press credentials.

As someone tried to give her a tape recorder. "Ten thousand dollars," that man said, jabbing it at her ribs. "Ten thousand if you get a tape of Cross."

She shot a drop-dead glance at the man and didn't take it. About that time the guard, one of several, unlocked the door and let her in as his cohorts held the mob from rushing in.

She didn't complain about the lack of rescue outside. But she'd hurt her hand somewhere in the crush, her neatly pressed coat was creased, a scab on her knuckle was bleeding, and she didn't want to think about her hair.

The newspaper dispensers just inside the building held the day's headlines. From the *Daily Star* . . . WHERE WAS SUPERMAN?

She couldn't stop to read it. She walked the travertine marble hall to the elevators in the close company of one of the security guards, almost as tight a security as at Stryker's Island. She didn't look back, but she imagined her colleagues' faces glaring jealously at her back.

A man in a suit shot her a sullen look as he exited the elevator. People in the hall had glum faces. Cross wasn't the only business in this place, and doubtless the other businesses and all their clients wished Cross were miles elsewhere and all reporters sunk in the harbor.

High time, she said to herself, trying to straighten her hair, high time to get the business settled, one way or the other, whether it was an engineering mistake or something else.

And yes, she thought as she exited the elevator on the thirty-second floor, it would be a good idea to talk to the investigators, too, and try to parlay what she did know into information coming from *them*. But for very good reasons, the investigators weren't talking: she'd tried this morning, and so had every other reporter in town, for days.

In the meantime either damage or justice was being done to the reputation of the architect and engineering firm, and the stories hitting the newsstands in the city and front lawns in the suburbs were already talking about the mayor and the fact that Cross & Associates had built very significant city buildings.

She walked in through glass doors stenciled in gold with the Pyramid and X of Cross & Associates, nice logo, beautiful offices, blue and gray, an anxious receptionist who lost no time in showing her into the inner hall, and into an office with corner windows, a magnificent view of the Metropolis skyline and the river, and a red-faced, balding, gentle-looking man who rose and offered his hand.

"Ms. Lane."

"I was a little surprised, considering the crowd out there, that you'd see me. Thank you."

"I know *you'll* be fair. That's all I ask, Ms. Lane."

"I intend to be fair."

He was an anxious man, even an indignant one. She never trusted the innocent look. She didn't even trust indignation. The reason con men worked so well was that they looked completely credible right down to the little signs, the shake in the hands, the distraught manner, the sadness in perfectly credible eyes.

She was after facts, not feelings.

"Ms. Lane, my life is being ruined. They're outside my house, the trucks, the whole circus. My phone is ringing with threats, my wife is terrified . . ."

"I can sympathize," she said, and truly could, but wouldn't. "Let's get at the facts, here. *Is* there a chance it was a roof failure the way they're saying, or what do you think happened? For the record, Mr. Cross."

"Honestly," Howard Cross said, and it was the face of a tired, soul-searching man, to all observation. "Honestly, I've been over the blueprints, I've double-checked our records, our orders, our materials, ever since that building came down, Ms. Lane. Can you understand how it felt, that morning, knowing something I'd built had come down on those people?"

"What did you think when you heard it?" It was a journalistic question, and she thumbed the switch on the recorder in her coat pocket and set it on the desktop, plainly evident to the man, and protecting him and her from mistaken quotation. "What was your first thought?"

It wasn't a glib answer. The thought process took a second. "My first thought? My first thought was, *This can't happen.*"

She was closer to believing what she was hearing.

"Why not?"

"I still have the model, Ms. Lane. Do you want to see it?"

"I'd very much like to see it."

Howard Cross got up from his desk and led her to an adjacent room, where numerous models lined the top of tall bookcases.

The model of the hotel stood on the reading table, conspicuous. It was eerie to look at it, whole and undamaged.

Cross laid hands on the model and moved half of it aside, showing the floors in cross section.

The support structure was exactly what Lex had described. A pyramid, upside down. But not just one pyramid. There were braces set into the outside walls, going the opposite way. Her eye could see the support and the integrity of the building, even if she'd had only a smattering of architecture in a collegiate Art Appreciation course. But she *had* only had a smattering of architecture, and therefore she kept a caution tag on her judgment of what she saw: a model was one thing. When scale and change of materials entered the picture—she knew that much—the equations changed.

Cross proceeded to point out what she'd already seen. And spread out pictures, details of the actual construction. Then he drew out of a vertical cabinet a set of blueprints, with the marks of use about them. "These are the actual ones," he said, and that seemed very credible.

He brought out materials samples, and talked about grades and quality. He brought out manuals showing the numbers which meant less to her than she wished they did, but Cross offered to show them to any expert of the *Planet*'s choosing and at no point acted as if he expected she couldn't follow him to his conclusions. He wasn't thinking about lawyers, and she wasn't dealing with a man with glib answers, only ready and thorough ones.

He wanted his story out there. And the question was whether the *Planet* was going to go out with a story directly challenging their rival's lead and supporting Cross & Associates' integrity.

Talk about trial by media.

"Did you talk to any reporter directly?" she asked him.

"By phone. Yes. But they wanted to know about my credentials. *Those* are my credentials." The wall of the office had been lined with certificates and photographs. This room, with its models of a good many major buildings of Metropolis, *these* were the credentials Howard Cross invoked, and he rattled off his professional associations as both architect and engineer with scarcely a pause for conscious thought.

Then he said, this tired, ruddy-faced man:

"Ms. Lane, call your experts. Call anybody you like. My reputation is everything. I've had two contracts fall through. My crews are being harassed. I had a man who's worked for me twenty years quit on me because he's scared for his kids and people are ringing his phone at night. I've got a building with the foundations dug sitting at a standstill. I've had more death threats than I can count and my E-mail's with the FBI. My wife is on tranquilizers and I'm next. I don't know what to do, Ms. Lane. I'm being killed in the press."

"Are you talking to the investigators?"

"I'm providing them copies of everything. Delivery records. Receipts. I put *quality* into that building! And there's no flaw in that design."

"Let me say two words to you."

"What?"

"Lex Luthor."

If a face that ruddy could go white, it tried.

"What were your dealings with him?" Lois asked. "Were they friendly?"

"He's in prison. Isn't he?"

"Did he ever threaten you?"

An intake of breath. "You know Lexcorp sued Premier over the contract for the Maernik."

"Yes."

"I got threats. Phone calls. Never the same party."

"What did they sound like? What did they want?"

"Just—pull out of the contract. Your wife will die. There'll be an accident. That sort of thing. I've had them before."

"Did you ever deal with Lex Luthor?"

"Not directly. Not pleasantly. Then—when they thought he was dead and we got into the lawsuit—" Clearly it wasn't a pleasant memory. Cross gave a twitch of his shoulders, a visible shiver, gazing at something in the past. "I got a phone call at three in the morning. A guy's voice. And it was something like,

'You won't last in this city.' And then he hung up. You know how it is . . . I was half asleep, I was still waking up. Things weren't registering real clearly. But it sounded like a voice I knew. And it took me a week to remember a cocktail party a long time ago. Luthor said it. Just brushed by—said that and walked off with a martini glass in his hand. That was what I remembered. And Luthor was supposed to be dead when I got that phone call. It was spooky, it was spooky as hell."

"What did you think when he turned up alive?"

"I thought I was real glad he's in prison."

"A lot of us are glad," she said, with personal reason to say so, and wondered if he connected her to the reporter Lex Luthor had been about to marry.

She hadn't wanted to cover the Lexcorp mess. She hadn't wanted her byline anywhere near Lex's business dealings.

Monique Simms had covered it.

"Let me say another name to you. William Smalley."

A frown. "Worked for me three months."

"Testified against you in the lawsuit."

"Lied."

"Competent at his job?"

"I checked his credentials real carefully," Cross said. "And he came in with references. I can show you the employee folder."

"Employee, not a partner."

"No way he was a partner. He was good at what he did. I hired him because I was sorry for him. Run of hard luck. Nasty divorce. The Maernik contract came up with a rush on it and we needed the extra hands." A pause. A hesitation. "Those things he said weren't true and we proved it to the client. I think he was a plant. *I* think he was somebody working for Lexcorp. And I fell for it."

"You know he's dead."

"Suicide. That's what they said."

"So's the reporter who covered the case. Monique Simms. Suicide."

She met the man's worried look with one she knew couldn't reassure him that she thought it was all a coincidence.

The recorder had run out of tape five minutes ago. She'd heard it click off.

"Thank you," she said, leaving matters at that grim point of insupportable hypothesis, and wished again that Jimmy were here. She had a small camera she used in desperation. But there were professional photos scattered all over the table. "Could you provide me a photo of the model? The cross section? Our staff artists could use it."

He swept up one, rejected it, selected another and gave it to her. "Print it, use it, just—write the truth. I've nothing to fear from the truth, Ms. Lane."

She didn't think he had. She wished she knew, on the other hand, what that truth was.

She wished she knew more of what she'd come here to find: the specific *cause* of the collapse.

But she was sure enough to tell Perry White that she had an interview the tabloids would pay in the five figures for, and she knew Perry. If he thought they had the truth, the *Planet* would set the standard. They were going to go head-to-head with the other news organizations over the Cross story.

"I'd be real careful," she said, "between you and me. I'd be real careful for a while. I don't think either case was suicide. But it would be real hard to prove."

"You *know* something?" Cross asked her.

"If I *knew* anything, my next stop would be the police. But I don't know. And I can't prove anything. Just—be careful."

"*You* be careful, Ms. Lane."

She led a charmed life where Lex Luthor was concerned. She'd heard it in that moment of alarm, when he'd believed she'd been in danger. Lex wouldn't kill her.

No one else on Earth could say that. And even she couldn't depend on it . . . for ten minutes running, or in Lex's next flight of madness.

"I will be careful," she said.

"Security will get you a cab," Cross said. "I'd walk you down myself, but—"

"I don't think it would be a good idea, your going down there. Is there a phone number where I can always reach you? Would you trust me with it?"

He wrote a number on a business card, and gave it to her. "Any hour," he said. "At *any* hour."

The building security guards had the taxi at the curb, and this time, on Cross' orders she had no doubt, escorted her to the cab past a horde of her colleagues shouting at her and cameras going as they opened the door for her.

She could imagine the video footage as she got in. She foresaw reports on the evening news that Lois Lane had been meeting secretly with Howard Cross—and she had to beat them with the evening edition. She trusted Frank's integrity, but she was all too aware now that *she* was news, and that if they hadn't anything else they'd go with clips of faces they could get. They needed visuals. Any visuals.

And she hadn't handled those questions well when she went into the offices. They'd taped her stammering over her answer about Lex. They'd taped her reluctant to talk after talking to Cross.

The cab pulled away from the curb, and past the driver's shoulder she had a view, in the rearview mirror, of a disgruntled lot of reporters—Frank foremost of the lot.

"Aren't you the reporter?" the cabby asked.

"Yes," she said, and had to suffer another interrogation. She didn't want to alienate anyone, envisioning in a moment of panic a cabdriver who'd transported her suddenly being besieged by reporters, a cabby on the evening news saying how Lois Lane had told him she hated Frank Borden and was taking out a contract on his life.

She wanted to be home. Her skinned knuckle was still seeping, and she blotted it with a tissue. She wanted to have that article done and on the stands in time to counter what they'd be saying about her.

She wanted Clark. She wanted to sit down with him over a quiet linguini dinner somewhere in Seattle, far away from the business at hand. There was a wonderful Italian restaurant at a downtown hotel. They'd been there, a little place, where they could sit in a quiet booth and not be recognized by anyone—

Maybe a quiet burger stand on a back roads highway.

She just wanted Clark. That was all. Was it too much to ask of the universe?

Probably. *She* had a story to write, and sore fingers and burgeoning headache and all—she wanted to get what she had on paper.

She sat in the cab outlining on her notepad the major points of her story, the diagram she wanted the staff artists to come up with—better a diagram than a photograph with something as technical as why a building stood or failed to stand.

There were families—Billy's was one—which had been vastly disturbed by the news that the hospital wing Billy and a lot of the other survivors were in had been built by the same architect.

Doubt like that was added stress those families didn't need, and one family, so Billy's mother had said, had gone so far as to insist a very sick man, not even connected with the tragedy, be moved to another hospital.

The doctors weren't arguing, apparently: it was so easy to transfer anxiety from something one couldn't do anything about onto some other issue one *could* do something about.

And almost before the dust had settled, the lawyers had closed in, looking for deep pockets. The Premier Hotel chain was a sure target for lawsuits. Howard Cross was.

The question was what a prospective jury might think; and hasty articles implying there might have been a design flaw weren't going to help the process of justice. Words settled into some mentalities like concrete, and once the buzz of accusation had started, some people wouldn't back off a position they'd loudly taken, not if a choir of angels showed up to prove the contrary.

If someone had wanted to *get* Premier, or Cross, or both, the economic damages could be astronomical. There were ways to make twelve ordinary citizens into hit men: a lawsuit for damages now wasn't going to run on logic alone.

And it shouldn't happen to Cross, if it wasn't his fault; it shouldn't happen to Premier and its employees and its stockholders, but it would, and mom-and-pop investors were going to bear the worst of it, as they already had, when Premier's stock went down. The list of economic casualties was already considerable: she hadn't asked Art, at the Business and Financial desk, what had happened to Premier stock the day of the disaster and after, but she could guess.

Cross, on the other hand, was a privately held corporation. It was going to be all his loss if he was sued. As he would be. He stood to lose his business, and his employees and suppliers would lose him, and Metropolis would lose a creative force that, along with Lexcorp, had helped shape the downtown skyline.

Without Cross, it would be Lexcorp, whose tower already dominated the skyline and reminded everyone of its creator.

Cross' offices were beautiful. But she'd lay odds Cross didn't own that building or the office park it stood in. Lexcorp's skyscraper was Lexcorp's property, all that rent, all those downtown square feet.

Ask where the money was, *ask* who was the powerhouse in Metropolis's economy, and who was a major employer, and who could move corrupt officials wherever they existed. And ask again what kind of economic damage might be done to ordinary folk if Lexcorp suffered another major hit to *its* reputation.

But she'd bet that Lexcorp stockholders had taken sharp notice when the *Star* article had linked Lexcorp to a lawsuit claiming contract violations on the part of Premier, and Lexcorp's allegations, in print, that the Cross design was flawed.

That was a thought.

She'd bet that it hadn't hurt Lexcorp stock. In fact, and granted that Lex Luthor was no longer the CEO, that news, prominently carried by Lexcorp's subsidiary, LNN, might well have improved the value of Lexcorp stock. Why, just ask LNN: Lexcorp in that lawsuit had been the voice in the wilderness saying that the hotel would be unsafe.

Now Lexcorp was right, wasn't it? Lexcorp had been proven right.

Never mind that Lex himself had been presumed dead and disgraced, and then alive and disgraced—Lexcorp wasn't Lex Luthor. It was a large corporation with fingers in a lot of pies, and a value apart from Lex's rise and fall.

The public perception that Lexcorp's engineering advice could have prevented the disaster, and that the hotel chain and the court had made a serious mistake in judgment, wouldn't hurt Lexcorp at all. But it would hurt Premier very badly when the damage and wrongful death suits hit the court.

It would definitely hurt Harold Cross—economically and personally. Angry crackpots calling his house at night. Lawsuits. Cross could go under, financially.

If Cross went under, that would leave Lexcorp alone, towering over Metropolis not only physically, but in terms of contracts and profits.

A lone *Planet* reporter might be building her own skyscraper of attenuated logic, but there weren't that many contractors of a size to rival Lexcorp and Cross. There weren't that many companies that could do what those two companies could do—set their stamp on the Metropolis skyline.

Motive, if there *was* some deliberate flaw introduced into the construction?

Motive was easy. Who stood to benefit was very evident. The method? In a business like Lexcorp's construction arm, there were engineers, workers, all sorts of people who might have been simultaneously on two payrolls, Lexcorp's *and* Cross & Associates'.

Lex, as she'd come to know, had never wanted for muscle and meanness to carry out his orders. If there'd been some flaw in the concrete, say, or if maybe the dimension hadn't been what they planned . . .

You could put in more gravel than there ought to be when you were pouring concrete, and what would result? She didn't know. She had to ask. She had a suspicion it wouldn't improve the quality at all. You walked along the boarded-up construction sites, and you mostly cursed the nuisance or worried about catching a heel in the cracks of the plywood walks. As she had on the frontage of the Maernik during its construction.

But wouldn't somebody see it if the newly poured concrete showed faults? Not if it was sunk deep in the dirt, not if you never saw anything but the top.

Cross had hired a minor talent, William Smalley, when the project overburdened his office; and Smalley had turned on Cross in testimony. That was *one* man who might have been on two payrolls: Cross & Associates' and Lexcorp's.

What if there were another person drawing double pay, not an architect, but somebody in the actual construction?

She really, really wanted to talk to the investigators.

And would, but this afternoon . . .

The cab rounded the corner onto Clinton, and there was the *Planet.*

And the horde.

It was worse. There were demonstrators with placards.

Protesting what?

She fished for the requisite fare.

"You sure you want to go there?" the cabby asked. "You got another door?"

There were doors in the alley, but not ones for alley access: they only opened from the inside. "Just pull up as close to the door as you can." She prayed for traffic to move, so she could get out and inside before questions got organized. She handed the cabby the fare and a generous tip. "Keep the change. Just get me—God! Don't hit anyone!"

A placard filled the window. It said WOMEN FOR EQUALITY. Another said NO DOUBLE STANDARD. Another was NO NUKES, and TAXPAYERS AGAINST FRAUD.

"Bargain day on banners," she said, shaken, bruised on already sore ribs from the lurch of the cab. The cabby got out as cameras tried to evade placards and focus on her and as placard bearers tried to get their message in front of the cameras.

The guy with the SALVATION banner had come. He attended trials and demonstrations. He seemed like a friendly face, against the push of cameras and microphones and questions. She was sore. She had a couple of pounds of gear in her purse and thought bitterly of taking a roundhouse swing with it, but that wouldn't do. It wouldn't do at all.

"Ms. Lane!" vied with "Lois! Over here!" from voices she knew, other journalists who, at the moment, weren't her close friends.

"What do you say about Lex Luthor?" someone shouted as she pushed her way to the door.

"Why are you dodging questions?" another yelled, as a banner crashed into her face. She fended it off with her sore hand, and then Carl, bless him, had the door open, and cops or guards from some source helped her through to the shocking quiet and sanity of the *Planet* Building lobby.

"Are you all right, Ms. Lane?" Carl asked.

"Yes," she said, and straightened her coat and her hair, and checked the fastening on her handbag just in case. She was outraged. The men who'd helped her in were standing at the doors, and they were, in fact, hired security. Carl had needed backup. It was *entirely* outrageous. And expensive.

"Thank you," she said, and marched into the elevator with, in her purse, the story she hoped would put the *Planet* ahead of the pack.

Her desk was awash in flowers. The *office* was awash in flowers. A large vase sat in the middle of her work space, and she moved it over.

And went to put her head into Perry's office.

"I'm back. I've got an interview with Cross. He sounds on the up-and-up."

Perry's resolve to quit smoking was wavering. He had an unlit cigar, and stuck it in his mouth and took it out again.

"How solid?"

"I saw the diagrams. I've got a piece for the art department." She took the photo out of her purse and laid it on Perry's desk. "I want that pillar there labeled CENTRAL SUPPORT PILLAR. Label that PARKING GARAGE. I'll get you the article in an hour. Hold me a spot."

"Good for you! Good for you!" Perry got up and patted her on the shoulder in that gingerly, afraid-she'd-break way he had, as if he wanted to do something demonstrative but that was the best his upbringing allowed him. "You get out there, you roll with that piece. —Where's Clark? Is he on this?"

"He will be." She'd put his byline on with hers. Pretend. Cover. Her brain was getting numb. At least this time he'd taken his coat.

She exited Perry's office into the well-wishes of Allie, who said she'd borrowed flowers, since there seemed to be so many, but there were cards. She'd saved the cards.

Cards. Courtesies to acknowledge. There must be a hundred of them.

"Lois the TV star," Ron said as she passed. "Admirers from coast to coast."

She'd have stuck her tongue out but she was a lady, and on the point of collapse, with a story yet to write.

She sat down and turned on her computer.

Someone had laid a newspaper on the side of her desk. The *Daily Star.*

SUPERMAN CLAIMS OTHER PRIORITIES, a front-page editorial said.

Questioned about his whereabouts during Metropolis's darkest hour, it began, *Superman claimed he was engaged in the former Soviet Union, raising the question—in this reporter's mind—where this city comes in the Man of Steel's loyalties. It might be objected that charity has no frontiers. We would answer that charity begins at home. It might be objected that free help shouldn't be questioned. We would answer that taxpayer dollars pay Superman's phone bills and afford him countless other privileges without an accounting made . . .*

It went on, subtly and unsubtly nasty, appealing to distrust, jealousy, isolationism, and coming to a conclusion that didn't quite mention what *really* set Edge off: the fact that the *Planet* got the interviews with Superman.

That was the article the reporters had been wanting her reaction to.

Post-its and While You Were Outs were a yellow and pink pile among the flower vases. She began to sort through them for time bombs, in advance of settling down to her article, eyeing two express mailers propped between vases and asking herself if she wanted to get into them.

Jimmy arrived beside her desk and quietly slipped a tabloid-format paper into her view. The *Whisper.*

MY SECRET AFFAIR WITH LEX. With pictures from her almost-wedding.

She snatched the paper.

"It's actually kind of funny—" Jimmy began.

She shot him a look that might fry eggs.

"—if you look at it that way," Jimmy said.

"Not likely," she said. Jimmy started to leave. She shoved the paper back at him. "Find a birdcage. Here's liner."

"Right," he said. "Want some coffee?"

"Please."

He was off. She sat plowing through Post-its.

The League of this, the Society for that, all wanting a statement from her.

Another message from Nightscape, wanting her on the air.

Message from the Women's Issue Forum, another from Equality in Journalism, both wanting her as a speaker.

Others from this and that fund, wanting her to call back, one message saying *Wanting Endorsement. Urgent. Disaster Fund.*

A While You Were Out from the DA, that somebody was using her photo in a fund-raising purportedly—and falsely—for the Maernik Disaster Fund.

She set that one aside—thump!—for a personal call to the DA. And she thought wishfully of a man in Suicide Slum who'd break arms for fifty bucks.

Bargaining for trouble, she picked up one of the express mailers and checked the sender's name—a national syndicate. It looked legitimate. She opened it.

It was. *We are interested in talking with you regarding a weekly syndicated column . . . .*

Wow, was all she could think. And didn't want to think further right now.

She opened the other mailer, seeking distraction from that stunner.

It was from something called Morton R. Wells Productions, and it began,

For combined book-movie rights to your story. Morton R. Wells Productions is willing to discuss an offer of one million dollars, for a novel to be written by Anthony Quinn Vardee, whose last book was six weeks at the top of the best-seller list, plus a major motion picture contingent on novel sales. We urge you not to grant interviews or rights to anyone without contacting us. Please phone us at your earliest convenience at . . .

A million dollars. Discuss an offer?

A million dollars?

Jimmy set the coffee on her desk. She sat stunned. Just stunned. Thinking . . .

Thinking it sure beat ten thousand from a tabloid reporter trying to bribe her.

She drew a long, steadying breath and pulled out the keyboard drawer, reminding herself she worked for the *Planet*.

Reminding herself she had a man's reputation in her hands, and in the tape in her purse. She took the recorder out and set it on her desk.

Rejecting the suggestion of flaws in the Maernik Hotel design, the architectural firm of Cross & Associates today came forward to state that after review of the blueprints and specifications they are convinced that the design was not at fault in the Maernik collapse. In an exclusive interview with Howard Cross, architect, the Planet *has obtained . . .*

"Hello, Clark," someone said.

She drew in a breath, spun the chair around, and he was there, walking in from the elevator, coat over his arm, blithe as if it were any day, any brief absence.

She was out of her chair.

Aware of the whole office watching. Reminding herself she'd told everyone Clark was on the job, in Metropolis, doing legwork for her story.

Oxygen seemed a little lacking in the room.

"Hi," she said, and snagged him by the arm, took the coat, hung it up, and walked him to the back hall, back by the copy machine.

She didn't, she told herself, know what he might have come from, or how he'd been getting along, but the look in his eyes and the oh, so gentle touch of his hands when they were alone told her she looked a little frayed.

"How have you been?" he asked. He, Clark, Superman, who'd been around the world holding up dams or something. His voice was soft, and went right to the frayed nerves and stirred up a dam break of her own that almost burst her restraint.

She drew a deep breath and didn't let it go. "I'm fine and you've been legging it around town getting information for me. We've got a shared byline on the Cross article and I've been to see Lex."

"Why?" That almost burst *his* restraint. It was a little louder a *why* than was safe in their quiet withdrawal. "Why on earth?"

"Because Lex was suing Howard Cross, who designed the hotel, and Lex lost. Or it wasn't Lex, it was Lexcorp, but I don't think there's that much difference even yet. But I can't prove it."

"Slow down."

"Lexcorp was contracted to build the Maernik. But when the truth came out about Lex, they lost the contract and Cross got it."

"That's a pretty slim thread. They're two big construction firms."

"But this was the contract Lex lost when he lost his reputation! I don't think he's forgotten it. I don't think he took it well."

"Granted he didn't take it well . . ." Clark looked a little set back. He'd come in with no briefing, straight off another set of problems, and he was clearly trying to fill in blanks off her non-inclusive report. "Why go out there?"

"Because I thought he might know what the center of the controversy was. And he did. He remembered the design, real well. He was scary, Clark."

"I know. And I don't like you—"

He stopped himself. He didn't say, *I don't like you going out there,* as if he had a right to dictate where she went.

"You're right," she said. "It *wasn't* a good idea."

"Did he threaten you?"

She shook her head. "Quite the opposite. We talked about the hotel. He was distressed when he thought I might have been in it when it went. I had the strangest thought—that if anybody he hired *was* responsible—I might have just killed that man."

Clark let go a slow breath and rubbed the back of his neck, not happy, not at all happy with the news.

"Two people are dead," she said. "Monique Simms? Suicide. She covered the Maernik lawsuit. William Smalley? Suicide. He came to Cross right at the time he got the Maernik job, testified against Cross in the lawsuit Lexcorp brought, and sometime after that—suicide."

Clark's frown was deeper, and worried. "You've been busy."

"*You've* been busy. That's what I've told everybody. You've been helping me track down details. Shared byline. And the media's been tracking me, every breath I take, and they want me to do a syndicated column, that's one thing, and there's this book and movie deal—they want to pay me a million dollars, Clark!" She was aware she was stringing things together without sense, and suddenly the whole sum of it seemed surreal to her, even threatening, to everything they'd mapped out together. "What do I do with a million dollars?"

He didn't answer that at once. Then he said, "You do what you want to."

"I don't *know* what I want." She'd expected another reminder about publicity. She'd expected to be mad.

But then she remembered that tabloid. Lex. MY SECRET AFFAIR. And didn't know whether it was a cold chill or a blush that hit her. *That* was what they'd go for. And she knew, in this man looking at her, waiting for her to come to her senses, she had something beyond all estimation.

"Oh, what's a million?" she said and, still shaky from the

thought of blowing a million dollars, found herself in very strong arms, against a very welcome warmth. "A million can't buy this."

"You're amazing," he said. The man who could go to Tibet on a whim or promise her a chip off a meteor's cold heart for a necklace only made her ask what she could do to keep ahead of him; but the man who could say, *You're amazing,* in that tone of voice, knocked her right off her feet and swept her up in the same move.

They were on their way to the moon standing right there in the hall, lips meeting, arms enfolding, just—he was there, and never would be away from her, not really *away,* no matter where in the world they were. He didn't take away from her: he added everything he was. And she was so overwhelmed with that it seemed the world and they were spinning together.

On the other hand, her feet weren't on the ground, and she wasn't sure his quite were, when someone cleared his throat slightly, murmured, " 'Scuse me, I've got to get a copy run."

Possibly Nathan the restaurant critic hadn't seen the brass band and the fireworks, or noticed very much at all of the goings-on. Nathan's passion extended mostly to food and wine, and the little gray man in the plain gray coat just never gained a pound or focused on much else.

Nathan went right past them into the copy room.

Lois let go a nervous laugh and squeezed Clark's hand. "I love you. You know that?"

Nathan adjusted his trifocals and looked at them from out of the room. "Oh. Clark. Lois. Hello. How did you find the restaurant?"

"Missed the reservation. The hotel, you know."

"Oh. Yes. Of course. It was that night."

" 'Spose we might try again?"

"I could do that, yes, I think I could."

On such a silly protocol, they excused themselves out of the vicinity and walked back up the short hall to the general office and the rest of the curious world, hand in hand—it was so natural to hold on to one another. "I'm sorry." She wasn't sure who had instigated the business in the hall. She thought she had. But he looked as bemused.

"Sorry," he muttered. "But can you *prove* anything?"

"About what?"

"About Luthor."

"No." Had that been the topic? Was that where the world had gone to starry space and them hanging above it all? "No." The Maernik. Luthor, in the cell. Barred shadow, and threat. "No, I can't. Just—it adds up, that's all. He's got motive, he's got all kinds of motives—"

"How did he do it? Who's the contact? Who's the hands and feet and what did they do?"

"*Anything's* possible with Luthor involved."

"But what can we prove?"

"That no one's safe." She gave an unmeant twitch of the shoulders, a shiver. "That money can get past the guards and wreck people's lives. But it won't wreck ours."

"No," he said. "But be careful. I don't like you talking to him. I don't like you coming to his attention. I'm sorry if it makes you mad, but that's the truth."

"I don't think I ever *leave* his attention," Lois said somberly, "and *that's* the truth." They'd reached her desk. She let go his hand and picked up her purse. "As long as I'm up for it, I'm going to go downstairs and talk to the press. Then I'm going to come back up here and write my article, and then you and I are going to supper. How's that?"

"Fine."

"We've got a civic function tomorrow night. *I've* got a civic function tomorrow night. That's our schedule for the week. And then you and I are going to take a day off and go to Nathan's restaurant and have an evening."

"That sounds good."

"Can you?" In the middle of the newsroom she couldn't ask him was he going back to Russia, or what else might take him away when she needed him. And she braced herself against a reluctant no.

"Yes," he said.

That fueled her determination for at least another hour before she'd fall on her face.

"What are you going to tell them downstairs?" he asked. "What is there to tell them?"

"Just the day's schedule, just that I'm going to the mayor's fund-raiser tomorrow night and I'm writing my article on the Cross statement today, which they can read in the *Planet,* and the investigation is ongoing. And meanwhile you can figure out where you're taking me to supper at five o'clock."

"I'll do that," he said. And seemed to wish he could say something else.

But she was going to do exactly what she'd said, and thought she might have the strength for it.

A woman who'd just spurned a million-dollar deal could do anything.

Chapter 12

Taking a world-famous woman to dinner in, say, Boston or Kansas City on a moment's notice wouldn't be the thing to do. The fact was, *she* was recognizable anywhere in the country and probably out of it, and a man who wanted to be inconspicuous had a problem.

But a little place like Lausano's, in the suburbs, that was a place a taxi could reach, and since Lois Lane's non-departure from the *Planet* by ordinary routes, like doors, would be too conspicuous, Clark did hire a cab, and gave the cabby instructions through the thick of rush-hour traffic, instructions that ducked down an expressway exit, under the underpass, around a corner, and down the boulevard for ten blocks.

Eddie Lausano had probably painted the murals. Certainly Eddie cooked the pasta, which was good, and Eddie's daughter did the desserts, which were sinful, and used real whipped cream.

And Lois was visibly fading, right into the bittersweet chocolate and raspberries.

No one had said a thing about the hotel. He'd advised Eddie, and there were looks from a couple of the tables, but no one came over, no one interrupted them.

"Got to get you home," Clark said, fingering her poor, scabbed hand. "Before you fall over."

"Rather go to your place."

"How would that look? On national television, no less."

"We *are* engaged." She offered a winsome if weary smile.

"But gossip you and I don't need. You've got to go home, Lois. The front door. The whole bit."

She sighed. Plucked up a raspberry with whipped cream. Sighed again. "I missed you."

"I missed you."

Another sigh.

"You did," he said, "really, really well."

"I'll bet you did, too." Eyes shut. She was falling asleep in her chair.

His eyes didn't feel the need of rest, but his mind needed sleep, needed it perhaps as much as any man's did. From the inside looking out, he never could answer that question.

It was always the question, what was ordinary, what he had in common with everyone else. And in what things he was different.

Lois let go because he was with her. He kept awake because he had to get Lois home, and only then, in his own apartment, he'd get some rest.

But the food had tasted very, very good. It had filled—maybe—a human need.

And for the company, he'd have stayed awake another week.

He paid the modest tab, left a good tip, and had Eddie call a taxi.

Clark Kent brought Lois Lane home and escorted her through the small stakeout of reporters. Lois was cheerful, and waved on her way in.

Clark Kent had also to leave, publicly, in a cab, glad for the post-sunset hour and the fact he wasn't the main target of the cameras.

And he was, by then, very glad to take that cab home, to a dim and slightly disorderly apartment, his own—which was usually in better order, but he'd left in a hurry days ago and thought, at the time, that he'd tidy up when he got home.

He was so mentally weary by the time he opened the door to his apartment that he didn't even consider the clutter. He tossed clothes into the laundry and showered—clear, clean water, and *soap*, beautiful, plain soap. He enjoyed the feel of it.

And enjoyed not moving fast. And not hearing the rush of the wind. And not being battered by cold rain, but by hot water.

And not facing any decision more dire than whether to go with Lois to the civic memorial tomorrow night and risk the cameras—he knew she'd desperately like him to go—or whether to stay prudently at home out of the public eye.

Go as a reporter, maybe, with Jimmy in tow: he wasn't news if he wasn't near Lois, and if he hung back with the other members of the press, he'd get questions from them about Lois, but none about himself so long as he played it all very carefully and didn't get drawn into commenting on the story they would be, like him, assigned there to cover.

It was probably a good idea: he'd feel better if he could at least be near Lois. He was just—anxious—about the pressure she was under, about the story she'd begun to uncover. Two people dead, one of whom had been an informant in the lawsuit over the Maernik, possibly a plant inside Cross & Associates, by what Lois had said at supper; and one who had been covering the story. He didn't believe in coincidence when the stakes grew this high.

Lois visiting Lex. *That* was enough to haunt him as he lay down to rest for the first time in days. She was on a lead and she'd taken measures to investigate that lead. As she'd always do. He had no complaints on that score.

Determination to do a little checking on his own, yes.

Quietly. Not to disturb her story. But—

He shut his eyes and drew a deep breath and chilled down the apartment a little.

Water flowed through his dreams. Water and wind.

And the bright orange flares of explosions.

Granny's face, with a bright, impish grin.

The girl with the cat and kittens. His young translator was trying to tell him something not too urgent, but he wished he knew what it was. It might have to do with Lois's problem.

But he was above the Caucasus by night, and stars were shining around the snowy peaks as they'd done when Alexander the Great had come through Persia, as they'd done when the Huns had swept through to the north, and when the skies had shadowed with metal wings. Up here, it was still the same.

Peaceful, between the storms.

The morning was gray, one of those silken gray days where the clouds seemed to hang just grazing the tops of buildings, where light seeped, rather than shone, down the canyons of downtown.

A police ribbon was still up at the site. Clark saw that as he walked up to the limit they allowed the public to approach the ruin. So were other ribbons up, a different kind of ribbon, remembrances tied on the chain link they'd put up to keep the curious out. Ribbons and flowers and pictures protected in plastic. One had a rosary. Another, a child's report card.

The street hadn't opened. What remained standing of the building was reckoned too unstable and the below-ground area far, far too dangerous to allow people even on the sidewalk next to it.

The Maernik wasn't the only damage. Businesses to either side had suffered, not only from falling concrete and subsidence of the sidewalk, and then from the emotional depression that attended the place, but now by the ruling that said the other structures were in danger from the standing walls and couldn't be occupied.

That was information he'd gathered from the *Planet*'s morning edition.

He walked up to the fence among others who'd come to stand and remember.

But the fence didn't stop him from a closer look. He took off the glasses that otherwise, with refractions off the structure of glass itself and the temperature from the surrounding air, bothered his close focus. He sharpened his senses, tuned out the thunderous world of distant traffic and jackhammers and people walking on the street, and probed with all the range of his sight and hearing, down into the shattered concrete and twisted steel, down past the wreckage of cars and girders, and down and down into the depths where the whole thing rested, down to that single pillar around which the garage and the structure above had been built.

He found what he thought was that area. It corresponded to the diagram in the newspaper he carried, folded, under his arm.

He found the signature of water and mud, both visually and with his hearing, as the building echoed, to his sensitized ears, with the thrum of Metropolitan traffic.

A lot of mud. It had been raining when the building had caved in, and there'd been that question raised, about the central pillar construction. Even in getting the boy out, where the inverted pyramid of the garage had rested against the earth, Lois had worked in water. So she'd told him. So she'd written.

After surviving all that devastation, Billy Anderson had nearly drowned.

A raindrop hit him. Others dashed across his vision, disturbing the air with large, cold streaks as he stood motionless as the stone itself.

He shortened and enlarged his focus. Mud from footprints had dried on the sidewalk beyond the chain link, in a dusting of powdered glass. A spot of rain hit the dried mud. And another.

Water certainly seemed to have been his curse lately.

Water was going to complicate arrangements for this evening, and maybe reduce attendance at the memorial.

Lois had begged leave from Perry to work by phone and modem today instead of coming in. She was going to beg, promise, and bribe her way into a last-minute appointment with her hairdresser and see if the manicurist could resurrect her nails.

He didn't think Perry would say no, not today. Not with the karma she'd gained.

And she'd gained karma with Perry for her absent partner at the same time, by sharing that Cross article byline: that had made it look as if he'd been in the city all along—a piece of subterfuge that troubled him.

It meant he'd better read that article really well, and that if there were leads still to follow, he should follow them for her—justifying that shared byline.

That meant, if he could, finding out why a former colleague who'd reported on the Premier lawsuit was dead, and why a principal figure in that lawsuit had suffered the same impulse to suicide.

That Luthor was in a prison literally within sight of all the resources of Lexcorp might be ironic justice; but Clark took very seriously everything Lois had said about that meeting, and took even more seriously Lois's fear that Luthor had settled on her as a focus.

That was *not* a comfortable thought. Luthor had shown signs of obsessive behavior *before* he'd undergone profoundly disturbing experiences. Luthor had never been able to resolve a problem by walking away from a conflict. He'd never been able to dismiss a possible slight. He'd never been able to take no for an answer, not in business, not in his personal life: Luthor had come to more than one setback because he'd offended someone he should have had better sense than to offend, and he then couldn't let the matter go: he had to pursue it, aggravate it, provoke response, which only made him madder.

Lex Luthor was not a man destined to be loved by those who had to deal with him. That would always limit him: he gained no loyalty—but then, he could buy certain talent.

Luthor had thought he could buy Lois. And she'd not only escaped him, she'd dragged the lure of her presence past him when he was in such humiliating circumstances, behind bars.

And Luthor had remained, by Lois's account, in good humor?

Then Luthor was *not* feeling entirely humiliated. He hadn't shown his nastier side, not once in that interview. So Lois had said.

It would be hard to prove Luthor's equanimity if *he* should visit. He didn't think he'd find Lex Luthor in such an expansive, helpful mood at all. And he knew Superman wouldn't.

No good to go over there, that was a fact. But a little investigation into Lexcorp activities at the moment might be a good thing. Lexcorp *said* all ties to its former CEO were severed. But he didn't buy it.

Meanwhile, resorting to the phones over at the Stillford Hotel, he had calls to make, to the President, to the State

Department. He sat there, listening to thunder rumble outside, thinking of Lois and her hair appointment.

It didn't seem, after everything else, fair.

No, he reported to the State Department, he didn't think the rebels, whoever they'd been, would venture back to that area too soon. The region hadn't, in general, known who he was, or why he was there, but he trusted there was the rumor in the mountains regarding one village with a very mean defense.

The ammunition was also out of the picture.

And, possibly by today, the bridge would be a fact the rebels would have to deal with.

But he left that on the lap of the State Department.

And had a solitary lunch in the Stillford's elegant small dining room, thinking to himself that it was going to be next to impossible to get a decent meal tonight: Lois would have butterflies, they were resisting being seen together, cameras would be following her around, and the rain was going to present a challenge to her to get to the Arts Center tonight without a soaking.

It was one job Superman couldn't quite guarantee, to stop the rain.

And to his frustration, Clark couldn't show up at her apartment to get a cab for her and help her shield herself from the rain, either. The stakeout would be at a pitch of activity this evening, such that if he was with her there, he would be fair game for the news services all evening.

He went to the lobby and waited for a letup in the downpour which had started outside, one of those chance events that made taxis scarcer than elephants on Metropolis streets. He found his hiatus and, having his umbrella and a good raincoat, he set out into the elements, thinking that a cab might be easier to find on Clinton than here.

It wasn't. He didn't really want to go to the *Planet*, to pretend he knew everything. Reentering that information flow would be easier tomorrow, with Lois to distract people from questions he couldn't answer.

And Perry, on Lois's assurance, believed he was working for the *Planet* during his absence from the office.

He narrowly missed snagging a cab. A frail-looking woman beat him.

And his course took him back by the Maernik site, which was running with mud, thumping with a sound that hadn't been there before. Pumps, he thought, to move the water that was running down through the high ruins, all that ragged tower of shattered concrete, and collecting below. He could more than imagine the conditions inside the ruin: he'd seen it, and still the workmen kept at it. The lingering operation was the recovery of certain personal effects from the rubble, and the slow search of experts hired by various lawyers for some hint of flaw or fault. Now and again they brought out a significant piece, evidently, to join a pile of broken furniture.

They hadn't even gotten down to the crushed cars.

A worker was coming out of the chain link gate near him. Clark flashed his press credentials. "Clark Kent, from the *Planet*. Anything turning up?"

"Not since days ago," the workman said, and wiped a muddy hand on his coveralls, hardly a mud-free surface. "Nothing much doing, but escorting engineers around. I can't talk about anything."

"I understand," Clark said, and did understand. These were busy, tired workers, not information officers. "What's the sound I hear?" He was sometimes doubtful, asking about subtle sounds, fearful of betraying his abilities. But this was a stranger.

And it seemed loud enough that ordinary people might hear it. "Is that a pump?"

"Yep."

"How much does it move?" Reportorial questions. Who, what, when, where, why? Automatic as breathing, and a conversation filler that might loosen more information. He owed Perry a story. Or five or ten stories. He took out the perpetually available notebook and pen.

"Three hundred gallons a minute."

"What do you think you've moved out, so far?"

"Oh, Lord, I don't know. Maybe a couple or three swimming pools' worth. It's a lot."

"Where's the water going?" He didn't see an outlet. But hadn't looked.

The workman pointed a grimy hand back at the open manhole. "Down there. There's a hole right to the sewer. Pipe's broke, clean off, but we connected the output down below, there, where guys don't have to trip over it."

"The pipe broke?"

"Mister." Clearly the workman was exasperated with questions, questions, questions. It was cold and probably he was on a short break with a cup of hot coffee as his goal. "Everything down there's *broke*. There just ain't much *intact.*"

"Is the water a problem to the salvage?"

"Oh, sure, it's a problem. But we'll move the water out. Level's dropping down there pretty fast since we turned the pump on."

"More rain won't help, will it?"

"Sure won't."

"What's your name?"

"Wall. Terry Wall."

"You work for the city?" There was a city number stencil on the yellow coveralls.

"Park Department. They got everybody on this duty."

"How many shifts have you worked?"

"Same as everybody. We lost count."

"Thank you," Clark said. "Thank you."

It was a story—a small one, but a good one. A good man, Terry Wall seemed to be. And the pump kept emptying the out-pouring of the heavens down into the depths of the ruin by way of the sewer system. He could see the connection under the side-walk now that he looked for it—connecting to the main sewer under the street. But—a fast glance at the pool of water in the ruin confirmed his suspicion—there was no hint of finishing the job soon.

Three hundred gallons a minute? That was a lot of water.

Thunder broke. Rain picked up, and the workman ran for cover. Clark walked on in his quest for a cab, his thoughts pre-occupied with images of the muddy terraces in the Caucasus, and the muddy flat through which a river ran.

It seemed as if he couldn't get away from water the last several days.

It seemed he'd been working and working and working and the problem kept coming back at him, with different dimen-sions. The dam. The high valley runoff. The bridge.

He walked on down the street, around to the *Planet* Building, where reporters staked out the place under a dismal shelter of umbrellas and improbable shelters made of raincoats. The cameras weren't so much in evidence.

He almost missed Carl's inevitable hello, being mentally in that high valley.

"Hello," Clark said, and took the elevator upstairs.

The newsroom was brightly lit, in full motion. "*There* you are," Perry said to him, and wanted him in the office.

Perry wanted him to cover the event tonight. It wasn't a society report the *Planet* wanted on this one, but a coverage with, Perry said, the delicate touch.

"Lois has got the recognition coming," Perry said. "And we don't want to lack class, you know what I mean? Like *class*. Like we were anybody else covering it, but this is *our* Lois, you know? I figure you can do it."

"Be objective?" He was doubtful.

"No." Perry jabbed an unlit cigar in his direction. "Be a gentleman. A *gentleman*. The *King* was a gentleman." A wave of the cigar aloft, at the autographed portrait. "I know you'll do fine. Won't stop you from sitting by her. You've got a good memory."

"I'd rather be in on a press pass," he said. He had a reputation for avoiding the spotlight, and he leaned on it. "I'd rather work."

"You're sure."

"Lois knows I'm not good in crowds like that." And because that gave him a little leverage and he didn't want to think of Lois having to manage alone, he added, "I think she'd really appreciate somebody coming over to the apartment, you know, help her get past the siege outside and into a cab. If I'm going to be in the press area—I think she'd really appreciate it if *you'd* sort of—escort her this evening. She respects you. She'd like that."

Was that an embarrassed flush on Perry's face? It didn't take supersenses to see. "Well, maybe *you'd* be better there," Perry said.

Clark shook his head. "Writing this article's something I want to do. It's what I *can* do for her and I can't sit there taking notes in front of all those cameras. It'd look bad. But if I'm there, I'd sure feel better if you were fending off the sharks and just helping her with the logistics. You sit with her. She thinks the world of you. She really does. She'd be very pleased if you were with her."

Perry drew in a breath and seemed to grow an inch taller. "I'll give her a call. Sure. Sure, I'll do it."

"I really appreciate it," Clark said, and went and nabbed Jimmy Olsen, who, at a vacant desk, was swabbing out a lens with a Q-tip. "You have a plain suit coat? Not a tux, suit and tie, but *class*. Perry wants *class*. I need a photographer."

"The Arts Center thing? The memorial?"

"At seven."

Jimmy looked more pleased than Clark would have thought he would be to be put on the society beat. It was the kind of job Olsen generally tried to duck, the smiling faces around the punch bowl, the mass shots of audiences, the stilted poses that froze and smiled for the camera.

"I can get a coat," Jimmy said. "Yeah, I'll do it."

The photos on this one would be something special. Jimmy was good. And Jimmy would come up with a coat. Best not to ask where, but Jimmy was resourceful.

Meanwhile he had to write his article, small as it was, just a tidbit of news, but fuel for the vast curiosity that drove a story like this, that kept the public hanging on every shred of information, unsatisfied and wanting conclusions and resolutions that might be months away.

Like . . . why? Why did a major building just fall down? Why was there no warning, no cracks, no sounds that might have advised of a problem developing? The unexpectedness of it was the still-worrisome question, and Lois's article on Cross & Associates had only redirected the concern. If the architectural design wasn't at fault, then what? If the design wasn't flawed, what about the ground underneath? Did the plan miss some hidden fault underlying the city? Had there been an earthquake? Were other buildings in danger? The public didn't feel safe downtown so long as the horror at the Maernik had no explanation.

Stones on the road in the Caucasus. Cracks in the dam. Cracks leaking water.

Water.

All that rain.

Maybe, he thought, maybe *that* was the answer. Maybe it *was* water.

He got up, late as it was, went to the art department, and looked at the original of the artwork that had run in the paper.

That central, supporting pillar, set in the bedrock.

All those wavy lines on the charts, that meeting in the tent with the Russians, the charts and the maps from Pyetigorsk . . .

Down on the river bottom, where water and sand had scoured the base from under a piling.

There was a question. There was a serious question. Underground water, possibly groundwater in excess of anything anyone knew was there.

It was 4:15 by his watch.

He had a suit at the cleaners; it had been there since before the disaster. He had to do some talking to Cross, but in the meanwhile he had to pick up his blue suit and the shirts he'd left before they went to the Unclaimed section.

"Where's Jimmy?" he asked Allie.

"Left," Allie said, "about half an hour ago."

Going after the dress coat, more than likely.

Perry's office was dark. Perry had had to do some cleanup and then would be going to Lois's apartment to pick her up.

As for himself, Clark wanted to get to the Arts Center tonight without having to resort to high speed. There were just too many people lurking about with cameras. That meant adjusting every schedule to accommodate travel by cab.

He took the elevator down to street level. It was raining buckets outside, at the moment. He couldn't find a cab to the cleaners, and walked, with dogged patience, telling himself what his father used to tell him, that walking was good for him.

Probably walking was good for the disposition. Probably it was educational, explaining to him why Lois occasionally arrived out of sorts. It was not good for the shoes, and water was running down his neck.

He picked up the suit, and his laundry, done up in plastic bags against the downpour, prepared to trek home through the gray downpour.

A cab appeared like a miracle in the rain, and he flagged it down, gave the cabby the address of his apartment, and settled back for a short ride. The windshield wipers fought hard against the flood that beat against the roof.

He didn't know the time. He looked at his watch, suspecting he was running late, but it still showed 4:15. He didn't know how—but he'd killed another wristwatch.

The forest green suit—it was sober enough. Black heels, dark stockings.

Lois straightened her hair, carefully, considering the downpour, and figured the hardiest of the press outside was cursing their luck.

She couldn't both cover the event and be in it. But she'd called in to get Jimmy for some photographs for a story she did want to do, a follow-up to her story on Cross. And Perry had intercepted the call.

The bell rang. She punched the intercom, heard Perry's cheerful, "Lois?"

"I'm on my way," she said. "I'll meet you."

He'd insisted on escorting her. It was the Southern courtesy idea. But it came welcome today, when rain complicated an already complicated process. It made her feel—well, moderately glamorous. Maybe not so harried and desperate.

She gave Elroy a rub of the ears, snatched her purse from the chair by the door, and went down, quickly, thanks to a ready elevator.

"You look beautiful," Perry said, looking proud of her.

Her mother was going to be there. Her father was. Her sister was stranded in Dallas on an overnight.

She'd be a nervous wreck, just contemplating the business of her family in front of the cameras—but there was Perry. Shining knight. Defender from the battering of photographers and the determination of her mother to get in front of the cameras with her daughter—

Perry, possessor of an umbrella and a taxi sitting at the curb with the meter running.

She ducked under the umbrella and ran with Perry to the cab. In the downpour only the hardiest of the reporters shouted questions at her: *Do you have a statement on the award?*

She called out a cheerful, "Thank you!" and ducked inside the cab, dry and safe. "Thanks, Perry. You're so good to me."

"Nothing but the best," Perry said, and settled into a comfortable quiet for the duration of the ride downtown, ten drowned city blocks as the streetlights came on, haloed in the falling rain.

The Arts Center turned up in a patch of twilight green, with its big globes of light shining like so many moons. It seemed a surreal night, the taxi hammered by the rain until it ducked down the drive and into the safe, dry parking garage.

Perry got out, Perry paid the fare, and she eased out, protecting her nylons and her coat from wrinkles.

Jimmy was waiting for them, in a neat brown suit, with his press badge and his cameras. He hooked a thumb back to the security personnel. "They're kind of touchy this evening."

"Ought to be," she said. "But I want that picture."

"Is that the big pillar you're talking about? The one that holds everything up?" Jimmy nodded toward the huge center column, down which the ramp spiraled.

"Yes. But—" Other cars had come in, one of them the mayor's, and the elevator was near at hand. Perry had gone over to talk to the mayor, and she snagged Jimmy's sleeve and drew him inside the elevator.

She pushed black 6, which was the lowest level.

"From down there, eh?" Jimmy asked.

"The design is just like the Maernik," she said. "Same architect. I want to get some shots and get up before the cars start getting into the shot."

"Right," Jimmy said, and changed lenses. "I'm ready."

The elevator stopped. The door opened on the stillness of the bottom level of the garage, and the huge pillar that was, essentially, the support for all the structure above. Earth surrounded this inverted pyramid, with a system of small braces helping support this section, which supported everything above. But this was the big one, reinforced with steel, an elegance that held the whole airy glass-and-steel of the Arts Center suspended above it.

Nothing, she thought, walking near it, could disturb a structure this solid. And it *was* solid. The very notion that something this massive could shatter was hard to think of.

But the Maernik was evidence that it could.

A small bomb, she asked herself? So meticulously placed that it might not be detected?

There was room for about thirty cars on this level. Might one carry a bomb of that size, park right up against the column? But Clark had said there was no bomb at the Maernik.

The elevator went up, called by some other user. It was quiet for a moment. Deathly quiet.

Just the thump of what she supposed would be the air-conditioning.

Jimmy's shutter clicked, slowly, in the low light.

"Funny sound," Jimmy said.

"Air-conditioning, I guess." It was more than the thump. There was a sound like air in a duct. "I guess they have to keep the air circulating down here. All that carbon monoxide, from the car exhausts." She punched the call button, for fear the elevator might be in heavy use soon as more guests began to arrive: she didn't want to get stuck in the basement with the car fumes.

"Got enough pictures?" she asked Jimmy.

"Hard to get a good one," Jimmy said. "The thing's so big. Hang on. I want you in the shot, to show the scale."

The elevator arrived. Jimmy snapped his shot and hurried over. He began changing lenses again, a photographer's amazing balancing act, a rapid clattering that looked like a total disassembly and reassembly of his equipment in the short time it took them to ride the elevator back up to the entry level.

At the entry, there was now a steady traffic of cars into the garage, more lined up waiting to get in, while a procession of

Metropolis's foremost citizens passed in eclectic order through the double glass doors that led into the huge, glass-walled foyer.

"There you are!" Perry said, and took her in tow. "Thought I'd lost you."

She didn't mention Clark. He didn't want attention from the cameras, and cameras clicked furiously as she came into the lighted foyer, near the auditorium, among the giant chromium sculptures by Fracassi—they always made her think of cranes, the feathered sort.

Mayor Berkowitz came to meet her and hesitated at her Band-Aid-covered hands. Touched her hand gently when she said—lying—it didn't hurt.

"Ms. Lane. I'm very glad to see you."

As cameras clicked furiously.

The place was filling rapidly with the elite and also with the heroes of Metropolis. She was gratified to see her companion in the dark, Jenny Whitmore, the EMT. "I've got to get your station number," she said to Jenny, and shook her hand. "I don't want to lose track of you . . ." But you did: things happened, and you meant to give someone a phone call, but things brought you together and separate lives drew you apart again, and all that held you together were terrible memories. She was overwhelmed by the dark for a moment, the dark she'd shared with Jenny.

"How's the little boy?" Jenny asked. "How's Billy?"

"Improving," she said, and recovered her sense of place and time as the mayor tried to get her attention for another introduction. "He's a lot better." She caught a breath that held light, and life, and survivors, feeling the sting of tears.

She introduced Whitmore to the mayor and his wife, with: "This was my partner down there. Her name is Jenny. She's a *full-time* hero. She's an EMT."

Strains of *The Star-Spangled Banner* came from the auditorium as Clark reached the press table, picked up his press release sheets, and slipped them into his pocket. Superspeed had gotten him to his apartment, and dressed, but he'd had an adventure getting a cab, which had meant a walk—in the rain—halfway to the Arts Center.

He drew a calmer breath, assured that he had his materials, he had his pass in order. On the opening strains of a choral arrangement of *America the Beautiful,* he made it into the darkened auditorium, and spotting the pocket of press and photographers in the usual place, to the left of the stage, he walked quietly along the side and joined them.

Jimmy was there, in a cluster of other photographers. Jimmy gave him a glance in the midst of a film change.

"Cab problems," Clark said quietly, and stood near Jimmy.

"We got here a little early. She wanted photos in the basement."

It was another of the Cross & Associates buildings. Of course.

The chorus had finished. He watched the mayor get up and take the podium, and spotted Lois, in her green suit, the green just catching the light from the stage. She looked beautiful. Incredible that she'd done what she'd done—but in his not-at-all-impersonal estimation—she was pretty incredible all the time.

Not the least because she'd want her fiancé beside her at a moment like this, and hers had an allergy to cameras. Perry was with her; he recognized her parents: they'd made it. That was good.

Her fiancé lurked on the sidelines, and she was just too far away, in the center of the row, for him to duck over and say, *I'm here, I love you.*

". . . in our city's calamity," the mayor was saying, and the curtain behind him began rising, on a large-screen display flanked with American flags. "Ladies and gentlemen, rescuers and survivors of this tragedy, a word from the President of the United States."

The screen came live, and showed . . .

Lex Luthor.

The audience stirred. Then gave a nervous, not quite-laugh at what one could take for a very ill-timed mixup of tapes. The mayor was trying to communicate with technicians backstage.

On screen, Luthor, Luthor as he'd become *after* his accident, was saying dead-on to the camera that the Cross design for the Maernik was flawed.

"Someone's mixed up the tapes," the mayor said to the audience, with a nervous laugh. "I apologize, ladies and gentlemen."

". . . a design that won't stand the test of time," Luthor said on-screen, to some unseen interviewer. On the tape, Luthor was sitting in an armchair with a martini in his hand. *When was this tape made?* Clark asked himself, recalling the chronology Lois had established in her article. *When was* he *sipping martinis and pronouncing on the Maernik design? It had to be before he went to prison. It* had *to be after the lawsuit . . . .*

"When they could have had an asset to the city," Luthor said, spinning the glass stem slowly in his fingers, "they picked a design that was flawed. Mistake. Mistake. It won't last the decade. There'll be a day people know the truth—perhaps tragically so. And will it prove I was right? Certainly. But at what cost? At what cost, do you suppose?"

"This is embarrassing," the mayor said. "Can someone cut that thing off?"

Lois rose from her seat and cast about as if looking for someone—Clark knew who that someone was, and stepped past the photographers, whose shutters were clicking. "Lois!" he said under the mutter of disturbance in the audience, and she came running, caught his arms.

"It's him!" Lois said. *"He's* done this! I don't know how, but he did it!" She was scared, her teeth all but chattering. "Clark, get Superman. This isn't a joke. He's not joking. People have to get out of here."

She was off to the stage, then, up the steps to the side, and crossing the stage to warn the mayor as the murmur from the audience became a buzz of disturbance and alarm.

Somebody *wasn't* changing that tape. It was beyond lack of competency. Clark went up the same steps and back into the curtains and the convenient dark.

"Ladies and gentlemen," the mayor said, over a rising commotion. "Please evacuate the building. Do not go to the garage. Go directly outside."

Superman passed the curtains and sent them billowing, the flags lifting and stirring as he stood beside Mayor Berkowitz, who was standing his ground by the mike and urging calm during the evacuation. Lois was beside the mayor. The rescuers, the firemen and police, in their uniforms, had forgotten about being honored and spread out to do their jobs, marshaling the audience toward the doors.

"Superman!" Lois said, short of breath, as if she'd seen him for the first time in the last minutes. "It's not a prank! Lex has *done* something. I don't know what, but he's done something. Cross designed this building. He designed the hospital annex and the Retirement Center!"

"Your Honor," Superman said to Berkowitz, "I'm going to take you outside. Lois, Jimmy, get out the stage doors!"

"The garage!" Lois protested, with no hint she was going to do what he'd asked her to do. The garage was where he didn't want her.

But he had the mayor to get outside, and did that, fast. Spotted stragglers on the way, among them the mayor's wife. He set the mayor down on the edge of the retreating and frightened crowd, in the driving cold rain, and went back to get them, but the firemen were getting them out safely: the mayor's wife, no young woman, wearing high heels and soaked by the rain, ran as best she could to reach her husband.

"Move across the street!" he called out, standing still for a moment and pointing so that they could see the lighted foyer of a nearby building he trusted Cross *hadn't* designed. He saw Mrs. Berkowitz reach her husband, safe, as all the crowd was safe, the firemen and police exiting the building last of all. Police who'd been on guard were already stopping traffic to protect the rain-blinded and frightened crowd as they streamed for other shelter.

He blazed back into the Arts Center with the hope that everyone was clear, now, and then knew he'd also left a crowd of newsmen in that building, and, *no,* not everyone was clear.

He streaked out the doors and into the parking garage—and intercepted Lois and Jimmy and a following crowd of reporters and cameramen on their way down the ramp of the parking garage.

"Out!" he said in no uncertain terms.

"There was a noise in the basement," Lois said shakily.

"I'll look!"

"I'm going!" Lois said, and caught hold of his arm, getting his attention. "I know what I heard!"

He could protect *her.* Not a horde of reporters. *He* could get in and out faster than they could get down in the elevator. But the key word, the one he needed, was *heard.*

"*Hush!*" he said. "Everyone stand still."

He listened in that moment of shocked stillness. And heard a sound he'd heard once before today.

A pump was working.

The reporters began talking again, not having heard anything, he supposed. But in that moment of Lois's attention elsewhere, he whisked downstairs, flying near the ceiling of the spiral ramp to avoid anyone trying to go down or up that ramp from the nether levels.

The sound was like a heartbeat to his ears.

And past the unfurling barrier of that central pillar and the distracting reflections of the parked cars, he chased that sound down to the very bottom, where only a few cars were parked.

Then he could look at the bare concrete floor, and see down to the depths. He could see the pattern of warmth from the building and the earth.

And he could see—and hear—the surge and swirl of *water* around the pillar.

Fast-moving water. Water . . . eroding the foundations, pushing sediment, moving earth. He didn't know for certain how it was getting in, but he knew how it could get out, in the middle of a city where an outflow like that would otherwise stop traffic.

A hundred gallons a minute. Straight into the sewer.

The sewer pipe at the Maernik had broken—everything's *broke,* the city worker had said. Broken pipes had obscured the evidence.

They'd found a broken pipe at the Maernik and tied into it to pump the water out. But there'd been a connection to the sewer main before the building had come down.

Had there been more than one tap into the city sewer? A way out—for water carrying a sludge of earth?

He sped up and up the spiral ramp, up to—he was far from surprised—a contingent of determined reporters, including Lois and Jimmy, coming down the ramp armed with cameras and recorders.

He landed right in front of them. "Somebody!" It wasn't safe to know all their names, even if he knew most. "Jimmy! Olsen! Get outside to the mayor, get him to a phone and have him shut down the outflow water from this building where it empties into the city sewer. Get him to get hold of the building supervisor! Shut the sewer down for the whole block. *Then* shut down the city water main for the whole block. In that order! Do you understand? It's urgent! Do the same for the lines into the Retirement Center! And the hospital!"

"But why?" Jimmy asked.

"What's going on?" was the chorus from a dozen throats, recorders and note-taking faculties ready.

"Undermining," he answered shortly. "Evacuate this building! Now! It's not safe!"

"Superman!" That voice would catch his attention above all others. "The hospital!"

He knew Lois's personal concern. He knew how scared she was for those kids.

He knew the cost it could be in fragile lives to order an evacuation that wasn't warranted: the hospital's frailest patients could die from being moved. Operations in progress would be stopped—maybe fatally. Lives in the neonatal units, the elderly, the critical depended on uninterrupted oxygen.

And he knew above and beyond all relationship to the press, his relationship to this woman—to a partner—didn't include leaving her behind. Not on this one. Not when she'd done the research and turned up the evidence that he'd been using to track this disaster: most of all not when she'd personally pulled those kids from the Maernik wreckage.

He swept Lois up in his arms, flung his cloak about her, and went, out the door of the garage, out into driving rain and through the thunder. She held tight, hair soaked, cold, and intent as he was, he was well sure, on getting where they were going, fast, before a madman let loose a disaster so callous, so heedlessly cruel a sane mind could scarcely imagine or track his reasons.

But Lex Luthor's target—that was the man whose win in court was timed with the collapse of Luthor's reputation, Luthor's control over his financial empire. Get them back. Make them suffer. The substitution of that videotape was no accident, and he wished he'd laid hands on the hireling who'd gotten it into the machine backstage and who'd kept it running past the mayor's exhortations to shut it off . . . if the machine's Off switch hadn't been disabled.

But he had other, more urgent things on his mind as he saw the hospital ahead and dived for the garage.

"The basement!" Lois gasped as he set her down. "The basement . . . check for a sound . . . like that one!"

"I can hear it," he said. "The same as the Arts Center." Lois's hair was dripping into her face, and he wiped it back. Every instinct said send her *out* of danger, but there were hundreds of helpless people upstairs, and he couldn't handle both crises at once. "Get upstairs. Tell the staff. Tell them to stop all surgeries they can. Evacuate the annex—*just* this wing. I don't know how, but Luthor's diverted water under the building. He's carrying mud out by the sewer, timing it to the weather reports." When he was in a hurry he'd tended to hold too hard, move too fast, and he was calm and careful with two fragile hands. "Tell the hospital authorities the same thing I told Jimmy. Shut down the sewer outlet first and shut down the water main second. Right now, water's all under this garage and we don't want it to drain out, do you follow me? That's how he does it: as long as the water's there, it helps support things while it's scouring the bedrock like sandblasting. He pumps it out fast—and there's no support left. *That's* how he's doing it."

"My God." Lois took another swipe at her dripping hair with a scabbed, shaking hand. "Can you save the building? Is there anything you can do?"

"Protect the patients. There's a joint where the annex joins the old part of the hospital." He saw her confusion. "There will be one, trust me! The main building should be safe, but get the patients as far from that joint as possible. Building engineers will know where it is. Get everyone out of the rooms on this side, into the main hospital, and don't let anybody go back after cars. Go!"

"Right!" Lois said, and ran for the doors that led inside the hospital corridors. She went through, out of sight, outside his protection.

Time was what he needed. Time was what the hospital needed, to move patients, some of whom were already suffering from the Maernik collapse. And he couldn't lose time worrying about anything but how to stop gravity from having its way.

If they could just stabilize the situation, he thought. If they could maintain the water level under the building, so that the water could help bear up the load of the building above, maybe they could pump in something more permanent to stabilize it. That was where he needed Cross, and any other expert Cross could bring in. Oil field mud, maybe, if there was any such thing within trucking distance of Metropolis. Or something . . . something to cradle the structure. Luthor's scheme relied on two things: in the midst of a city, a building got its pure water from one main and spilled its outflow water into the city sewer—and there was nowhere for a building to get or dispose of water but those two conduits.

Create a water-filled cavity under a building by diverting a huge amount in under the foundations, scour the mud out into the sewer, keep inflow and outflow balanced so that the water stayed at a certain pressure—that set up the situation. Then shut down the inflow and pump like mad: the water would empty, the building would have a huge hollow under it, and concrete gauged to have a backing of earth would crack, fail, shatter under more weight than it could bear unsupported. Like a house of cards, once the structure failed at the foundations it went out of balance, and everything came down. Concrete all up and down the structure cracked, steel bent, glass shattered and shards flew like spears.

Like the Maernik; like—

A van whipped up the driveway out of the rain and into the garage. He moved to stop it, thinking it might be some patient's unsuspecting family.

But another van screeched to a stop behind it, and both vans were full of reporters. Doors opened instantly. Reporters and cameramen of every news organization in the city started bailing out. With the doors open, lives and limbs were in jeopardy if he shoved them.

"Out!" he said. "Back up! The place isn't—"

A sudden thump, a jolt. A crack ran like lightning across the floor, up the wall.

The first reporters out froze in panic, beside the two heavy weights of those vans, weights the unstable floor didn't need, as others scrambled to get out of the threatened vehicles.

"Leave the vans!" Superman shouted at them. "Get out of here!"

A second crack appeared, right under the vans.

Like the dam. He was dealing with unstable concrete. Water. And imminent devastation.

"Run!" Superman yelled, and dived for the deepest part of the garage, down the spiral, down past mostly vacant levels of the structure, past the scatter of remaining cars, down to the lowest floor, in which cracks were proliferating like gunshots and concrete was separating from the structural web of rebar, dropping away into dark holes.

He heard through all of it the same sound as at the Arts Center, thump-thump, thump-thump, like the beating of a giant heart.

And from this vantage he could see the pool of water underneath the concrete floor, a pool half filling a hollow that shouldn't exist at all.

The destruction was further along here than at the Arts Center. If the water here was half gone, that meant the water under the building was draining fast, the strain was increasing to the point of disaster, and it could come at any second—or at the next car to drive into the garage upstairs.

Someone had to be manning a pump to get the water in and one to get it out: even running unattended most of the time, an operation like this had to come from somewhere, and there had to be equipment and power to run it. There had to be pipes, and pipes led to pumps—

His vision tracked one large pipe to an area that to his eyes looked as if it just quit in the middle of the hollow under the building. He saw another pipe that started on the other side, deep in the water-filled hollow beneath them, apparently attached to nothing, down there where water had scoured through the cavity.

He'd asked the mayor to get the source and outflow shut down. But too much had already gone. He needed the inflow continued, the *outflow* cut off to bring the water level back up, and he feared to leave it even to get to a phone.

A crack shot across the floor. Concrete fell—just a little concrete. But the process was approaching critical, and it was a nightmare. Like the dam he hadn't been able to save, the devastation he hadn't been able to stop. Down here, with his hearing, the beat of that outflow pump was like the beat of a wounded heart, bleeding water away into the sewers, leaving hollowed-out space where the building design required solid earth beneath its concrete supports. Stone or concrete weighed vastly less underwater, almost as if it floated: when the water that had hollowed out the earth was suddenly removed, as was happening now, the unsupported concrete endured stresses in places it was never designed to bear weight. And one crack happened. And another.

Two pumps—one bringing water in from a city main, one carrying earth-laden water out from under a building into the sewers, kept a balance of forces, substituting water for solid earth, scouring stone, eroding a water-filled cavity where no cavity should be. Then, at a certain stage, the inflow pump was cut off, while the outflow pump kept shooting the water out—choosing, but not precisely, the time of collapse: the time at which weight-bearing concrete *cracked*.

The process here was three-quarters complete. He could fuse that outflow pump to slag with his heat vision and stop it, but he couldn't see it from where he was, and the central support pillar was losing more and more substance around it. He needed desperately to stabilize the area, as concrete continued to drop in chunks from a floor increasingly lacking support.

All those patients . . . it was a nightmare, with nothing to take hold of, no leverage, no time.

But a vertical barrier like the dam in the Caucasus was one problem, with gravity working against the situation.

This flood underfoot, this crumbling away of supports, had gravity working *with* it.

Different equation.

This time . . . cold . . . increased solidity . . . even if it cracked the concrete . . . would hold the building. The hospital. The patients.

He carefully bent rebar in a gaping hole in the flooring, where concrete had dropped, wanting no sudden shocks to the precarious structure, and dropped down into a dark hollow smelling of water and earth and wet concrete. He drew in air and breathed it out, supercooling it. He dived through the water: the little warmth it had was energy; and he took it in as fast as he could. He drew energy from the air he took in when he surfaced, bringing the oxygen and nitrogen atoms to a quieter and quieter state, as the energy that had kept the atoms agitated, the energy that permitted *any* movement of matter, flooded into him. He rose into the light and breathed the air out again, over the disintegrating floor, the steel, the vacancy that was exposed as concrete continued to drop away in chunks and slabs.

Cold. Cold that contracts most substances but expands water into a solid, like slowly flowing rock, and makes its volume larger.

Cold so sudden and so deep that as he rose above that pit a mist went up about him, and a rime began forming on every surface. The moisture in the air from the rain outside was creating thicker and thicker frost on everything, ice on parked cars—ice underneath, around all the places where the building's supports were sunk in fluid water, rock and earth.

It looked like Antarctica, the ice steaming in the wet air coming down from the spiral ramp.

Nothing on that lowest level could move.

But he could. And he wanted the persons responsible. He wanted them with a passion—but not more than he wanted the hospital and its occupants safe.

He shot out of that level toward the upper structures and met reporters. Cameras were rolling. Someone was trying to back up the threatened van.

Thump! went the concrete, and a tire went in. The whole van jolted. Reporters scrambled and tried to get their colleague out.

"Get *out* of here!" Superman said, grabbed two by their coats, went back for the van and the equipment—worth reporters' jobs if they lost it—and set it, wheezing on its shock absorbers, safely outside. "I know how they took down the Maernik!" he said. "And I'm on my way to the Sun Tower Retirement Center, ladies and gentlemen, where there may be another of these set-ups, if you want your story. This garage ought to hold up, at least until they get jacks and timbers in here."

There'd been a terrible shock. A jolt like an earthquake. Screams had rung through the corridors of the hospital, as patients and relatives, nerves strung tight from what they'd survived, believed the floor might go in the next heartbeat.

If they'd doubted her warning and her advisements in the least, Lois thought, they'd have believed her now: but Lois Lane on her own, the hero of the Maernik, had credence with the hospital staff, and they'd moved on her word alone.

Since the floor hadn't collapsed, since they still had time, the evacuation still went on at a pace as slow as nightmare, relatives helping patients, staff assisting those who could walk, patients helping patients, and wheelchairs, gurneys, everything they could possibly press into service.

They'd put Billy into a wheelchair. They'd *just* gotten the wheelchair, though Billy's father was wanting to carry him, against the nurses' advice. Lois would have carried him herself, except that Superman was downstairs—and there wasn't a chance the building would really fall. He'd stop it. She told herself that through the jolts, and despite the crack that split the wall in the hallway.

She told herself that when, with Billy in the wheelchair and his father pushing it, his mother walking beside, they hurried toward the end of the hall.

"We'll make it," she said for the hundredth time. "It's all right. We'll make it."

A rush of air sent paper charts fluttering and flying. Frayed nerves twitched, and patients and staff gave small yelps of alarm. Superman had appeared on the floor, hand upheld in that calm down gesture that told her everything.

"The building is shored up," he said to everyone around him. "Slow down, take it easy. Get to the other wing, but take your time. It should stand. Get building engineers to look at the basement and get jacks and timbers in there. Get Cross on the phone. He'll have the best advice."

"What—" —*happened?* she was trying to ask.

But with another rush of air and flutter of papers scattered by his arrival—he was gone.

"Are we okay?" Mrs. Anderson asked faintly. "Are we safe, then?" And Billy asked, kid that he was, "How'd he *do* that?"

"He's just pretty fast," Lois said, shoring up her own confidence, and with Billy and the Andersons continued the trek to the end of the hall, where they were setting up cots, laying down mattresses, filling vacant rooms with the most serious cases, on this floor and on others.

But Billy wasn't on the list of the criticals anymore. And when he left this hospital, as he would, soon, he wouldn't be Her Kid anymore.

They crossed the bright metal joint that marked the end of the annex and the beginning of the old building, out of the threatened area, and nurses and orderlies were arranging places for everyone, stacking them up like planes at the airport, directing a calmer, less frightened traffic. Lois felt a little wobble in the knees, even so, but somebody said,

"Hey, it's that reporter lady!"

And somebody else said, "That's the one that got those kids out," and an old woman in a wheelchair, among those jammed into the hall, reached out and patted her arm as she stopped with the Andersons.

"Way to go, honey," the old lady said.

It was a nest of rats, two-legged ones, in the building next to the Civic Center, three men who looked up as Superman plunged through an office basement wall, following electric lines and

pipes that weren't, he was willing to stake his good reputation on the guess, a reasonable adjunct to the Metropolis Arts Center's original plumbing.

Very large pipes went underground from there, to and from, and involved two big pumps and a tie-in to the sewer line. Just the same as they had in the now entirely frozen basement of the Sun Tower Retirement Center—which had only begun to drain, and which had suffered no damage: the residents might not even know what had happened, except that the air-conditioning had suddenly mandated an extra sweater or a recourse to the heating system. The furnace might not work. But the retirees could sleep securely in their building tonight and read about it in the papers.

Meanwhile a reasonable individual could ask what three men were doing sitting in the dark in a building with two huge pumps and a lot of pipe—pumps which weren't doing anything, since the city had shut down the sewer and the water main. But evidently they'd thought they'd be safer to sit tight, with all the commotion around the Arts Center. They'd just sit safe and quiet in the dark and leave in the small hours before dawn.

So they might have thought.

Wrong.

"Good evening," Superman said. "Friends of Luthor's?"

"That's our *wall!*" one protested indignantly, still crouched in the little nest of boxes and crates—and pipe and other such evidence. "You can't just bust down our wall! We got *rights!*"

"Sorry," Superman said, and nodded back over his shoulder to the dark, the rain, and a grim, raincoated line of Metropolis's finest.

And at the mayor and a municipal judge, both drenched, both of whom had been with the police at the Civic Center. And neither of whom were in a forgiving mood.

"Talk to them," Superman said. "Tell *them* about it."

One man was reaching into the shadows at the side of the pump.

Superman reached faster, stopped the hand on its way to the Uzi, bent the weapon into modern art, and took the owner up by the back of the coat. The others thought they'd scatter out through the building.

He took the would-be gunman out to the police, in the rain, the man protesting his innocence all the way. The other two had run, escaped inside the building.

He could see them. He waited, just to know which way they'd dodge.

To the service area and the van they had behind the garage door. He could see that, too.

And moved, as fast as the flash of lightning in the heavens.

Glass was a cheap repair, compared to a door. Lives were *not* cheap, and they'd already demonstrated they were armed. He zipped through a window just wide enough for him, in a shower of glass virtually powdered by the impact.

They were getting into the van, with the notion they were going to drive out a shut garage door, no doubt.

He landed beside the driver.

The man yelled, shoved the van door at him and ran for the door.

So did his colleague. A shot came back at him.

"I don't think so," Superman said, and rounded the back end of the van. He collected the gun and flung it straight up, where its barrel lodged firmly in the sheetrock, out of play. Then he nodded toward the garage door.

"Open the door," he invited them. "Go ahead."

They scrambled to do that.

There were rain-soaked and grim-faced police on that side, too, police who wanted the perpetrators of the Maernik disaster very, very badly.

The rental agreement on the office complex would be immaculate, Superman was sure. So would the rental agreement on the office building next to the hospital, and the warehouse near the retirement tower. Nothing in documents involving those adjacent buildings would ever touch Lexcorp, oh, no, nothing so easy.

Nothing would indicate how, somehow, the arrangements traced back to a madman locked behind penitentiary bars with no contact with the outside world.

But Metropolis was not in a forgiving mood. And if these men wanted to share a berth on Stryker's Island with Luthor, having failed in the rest of Luthor's murderous plan, they could likely find a ticket to that same prison.

It remained to see how silent they'd stay, when that prospect stared them in the face.

But he didn't think, even if these men talked, that the contacts they named would lead high enough. A man named Smalley had died. A reporter, Monique Simms, had died. No one had put those two facts together until Lois had started prying and searching into the Maernik.

If they did find a connection to higher-ups, there was a strong likelihood there'd be other mysterious deaths—if they didn't move fast enough.

In the meanwhile . . . ice . . . would keep its iron grip on the threatened structures; and jacks and shorings would prevent a collapse. Ambulances would move less critical patients to outlying hospitals, where the threat to that one wing had put maybe twenty hospital rooms out of commission.

All the same, he'd keep an eye on the hospital tonight, maybe help the workmen who'd be bringing in heavy-duty jacks and shoring timbers. He'd have to be sure that water stayed frozen. That was another matter.

He left Luthor's hired help to the police and the municipal judge and lifted himself, almost leisurely, into the night sky.

The hospital had been, of all, the most threatened. Luthor had planned that brutal strike at the very moment the city was honoring its heroes. The Arts Center would have gone next.

And while the city was still reeling from those disasters, the giant Sun Tower would have gone.

The mind that could have conceived and carried out such a scenario deserved to be behind bars for a long, lonely life.

Lightning flashed as he flew slowly over the hospital, reassuring himself that it was still standing, safe and secure as the ice could hold it.

He saw streets glistening with rain and reflecting red lights. Ambulances were waiting at the emergency room doors . . . as he supposed, to carry the patients Memorial no longer had room for to hospitals about the area. There were flatbed trucks, already bringing in timbers and truck jacks.

Lights still shone from the windows on all the floors, even the threatened annex.

Beautiful lights, he thought. Power was still on. He'd get the cars out of there tomorrow morning. People's property would be safe, too. That had its importance, in the scale of things.

He flew past the front of the hospital, checking for cracks, listening, below the sounds of the city, for any further difficulties, and heard none.

He landed there, in front of the doors, expecting to go in more quietly this time.

Looking for someone.

But she was there, waiting next to the rain-spattered window, where she had a view of the approach to the main doors. She saw him and left the window.

He waited as she came out the glass doors and walked out under the portico.

"Hi," she said.

"Everything all right?"

"Pretty well buttoned down." Her hair was a mess. She raked it back, and suddenly the weariness showed. "Taxis melt in the rain. You never find them."

"Want a lift?"

"Sure," she said, as if, for anyone watching from the lobby or the window, they were casual acquaintances.

And as if they were casual acquaintances, he folded a corner of his cape about her and carried her up, up into the rainy sky.

They were somewhere only in the witness of passing planes when he hugged her close and kissed a weary, sleepy partner very tenderly.

"Do you know how Lex did it?" she wanted to know. The reporter—wanted to know. She had a lead on every reporter in the city—except him.

"Yes," he said, and to stop the question, kissed her twice. And a third time. It was easy to forget time and storms with her arms around him. There was, for a rare moment, company up here, above the world.

But the thunder rolled, and the rain sheeted down as they flew into the outpouring of a cloud. And he'd answer her questions later.

Getting her home and out of the lightning was his first priority.